FOREVER AZATHOTH

FOREVER AZATHOTH

Parodies and Pastiches

Peter Cannon (signature)

PETER CANNON

HIPPOCAMPUS PRESS

NEW YORK

"Azathoth in Arkham" was first published in *The Azathoth Cycle* (1995), "The Revenge of Azathoth" in *The Azathoth Cycle* (1995), "The House of Azathoth" in *Cthulhu Codex* No. 8 (August 1996), "Azathoth in Analysis" in *Tales of Lovecraftian Horror* No. 9 (Lammas 1998), "Bride of Azathoth" in *Parts* No. 15 (May 1999), "Son of Azathoth" in *Forever Azathoth and Other Horrors* (1999), "Cats, Rats, and Bertie Wooster" under the title "Scream for Jeeves; or, Cats, Rats, and Bertie Wooster" in *Crypt of Cthulhu* No. 72 (Roodmas 1990), "Something Foetid" in *Crypt of Cthulhu* No. 77 (Eastertide 1991), "The Rummy Affair of Young Charlie" in *Scream for Jeeves: A Parody* (1994), "Tender Is the Night-Gaunt" in *The Mammoth Book of Comic Fantasy* (1998), "The Sound and the Fungi" in *Forever Azathoth* (Subterranean Press, 2011), "All Moon-Beasts Amorphous and Mephitic" in *Crypt of Cthulhu* No. 90 (Lammas 1995), "The Undercliffe Sentences" in *Made in Goatswood* (1995), "The Arkham Collector" in *Return to Lovecraft Country* (1997), "Old Man" as "Le Vieux" in *Rêves d'Ulthar* (2002), "Nautical-Looking Negroes" in *Lore* No. 5 (Summer 1996), and "The Madness out of Space" in *Eldritch Tales* Nos. 8 (January 1982) and 9 (April 1983).

Published by Hippocampus Press
P.O. Box 641, New York, NY 10156.
http://www.hippocampuspress.com

Cover and interior illustrations by Jason C. Eckhardt.
Cover design by Barbara Briggs Silbert.
Hippocampus Press logo designed by Anastasia Damianakos.

First Edition
1 3 5 7 9 8 6 4 2

ISBN 978-1-61498-024-7

CONTENTS

INTRODUCTION

In rereading the stories in this volume, most of which I wrote in the 1990s, I was struck by a couple of details that serve to show how much the world has changed in the years since. In "Son of Azathoth," two characters meet in a library in a dispute over a card catalogue drawer. Granted, this confrontation takes place in the 1970s, at the beginning of the electronic revolution. More strangely, the two principals of "The Arkham Collector" exchange personal letters through the U.S. mail circa 1995. The latter tale refers once to online matters, but otherwise you'll find no mention of anything related to the current digital age in a collection of what for the most part are period pieces. You'll also find, as befits an earlier, more reticent age, no bad language. Sex and violence are largely offstage, the way Lovecraft himself preferred it, I might add.

Starting in 1993 with "Azathoth in Arkham," I produced one installment per year of *Forever Azathoth,* the serial novella that gives this book its title. A sequel to "The Thing on the Doorstep," it plays variations on Lovecraft's mind-swapping idea. It also parallels the history of Lovecraft fandom and scholarship, with ambitious Miskatonic University student Vartan Bagdasarian doing for Edward Derby what S. T. Joshi has done for the Providence gent. Those of you familiar with those classic TV cartoon characters Rocky and Bullwinkle will understand why I view *Forever Azathoth* as a sort of horrific "Fractured Fairy Tale."

Back in the days when we Lovecraftians were feeling defensive about our hero, I decided a good way to try to raise his profile was to link him with more established writers. (My Twayne critical study, *H. P. Lovecraft,* is full of such literary name-dropping.) An infatuation with British humorist P. G. Wodehouse led to the three "Wodecraft" tales, starting with "Cats, Rats, and Bertie Wooster," a retelling of "The Rats in the Walls" from the perspective of Wodehouse's gentlemanly dimwit, Bertie Wooster. Sherlock Holmes fans will note the nod to "Silver Blaze" at the start. Arthur Machen fans will pick up on the passage, as Bertie and Jeeves approach Exham Priory in Bertie's two-seater, where I crib from the Welsh master of the weird.

The second Wodecraft tale, "Something Foetid," thrusts Bertie and his man Jeeves into the plot of "Cool Air," though at one point the dialogue veers off into an hommage to John Cleese's *Fawlty Towers.* (How fortunate that the landlady's son shares the same name, Manuel, as the Spanish waiter who so often exasperates Basil Fawlty in the BBC TV series.) In "Something Foetid," my favorite of the three, Jeeves acts as more than just a wise counselor, playing an underhanded role in the denouement, which involves one of the manservant's so-called sartorial tyrannies (in this case, disapproval of the young master's new suit). "The Rummy Affair of Young Charlie," a cross between a bit of *The Case of Charles Dexter Ward* and "The Music of Erich Zann," also owes something to Larry Shue's play *The Nerd.* The presence of a certain "Mr. Altamont" may intrigue Holmesians.

The next two stories meld Lovecraft with two mainstream American writers who were his contemporaries, F. Scott Fitzgerald and William Faulkner. Fitzgerald's characters from his 1934 novel, *Tender Is the Night,* join Randolph Carter on his quest for Unknown Kadath in the Cold Waste in "Tender Is the Night-Gaunt." The fungi from Yuggoth invade Yoknapatawpha County in "The Sound and the Fungi." A fondness for the works of British author James Herriot of *All Creatures Great and Small* fame led me to pen "All Moon-Beasts Amorphous and Mephitic."

Two tales pay tribute to contemporary masters of the horror genre. The petty annoyances a professional horror writer often has to endure, as wittily described by Ramsey Campbell in his *Necrofile* column of the period, provided the spark for "The Undercliffe Sentences," a spoof at one level of Campbell's "The Franklyn Paragraphs." Martin Amis's novel about authorial envy, *The Information,* was also an influence. T.E.D. Klein and the late Jon White, a New York City book critic and collector, are the models for the characters in "The Arkham Collector."

"Old Man" is my posthumous collaboration with Lovecraft. Unlike August Derleth's tales of the same ilk, mine actually contains plenty of Lovecraft's own words, in particular passages from his letters describing the Kappa Alpha Tau, the fraternity of cats that brightened his last years at 66 College St. on College Hill. Indeed, you could say I have merely stitched together, Frankenstein-like, chunks of Lovecraft prose, the closing crime twist my only original contribution.

A two-page outline by Robert M. Price helped inspire "Nautical-Looking Negroes," a sequel to "The Call of Cthulhu." Bob's theological musings, in particular his book *Beyond Born Again: Toward Evangelical Maturity,* were also an influence. In addition, I owe Bob thanks for suggesting I expand Captain Baker's exhortation to the crew of the *Polestar* before their attack on the fiendish Inutos. This novelette is my attempt at an old-fashioned pulp adventure tale, complete with racist white males—though for the scantily-clad, attractive young woman who typically serves as a sacrificial victim to the gods, I couldn't resist substituting an overweight, middle-aged man in his underwear.

"The Madness out of Space," my first work of Lovecraftian fiction, keen observers may notice, is not included in the Subterranean signed limited hardcover edition of *Forever Azathoth*. I've added an afterword for this appearance.

Finally, readers should know that the contents of this volume vary from the Tartarus Press edition published in 1999 under the same title. I've dropped the five stories inspired by Lovecraft's best friend, Frank Belknap Long, and added four others in addition to "The Madness out of Space." Long fans, however, will recognize Frank in the character of aged Atal in "Tender Is the Night-Gaunt" as well as his wife, Lyda, in the figure of the copyeditor who torments the hero of "The Undercliffe Sentences."

PETER CANNON
New York City

Forever Azathoth

I. Azathoth in Arkham

While it is true that the late Edward Derby was my father's best friend, I hope to show by this statement that I, Edward Derby Upton, his namesake, have no especial reason to be proud of the fact. I confess that I never much cared for "Uncle Eddy." The brilliant child scholar and *fantaisiste* was, I quickly realized as a child, too focused on his own affairs to take any real interest in mine. Later, as a youth keen on such manly sports as boxing and baseball, I found Derby too flabby, too feminine. At Harvard, where I read the writings of Freud and Jung, I recognized that the immature misfit bore all the hallmarks of a classic narcissist. Heaven knows what my father saw in Derby, unless he got a vicarious thrill out of the younger man's career as a poet of the morbid and the macabre, having had leanings himself toward art of a somewhat grotesque cast. If only my foolish father had had the sense to drop him when he married that awful Waite woman and started to behave like a lunatic, then the tragedy that was to bring me and my mother such grief might have been averted.

When on impulse a senior partner in one of Arkham's most prestigious architectural firms drives over to the local funny farm and blows out the brains of his best friend, it is natural to attribute such an act to madness. Of course, the shock of discovering the badly decomposed body of that friend's estranged wife clutching a deranged note urging him to that very act might have been enough to unhinge the mind of any but the thickest-fibred. My wits certainly wavered when Soames, the family butler, phoned the Delphic to inform me of the ghastly prank or whatever it was that lay on the doorstep of our house in Saltonstall Street that winter morning. I instantly left for the North Station, to catch the next train to Arkham. Outside the family homestead I found the footman hard at work scrubbing the stoop. Inside everyone was in a state of alarm, as the upstairs maid had only just realized my father was missing from his bedroom, where he had been resting after suffering a series of fainting spells.

Within an hour we had learned the grim sequel. My father called from the station-house to announce that he had turned himself in to the police, who were holding him for the murder of Edward Pickman Derby. His tone was sober and determined, not at all the voice of one who had lost his reason. By the time I arrived Judge Hand, a distant cousin of Learned Hand and well known to my father as a fellow member of the Miskatonic Club, had already set bail. The prisoner was free to leave in my custody, despite the serious charge against him—first-degree murder. In person, my father appeared his usual calm and dignified self. On the return ride home he muttered about black zones of shadow close to our daily paths and striking before reckoning the consequences, but otherwise said nothing.

As we pulled into the driveway, he promised to write down as soon as possible a full account for me and my mother explaining what had led him to "avenge" Edward Derby. I have yet to discover any such document among his papers. Perhaps he shrank from revealing to us untold terrors that would threaten our sanity. Or, what is more likely, the poor fellow never had the chance to put pen to paper, given even greater calamity to come.

Two days later, despite the ordeal he had just been through, my father, ever loyal to his friend, insisted on going to the hastily arranged double funeral of Edward and Asenath Derby. While some Innsmouth folk and a few of the "intelligentsia" from the university were there, as I later heard, to witness the twin-casket ceremony, my father was the only respectable citizen of the town in attendance. That afternoon in Cambridge, where I had returned to my club, I received another frantic phone call from Soames. My father had fainted at the end of the graveside service, the man reported, and a couple of the college "sophisticates" had been kind enough to bring him home. Reviving after a sudden seizure, he had flown into a violent rage lasting several minutes, until just as abruptly he had collapsed into a catatonic silence. Before he could do further damage to himself or to others, the stalwart butler had with the aid of the footman taken the liberty of securing his hands and feet. With the arrival of the family doctor, alerted earlier, my father had been bundled off under sedation in a closed car to the sanitarium, where he was presently undergoing observation.

Again I took the next available train to Arkham, my first duty being to comfort my distraught mother, my second to learn all I could about my father's condition and what, if anything, could be done for him. As a student of psychology, I was in a position to understand something about mental disorders. To my dismay, the doctors at the Arkham Sanitarium were to diagnose my father as a paranoid schizophrenic. A hopeless case, he would never be fit to stand trial. Instead he was bound to live out his natural days in a straitjacket, for the time being incarcerated, irony of ironies, in the padded cell lately vacated by Edward Derby.

At first my mother and I made regular visits to the sanitarium, but we soon stopped going altogether when it became clear that the once loving husband and father had no idea of our identity. At best he would smile at us from behind the protective bars with an idiotic leer. This pathetic speechless creature, I was forced to conclude, no longer had any more relation to me than an ape or a gorilla. In later years only the faithful Soames was known on occasion to look in, talking of family matters as if his old master could still comprehend them.

Fortunately, funds were plentiful for my father's maintenance. His partners at the architectural firm were not ungenerous in their disability pension, but this was pocket money in comparison to the fortune that in due course my father came into as principal heir to the Derby estate. Family lawyers early on had wisely contrived to cut Asenath out of any interest in Edward's assets. While certain complications did arise to do with Asenath's mysterious death and her equally mysterious prior disappearance, as well as with my father's central role in her husband's demise, the jury ruled—advised by Judge Hand, who presided in the case—against her Innsmouth relatives in their suit contesting Edward's will. By this time I had attained my majority and was within sight of my Harvard graduation. As my father's guardian, I was free to administer the ample income as I pleased.

After taking my degree I returned to Arkham to live with my mother, whose health had been in decline. Thinking a change of scene would soothe her nerves, I gave the tenants of the Derby mansion, which my father had inherited, their notice. By year's end, after selling the old Crowninshield place, another legacy of the Derby estate, we were ensconced in our new home, which Edward had had renovated in authentic period style shortly before his confinement. In addition to our own servants, we hired a number of the staff formerly employed by old Mr. Derby, who were only too eager to resume their duties under a familiar roof. The Depression had hit bottom that fall, and any sane person would have opted for domestic service over the bread line.

In my new circumstances, I decided to defer a professional career. My mother, despite her various ailments real and imaginary, proved fully capable of running the household. With no responsibilities to speak of, I alternated my routine between the Miskatonic Club, where I exercised daily in the gym, and my library, where I pored over the latest psychological journals and books. I had the notion that the theories of Freud and Jung might offer some insight into my father's sorry mental state. They might even, I hardly dared hope, suggest a cure. But I was doomed to disillusionment. Freud was too dogmatic, I eventually realized, his theories of infantile sexuality no more "scientific" than the postulates of Marxism. As for Jung, his archetypal analysis, I reluctantly concluded, just made basically well-adjusted if underconfident individuals feel a little better about themselves. There was no more real substance or solace in the ideas of these "geniuses" than in the teachings of orthodox religion.

For a while I admit I was aimless, ceasing to go to the club and lacking the intellectual spark that had once fired my independent studies. What saved me during this dark period from lapsing into total apathy, as it turned out, was none other than—the poetical works of Edward Derby. I had kept the presentation copy Derby had given my father of *Azathoth and Other Horrors,* though I had never bothered to open it. (Indeed, for a long time I mistook the title for *Asenath and Other Horrors.*) Having never been fond of contemporary poetry, I cannot now say what prompted me to take this book off the shelf, other than a need to try to alleviate my suffocating boredom.

Since the title poem occupies half the volume, I will cite only enough of the opening to convey the striking flavor of the whole:

> At infinity's center, last amorphous blight of nethermost confusion,
> You bubble and blaspheme, the boundless daemon-sultan;
> Shapeless and ravenous, you gnaw amidst the muffled, maddening
> Beat of vile drums and the thin, monotonous whine of accursed flutes.
> Headed for those unhallowed pits where no dreams reach,
> Onward through shoals of shapeless lurkers and caperers in darkness,
> Vacuous herds of drifting entities paw and grope and grope and paw:
> The nameless larvae of the Other Gods, blind and without mind,
> Possessed like you, Azathoth, of singular hungers and thirsts.

Where on God's green earth, I wondered, did Derby come up with these outré images? My distaste for his personality, I should say, did not prevent me from appreciating his verse. It touched me in some unaccountable way, as great literature is supposed to. The bizarre name Azathoth in particular intrigued me. Was it a corruption of Asenath? (Maybe I wasn't so far off the mark after all when I confused the title.) The copyright page, however, bore a date years before their first meeting. Here was a puzzle that

piqued my curiosity as nothing else had in ages. I resolved to do a little research, to go by week's end to the university library, where I was certain I
could dig up some data on the poet-prodigy's sources.

At the Miskatonic library, where Derby himself must have spent many
an hour as an undergraduate, I explained my purpose to the head librarian,
Dr. Henry Armitage, who let out a low whistle when I mentioned that I
possessed an inscribed first edition of *Azathoth and Other Horrors*. He be-
lieved the name Azathoth to be Hebraic in origin, but doubted I would find
it listed in any of the standard linguistic references. Others had already inquired on the topic. The librarian remarked that Derby's local celebrity had
been growing quietly since the publication of his collected nightmare-lyrics
in his eighteenth year, and even more so since his tragic and sensational
death at age forty-two. Almost incidentally he added that he knew of an informal group of Derby acolytes that gathered every so often on campus. If
I was so inclined, why not check the bulletin board in University Hall for an
announcement of their next meeting?

I did not linger at the library, but after thanking Dr. Armitage for his
help hurried over to University Hall, where there was posted just what I
was hoping to find: a notice of a classroom get-together for the following
evening of the "Dead Edward Derby Society." What a stroke of luck! As
excited as I was by the prospect, however, I decided it would be best to re-
frain from revealing my own tie to the poet. Back home, when I outlined
my scheme to Soames, he agreed that this would be the soundest policy.

When I introduced myself as "Ed Upton" to the dozen or so students
who had assembled at the appointed time and place, no one betrayed any
particular interest. I will not deny that I felt somewhat self-conscious. For
one thing, I was dressed in expensive tailored clothes far beyond the means
of the average undergraduate. For another, my college days were by then
more than six years in the past. Although obviously older and more com-
fortably off than the rest of the Derby *aficionados,* I was relieved to be
treated like any other new participant.

At a signal from the acting moderator, we pulled our chairs into a circle
and each person spoke briefly about what Edward Derby meant to him or
her. Some raised questions, to which others supplied answers. When it was
my turn I asked the question of most concern to me: who or what was
Azathoth? One person was sure Azathoth was purely Derby's invention.
But if so, said another, what did that tell us about his childhood? (I nodded
in approval at this acute comment.) One girl brought up the gender issue:

should Azathoth be referred to as he, she, or it? Someone else suggested that the name, along with Derby's other exotic concepts, came out of ancient and arcane books, like the *Necronomicon*. Everyone had heard of Abdul Alhazred's *Necronomicon*, a copy of which was rumored to be the prize of the library's rare book collection. Since a bungled burglary attempt a decade earlier, however, no one was allowed to view it. Not only did Dr. Armitage keep the forbidden tome under lock and key, the moderator asserted, he had even removed its slip from the card catalogue.

Thereafter discussion broke down into smaller groups. When I let out to my neighbor that I was an Arkham native, he asked me whether I had been around when Derby was killed. All of a sudden I was on the spot. As I pretended to cough, another student said he thought the name Upton sounded familiar. People stopped talking; eyes shifted in my direction. Realizing I was cornered, I decided there was nothing for it but to confess that I was indeed related to that Upton, the one who had murdered his best friend, the author they all so admired. For a long while the group to a man sat in stunned silence. A girl finally spoke up and expressed her sympathy for what must have been a dreadful personal experience. Others began to join in, producing a veritable chorus of "how awful" and "what a shame" and "sheesh, I'm sorry."

I recovered sufficiently, if not to address the painful circumstances of Derby's death and my father's dementia, then to satisfy my listeners as to details of their idol's career in his sunnier, pre-Asenath days. I took care to say nothing derogatory, playing up those aspects of his boyish personality that I knew would most appeal to youths who in all probability were no more advanced in their social development than he ever was. It would not be inaccurate to claim that I dominated the rest of the proceedings. At the end of the session, carried away perhaps by the warmth of my audience, I impulsively proposed to host the next meeting at my place, the very house where Edward Derby had grown up! The gang enthusiastically accepted my offer, and a date was set for the following week.

When I told my mother that a group of new friends would be coming over, she was not pleased. She had become rather a recluse in her old age, and had difficulty with the prospect of facing, as she put it, a crowd of crude college kids. As always, however, she deferred to my wishes when she saw that I was adamant, though she vowed not to set foot outside her bedroom during the affair.

While an impartial observer would no doubt have deemed the event a great success, I cannot rule out that my mother's subsequent breakdown did not follow in some way from this, for her, highly upsetting episode. The maid who served the tea and sandwiches should never have given her that overcolored report on the table manners of some of the guests, while it was indeed unfortunate that one Derbyite, apparently overwhelmed by handling a clock of colonial vintage that had actually rested on his hero's mantel, should have dropped it on the marble floor.

Such conflict was obviated in the future by the family doctor's opinion that my mother should remain indefinitely at the Arkham Sanitarium, where she had a private room in one of the cheerier wards and could wander the park-like grounds at will. Whenever at her physician's discretion I visited her at a halfway home outside the hospital, I made a point of not mentioning the Derby Society meetings that we were now holding with increasing frequency at the house. Furthermore, I did not tell her how I was finding my calling as spiritual leader to a flock of young people, many of whom were sorely in need of adult guidance. In recognition of my senior status, as a token of their esteem, they had even dubbed me "Grandpa."

When my mother died during a routine operation days before the Harvard-Yale game (which I missed for the first time since boyhood on account of a gang outing), I was not as depressed as I might otherwise have been. For once I felt my life had purpose. For once I had gained something that riches could not buy—the uncritical respect of sensitive persons. In all honesty, their company had come to mean more to me than that of the club bores and Ivy League jocks with whom I was used to associating by virtue of birth and breeding. No matter that the imaginative work of my father's late friend provided an easy escape. For them pretending that the fantasy worlds of *Azathoth and Other Horrors* were real was a form of therapy, a way of coping with the typical fears that arise from an awkward adolescence. And so I humored my companions, assuring them that their harmless pastimes went even farther than the degenerate doings of the decadent set that had flourished during Edward Derby's heyday.

After New Year's, one fellow suggested that instead of getting together to talk over spaghetti (I had had to modify the fare served *chez* Upton to accommodate most members' less than refined tastes), we do something truly "daring"—like holding a midnight vigil at the poet's grave. We had to mark the anniversary of his death in February in some fashion, he declared. Why not sneak into the cemetery and perform an appropriate ceremony in homage? While this suggestion struck me as a trifle ghoulish, I held my tongue since everybody else agreed it was a wonderful idea. We did not call ourselves the Dead Edward Derby Society for nothing.

That fateful night before Candlemas, nearly a score of us met at an obscure corner of Arkham's Christchurch Cemetery and, one by one, climbed over the iron-spiked fence. Since it was also the anniversary of the onset of my father's mental illness, I could not help having mixed feelings. (On his return from the sanitarium that day, Soames had said that the patient was neither worse nor better than usual.) As we stumbled in single file across the hard frosty ground, we were grateful that the sub-freezing temperature reduced the risk of interference from watchman or guard dog—and of nasal assault by pestiferous graveyard odors.

With the aid of a flashlight we located the family plot where the Derbys had been buried for eight generations. A modest shaft marked Edward and Asenath's final resting place, uniting them in death as they had never been in life. Some of our party lit candles, others incense. From memory I recited an extended passage from "Azathoth," Derby's longest and most popular poem. After intoning the last line, I quipped that I was still as much in the dark about Azathoth as I was when I first joined the society. From behind I heard a hiss that sounded something like "ignorant swell." After a second I recognized it as the voice of our newest member, a scholarship student from Innsmouth. She went on to say that it was lucky for us all that we had no clue as to the true nature of Azathoth—or Asenath, for that matter. Her older sister, she added, had worked for Asenath, who had in fact been much more "talented" than her weakling of a husband.

This challenge to Derby's artistic integrity left the rest of us standing (and shivering) in shocked silence, until finally someone was bold enough to ask what was so great about Asenath. Well, for one thing, the Innsmouth girl replied, Asenath had had the ability to exchange minds, which was a far from simple exercise. It was really more an art than a science. It required a lot of "creativity." Writing a poem full of funny names was child's play by comparison. A few of the group indulged the newcomer by debating her outlandish claims, but when she announced that Asenath could work her will from the grave we decided it was time to head home. As we retraced our steps through the time-worn, rime-encrusted headstones, I had to admit, as much as I hated to, that a figure like Edward Derby attracted his share of kooks. I was following right behind the Innsmouth girl, and despite the frigid air I could detect the faint but distinctly putrid smell of rotten fish.

The next morning the director of the sanitarium rang up to report that the doctors had observed a significant change in my father's behavior. After describing these latest symptoms in brief, he asked if I wished to come in and observe the patient for myself. I answered that I had to think about it, so startling was this news, but would get back to him shortly. As soon as I was off the wire, I summoned Soames.

"Soames, the most amazing thing has happened."

"Yes, sir."

"My father's taken a new turn. It's incredible, but evidently he now believes that he's you!"

"How odd, sir."

"Rather than being violent or passive, he acts frightened or bewildered, I've been told."

"Very curious, sir."

"What do you make of it, Soames? This could be a sign of the end of his psychosis. For a start, maybe they'll let him out of that straitjacket."

"There may be some slight promise of hope, sir."

"You saw him yesterday, and yet you noticed nothing extraordinary?"

"That is correct, sir."

"Then the change must have occurred shortly after your visit."

"So it would appear, sir."

"Queer that he should start mimicking you, but then you've been the only member of the family, as it were, to visit him over the years. By the way, Soames, it's mighty decent of you. I wish I had your fortitude. I know I should've kept up my visits, but it's just so hard for a son to see a father's once noble mind so sadly o'erthrown, as the poet says."

"I quite understand, sir."

"I'm considering driving over to the sanitarium right away—though I could wait until the issue becomes clearer. What do you think?"

"I think the issue is about to become very clear, sir. Yes, you could depart immediately, but on the other hand it would be no tragedy in my view if you were to change your mind."

Soames was smiling. Soames rarely smiled. It was a goofy smile. An unpleasant smile that vaguely reminded me of—

"I suppose I owe you an explanation, Upton, or shall I call you Soames? I think the sooner you get used to your new name the better, don't you?"

"I know I don't have to waste my time convincing you of the possibility of personality exchange, so I'll answer the obvious questions first. Why, might you ask, didn't I get into the head of an employee of the sanitarium? Ha! Do you realize how strong-willed those doctors and nurses and orderlies have to be to survive. No? Well, I guess you've never spent a lot of time in the nut-hatch like me—or your parents. Oh, sorry. I guess madness in the family is a sore subject.

"Why did I wait so long, seven whole years and more? They never did move me from that wretched cell where they locked me up when I was in Derby's body, by the way. Wasn't it kind of monotonous? Well, if you'd read the stuff I'd read in the *Necronomicon* you'd see why it was worth waiting for the chance at eternity. Besides, I wanted to be sure I was ready to hold on for good on the first try. I've learned a few things since I made the swap with that half-human daughter of mine.

"Early on I'll admit I had you targeted. But, damn it all, you were smart enough to keep your distance from the loony bin. So I had to get to Soames first, though he'd be a hard egg to crack. You remember he was the one who dealt with the mess on your doorstep that sent your old man into a swoon. Soames was tough, real tough. But he was getting on, and by his last visit it was a cinch to kick his consciousness out and throw in my own. He was too feeble to put up the kind of struggle your dad did. Yeah, your old man may have been faint-hearted, but at least he had the guts to fight back. Frankly, I don't expect the same trouble from you. A life of luxury has softened you like a sponge.

"As for your future, I'm afraid I have to give you the boot. Why should I keep an old geezer like you around when I've got an able-bodied footman ready to take over your spot? This new European war is bound to spread, and before everybody runs off to do his patriotic duty, I'm going to see to it that I have adequate help. Your exit won't be the only change. Believe me, your pals are going to be in for a big surprise at the next Derby Society meeting. What a pathetic crew! Before I made the switch yesterday, you should've heard Soames grumble about their pitiful antics.

"Yeah, I know it may be rough landing a new job at your age, old codger. I might have a lead for you, though. Soames happened to mention that the Miskatonic Club shoeshine boy's quit and joined the army. It seems Judge Hand was worried about getting a replacement, but don't worry, next time I drop by the club I'll put in a good word for you with the judge."

II. The Revenge of Azathoth

What lay behind my decision to leave the Midwest to attend college in Ark-ham, Massachusetts, was my love of the marvel-shadowed, subtly fearsome writings of the poet and *fantaisiste* Edward Derby, whose abbreviated, leg-end-haunted life had been spent brooding beside the darkly muttering Miskatonic (at least according to his early, more pastoral verse celebrating his native New England). I had been a Derby enthusiast ever since coming across in my twelfth year a copy of his collected nightmare-lyrics, *Azathoth and Other Horrors,* published in 1908 when his reputation was at its peak. Af-ter devouring this, his only book, its every line redolent of adventurous ex-pectancy, I tracked down and read all his other available work, gleaning what little biographical data I could from the editorial pages and letter col-umns of the specialty magazines that had carried his poetry and prose in the teens and twenties.

While he was never prolific, Derby's output over the years fell off steadily both in quantity and quality—though some misguided critics will argue that the late epic, "To Asenath," is the equal of "Azathoth"—until about 1930, when original contributions under his name abruptly disappear from all the usual venues. Curious about this anomaly, I was on the verge of writing to the author himself in care of *Whispers,* the journal where his work most often appeared, when I learned of his tragic passing at age forty-two—gunned down in cold blood by his best friend in an Arkham insane asylum. This lurid story, with all its gruesome and distasteful details, was widely reported in the national press, including the newspaper of the small university town where I was living with my family and attending junior high. Sickened and dismayed, I vowed to work extra hard at my studies in the hope that my parents, both professors at Sauk City State, would allow me to leave Indiana after high school for Miskatonic University, where I envisioned myself engaging in ground-breaking scholarship that would se-cure the reputation of my late literary idol.

Graduating a year early at the top of my class, I entered Miskatonic in the fall of 1939 as a freshman. Since my interest at the time was primarily bibliographical, I was disappointed to learn that the library contained no Derby material, beyond a couple of first editions of *Azathoth and Other Hor-rors.* (While the publisher, a small press in Cambridge, had reprinted the volume at intervals over the years, it was a pity they'd never seen fit to issue a second collection before going bankrupt in 1931.) Who possessed Derby's original manuscripts was a puzzle, assuming they still existed. Who controlled the estate was also a mystery, though I was too young and naïve to appreciate the importance of this.

What I did find, however, was a number of other undergrads who shared my preoccupation, drawn to Miskatonic because of the university's associations with the poet. In short order we formed the Dead Edward Derby Society, meeting every week or so to discuss his work or to read our own, Derby-inspired writings. (I myself, I hasten to add, have no talent whatsoever for either fiction or poetry, critical and textual analysis being my métier.)

Any student who had known Derby, or his wife Asenath, had long since left Miskatonic. If any professor had had an affiliation with the couple, he did not respond to the notices we posted around the campus advertizing our get-togethers. One October evening, however, there appeared in the vacant classroom where we customarily gathered a gentleman who markedly stood out from the rest of us. He looked to be in his late twenties, though a certain formality of manner conveyed the impression of greater age. Judging from his clothes, I would have said he was a banker or member of some otherwise highly respectable profession. I confess that when he introduced himself, in a cultivated Boston accent, I didn't take any special note of his name—Ed Upton.

What first struck me about the stranger was his interest in Azathoth, the godlike entity of Derby's lengthy narrative poem that is the centerpiece of his volume of collected verse. In the course of our general discussion, Upton raised the question of who, or what, was Azathoth. Someone suggested that Derby had made the name up; someone else claimed that he had found it in the *Necronomicon,* back in the days when anybody could walk into the library and consult that mythical tome. (Near the start of the term it so happened that I had asked the head librarian about the etymology of the word *Azathoth,* which he suspected had an Egyptian origin, but on the whole this line of inquiry was not one I considered very significant relative to others. Thus I declined to add my two cents to the debate.)

It was sometime after we had broken up into smaller groups that I suddenly became aware that all conversation had come to a halt, the only sound being our older visitor coughing violently. "Yes, yes, I'm related to that Upton," he finally blurted, after wiping his mouth with a handkerchief monogrammed EDU. "I'm the son of the man who murdered Edward Derby!"

It is to Edward Upton's credit that so soon after this melodramatic and painful personal revelation he was able to master his emotions and go on to regale the company with stories of Derby's early exploits. Fascinating stuff! His career before he met and married Asenath, in 1929, was not well documented, so this was a most welcome and unexpected source of Derby data. To cap off the meeting, which ran an hour longer than usual, Upton invited everybody for next time to come to his house, which had formerly been the home of the Derbys. Needless to say, the gang jumped at the proposal.

On the appointed afternoon the following week, ten of us "Derbyites" rendezvoused in front of Upton's house, a Georgian-period behemoth (which we were to dub Derby Manor), located on one of the finer avenues of the genteel Yankee neighborhood that abuts the Miskatonic campus. At the door our knock was answered by an elderly butler with an English accent who showed us into a drawing room, where he instructed us to wait for his master. This lofty room was furnished with an array of splendid antiques, but what chiefly attracted me was a pair of Copley portraits, identified as Theodore Howland Derby and his wife, Fanny Osgood Derby. Evidently our host owned not only the house where the poet had grown up but also most of its original contents. Might not there be a cache of manuscripts secreted somewhere—say, in a Chippendale secretary?

Before I could pull open and inspect any drawers, however, Ed Upton joined us, apologizing for keeping us waiting. "Sorry, boys, but my mother hasn't been feeling well. She's upstairs and would be most grateful if you kept your voices down." He gave a feeble smile. "Anyone for tea?"

A maid appeared bearing a silver tea service on a tray, supplemented by a plate of sandwiches. Accustomed as we were to dorm fare, we partook heartily of this repast as we chatted about things Derbyian. Our host seemed to be enjoying our company, though he was reserved to the point of shyness. I tried to draw him out by asking him about the prose fragment entitled "Azathoth," which had appeared in *Whispers* years after the publication of *Azathoth and Other Horrors*. The concept in this fragment varied significantly from that in the poem. Was it a later refinement, or did it represent an earlier stage, predating the poem's composition?

"I don't know," was Upton's reply.

After tea our host was kind enough to take the group on a tour of the house, showing us Derby's former bedroom, study, and library. In a dimly lit hallway on the second floor Upton motioned to us to tiptoe, single file, past what we later concluded must have been his mother's bedroom door.

At this juncture, I admit, my scholarly impulses got the better of me and I snuck back into Derby's study, where I had noticed a cupboard that looked promising as a manuscript repository. A quick peak was all I wanted, but the cupboard doors were stuck. When after about the third tug they abruptly flew open, I lost my balance and staggered against a table, knocking over an old clock. I just had time to shut the cupboard and cover my tracks, as it were, before the crash brought the rest of the company back into the study. I apologized for my clumsiness, mumbling something about a fascination with antique timepieces. To my vast relief, Upton didn't insist I pay for the damage as he ushered us downstairs, though he did say it was perhaps best to cut our visit short. Happily, at the door he extended an invitation to return the following week, this time for dinner.

Over the remainder of the fall semester, in my capacity as unofficial leader of the Dead Edward Derby Society, which I had naturally assumed, I encouraged everyone to take advantage of the hospitality offered us at Derby Manor. Frankly, I had to cajole some of the gang, who either had a problem with the strange and unfamiliar foods served at meals there or, more seriously, with "Grandpa" Upton himself, who behaved as if he were decades older than his actual age. I conceded that our patron was at times a stuffed shirt, but then one had to make allowances for a person who had suffered such terrible family tragedy. Sadly enough, there would soon be cause for further grief. In late November Mrs. Upton, whose absence I will say did make our second visit to the manor more relaxed, was to die in the hospital, evidently after a long illness. Ed said little about it at the time (by then we were on a first-name basis), but his mother's passing surely took its emotional toll.

In the meantime I resolved to take a more subtle approach in my quest for Derby manuscript materials. Although I had gotten only a glimpse, the cupboard in Derby's old study had indeed been stuffed nearly to overflowing with papers. These, I was convinced, were the drafts and proofs of countless poems and stories, many no doubt unpublished, of America's foremost modern *fantaisiste* after James Branch Cabell. I was gaining confidence that Ed would ultimately give me access to this treasure trove, for he had already taken my advice on adjusting the menu for our meetings, having his chef prepare more spaghetti and meatballs and less cream sauce and caviar.

At our first get-together after Mrs. Upton passed away, knowing of Ed's continued interest in the nature of Azathoth, I introduced a new topic that I hoped might lead to other things: textual problems in Derby's long narrative poem. In the first stanza the "daemon-sultan" is described as "boundless," I said, but elsewhere he is called "mindless"; a few lines later we are told the "Other Gods" are "without mind," virtually a synonym for "mindless." Is this sort of redundancy deliberate, I speculated, or could it represent a slip of the pen—or the proofreader? One could only be certain, I hinted, by comparing the printed text with the original manuscript.

"Funny you should mention it, Vartan," said my host. "In that room where you dropped the clock, I don't know if you remember, there's a cupboard where Uncle Eddy kept a lot of papers I've never bothered to look at. Maybe some of them could be stuff he wrote."

There was a silence as I waited for him to make the obvious offer. Finally, I spoke up, and in as casual a tone as I could muster, suggested that I'd be glad to save him the effort of examining the cupboard's contents, not that I wanted to impose or anything . . . He said that would be most considerate of me. Another silence ensued.

Well, the long and short of it was, right before Christmas vacation, Ed finally allowed me to come over, alone, with the express purpose of poking into Derby's cupboard. I didn't object to the butler's "lending a hand," though I suspected his presence was really to ensure that no loose papers strayed into my pocket. I still had plenty of work to do to win the trust of the man who, I'd come to realize, controlled the literary rights to the Edward Derby estate.

It would be a gross understatement to say that this first superficial inspection fulfilled my wildest expectations. Balboa gazing at the Pacific, Coronado stumbling onto the Seven Lost Cities of Quivara, Ponce de Léon bathing in the Fountain of Youth, could not have felt as fortunate as I did in those first ecstatic moments of discovery. In addition to such minor items as stacks of amateur journals and old magazines, including a complete run of *Whispers* to 1930, there were piles and piles of handwritten manuscripts—the overwhelming bulk of which I could tell had never seen the light of print. In the hour or so I spent exploring this gold mine, I couldn't help imagining a rosy future—of settling permanently in Arkham, of founding my own imprint (Sauk City House after my home town? No, better was Azathoth House), of preserving the entire Derby oeuvre between cloth covers, of having my name as editor on every title page. A corrected edition of *Azathoth and Other Horrors* might be my first project, assuming I could secure reprint rights . . . Reflections on the permissions issue brought me back to earth.

When I reported my initial findings to Ed, who seemed pleased, I refrained from sharing with him the full scope of my vision for the Derby manuscripts, in particular my own principal role in their disposition. We did agree, though, that everyone would benefit from his eventually donating them to Miskatonic University, where they could be properly stored and made available to scholars, while he could take a hefty tax deduction. For the moment I was satisfied to put my more ambitious plans on hold, my first task—a formidable one—being to catalogue every scrap of paper from Derby's hand I had uncovered. Luckily, Ed was receptive to this idea.

Early in the new year, after vacationing in Indiana, I established a routine of coming over on Saturdays to the manor, where I was permitted to sit at a desk in Derby's old study to perform my labors. Relations between my patron and myself grew ever more cordial. The butler stopped checking up on me after the initial visit, while Ed was even able to jest about putting the clock I'd broken out of my reach, on the mantel, as soon as it came back from being repaired in Switzerland.

This honeymoon period, regrettably, did not last. The gang had continued to meet as usual for dinner one evening a week at the manor, while making a special midnight outing to Arkham's Christchurch Cemetery on the anniversary of Derby's death. Some rather absurd and ill-informed remarks at the grave from one of our newest members regarding Derby's literary merits versus his wife's alleged psychic powers may have left a bad taste in Ed's mouth, but this in itself could not have accounted entirely for the extraordinary scene a few days later at the next gathering.

We got our first glimmer that things would be different when our knock at the door was answered, not by the aged Englishman, but by a surly younger fellow whose speech betrayed his townie origins. In the living-room "Grandpa" greeted us in a rough, boisterous manner, far from his normal mild and timid tones. Where in the past he had been content to be more an observer than a participant, he now charged like a bull into the conversation, making all sorts of outrageous comments.

"Hey, kids, you ever seen a shoggoth?" he declared. "I know where you can find a pit full of the cuddly critters. Kamog! Kamog! Heh, heh."

When the girl who had taken umbrage at the grave told him he had better be careful what he said about shoggoths, Ed asked on whose authority she said so.

"I'm from Innsmouth," she replied, as if that explained everything.

Ed laughed again. "Yeah, tell me about Innsmouth," he said, leaning over and pinching her ample buttock.

Ed laughed again. "Yeah, tell me about Innsmouth . . . "

"You pig!" she said, slapping away his hand.

"You fish!" he retorted, giving her another pinch.

Those of us watching this exchange were stunned. What was so shocking was not so much our host's advances in themselves—though it was puzzling that he should flirt with such a homely girl (granted, coeds constituted a definite minority of the society and we were glad for whatever female company we could get)—but that these advances were so out of character. In the months we'd gotten to know him Ed had struck everyone as being wholly neuter, or at any rate a gentleman who would never treat someone of the opposite sex so crudely.

Matters did not improve over dinner. Ed and the girl swapped further barbs, each trying to upstage the other. At one point they quoted passages from the *Necronomicon* for the other to identify, leaving out the rest of us who hadn't had the privilege of setting eyes on that forbidden book. When the girl reached for her third hamburger, Ed remarked she might do better to put it back on the platter, given her obvious tendency to put on the pounds.

"Suck your own tentacle, buddy!" was her reply.

The group was ready to leave immediately after eating. As he said goodbye, Ed suggested apropos of warmer weather in the spring that we all ought to go on a camping trip to Chesuncook, Maine, where he knew a great spot in the woods, very secluded. His raucous laughter was the last thing we heard before the door of Derby Manor slammed behind us.

While some of us did show up the following week, it was clear that the visits of the Dead Edward Derby Society to the Upton household were numbered. Ed never explicitly discouraged our coming over, but his behavior only got more and more out of hand, to the point where finally everyone dropped out. The consensus was that a free meal wasn't worth the insults. Nor did a prospective camping trip excuse his arrogance. Where before Ed had never visibly condescended to us, he now didn't hesitate to rub in our faces the fact that he was a Harvard man and we were mere Miskatonians. A natural aristocrat he may have been, but that didn't give him the right to lord it over us, those of us of humbler background asserted.

To take the most charitable view, I wondered if the loss of his mother might have unhinged him in some delayed fashion. In late February we noticed his father's obituary in the paper, and though the crazed killer had been confined to the Arkham Sanitarium since 1933, we figured his passing could also have contributed to the son's further mental decay. At any rate, I didn't abandon my Saturday routine, while for his part Ed betrayed no sign that he objected to my researches. He did, however, no longer call me by my first name, using my last name instead—Bagdasarian—which he habitually mispronounced, possibly intentionally. To be perfectly honest, I was willing to put up with almost anything for the sake of access to Derby's papers. I had run across several variant versions of "Azathoth" (the poem, not the prose fragment), which would take me many pleasurable months to collate.

I was not, as it turned out, the only Derbyite who refused to be intimidated by Upton's antics. To my surprise, I arrived one Saturday morning at the manor to find there the girl with whom he had sparred, Wendy Babson. I scarcely knew her, though she was about the last member of the gang I would have expected to have kept up with Ed. Wendy admitted that the two of them had recently buried the hatchet, on account of their common link with Innsmouth. Because Innsmouth had been regarded as the armpit of the North Shore ever since the winter of 1927–28, when half the population was arrested on unspecified morals charges in a predawn raid, I couldn't imagine what Upton's connection could be with the place. I decided it was best not to ask.

As the only regular visitors to Derby Manor, Wendy and I ended up forging a kind of alliance as the months went by, exchanging confidences as well as household gossip. From the new butler, for instance, she learned that his predecessor was presently employed at a local men's club (none too happily). Despite her claim that she and Upton were reconciled, she still carried an enormous chip on her shoulder. Her resentment, she told me, dated back to the period when her older sister, Eunice, had worked for Asenath. Asenath had been forced by Derby, her callous husband, to fire Eunice along with two other devoted servants from Innsmouth. Incidentally, Wendy revealed that her knowledge of the *Necronomicon* was second- or even third-hand, derived from her older sister, who may have gotten all she knew about the dreaded volume from Asenath.

Why Upton sought out Wendy's company was the mother of all mysteries. Besides being fat the girl had a hygiene problem, as did many Innsmouth natives, rumor had it. What was the appeal of this unattractive slob for a man of his position? More than once, to my embarrassment, I overheard him cursing her as a "common Innsmouth slut."

Upton's treatment of myself, brusque and businesslike at best, started to deteriorate rapidly after I got back to Arkham in the fall. Once, after a particularly bitter fight with Wendy involving candlesticks, he threatened to bill me for the cost of fixing the clock I'd wrecked unless I got cracking. Another time, after returning home in a rage because his brown shoes had been polished black at his club by none other than his inept former butler, he called me a wog and an oaf and swore he'd hire a professional if I didn't finish the job soon. When I later asked Wendy what accounted for Upton's impatience, she said she suspected that he now planned to sell the Derby documents. Broken down into small lots, the papers could bring a pretty penny from private collectors. This was disturbing news, to put it mildly. If true it could mean that Derby, though best known as a poet, might never be recognized for what I was coming slowly to realize was his greatest achievement—his short fiction. From reading the manuscripts of scores of unpublished stories I now viewed him as nothing less than the Joseph Hergesheimer of fantasy.

Casting an increasingly long shadow over the uneasy truce at Derby Manor, as over everything else in 1940, was the war in Europe. Any sane person could see that it was only a matter of time before the United States entered on the Allied side. Though my family had emigrated from Iraq when I was a child, I was as eager as any native-born American to serve my country. On the other hand, I wasn't terribly upset when in registering for the peacetime draft I was not classified 1-A on account of my poor eyesight. For the moment I could focus on my researches without fear of disruption. Upton, in contrast, was in fine physical shape (he had resumed a program of exercising around the time his personality had coarsened) and became extremely agitated whenever the subject of the draft came up. It was not that he was afraid of death, he averred, but that he dreaded being shipped overseas for an indefinite period when there was so much to do at home. (Just what he had to do at home that was so important was never clear, in my opinion.)

In any event, I couldn't complain, since schemes to avoid the draft distracted Upton from bugging me about my progress, or lack of it, on my cataloguing chores. During most of the spring semester he was busy trying to twist the arm of a judge he knew with influence on the Arkham Selective Service board. When I returned to Miskatonic for my junior year, it was evident that his campaign had failed, for in a last desperate measure over the summer he had, to qualify for a marital exemption, married Wendy! His relief was palpable, and it wasn't long before he started turning up the heat on me again. If I ever finished he vowed he'd take me for a personal tour of his favorite place in the Maine woods as a reward. Then the Japs bombed

Pearl Harbor, and all bets were off.

Upton's call-up notice arrived the day after Singapore fell. What happened next is rather confused, and if it hadn't been for the string of military catastrophes in the Far East no doubt this new affair would have grabbed the headlines just as the sordid story of Derby's murder had nearly nine years before. As on so many past occasions, Wendy was my primary informant.

According to her, the night before Upton was supposed to leave for Parris Island, he complained of a headache. Shortly thereafter he collapsed in a fit of mirth, losing consciousness. She called an ambulance and he was rushed to the hospital, where he languished in a coma for days. When he finally woke up, he could neither speak nor walk and accepted only liquid nourishment. With her permission, he was transferred to the Arkham Sanitarium.

Had Upton faked the whole thing? I don't think so. If the man had been playing possum surely he would have put up more than the feeble resistance he apparently did when on the second night of his incarceration he was strangled—by a venerable visitor who seemed scarcely capable of knotting his tattered winter scarf around his victim's throat. Yes, the old butler—Soames as he was called—had taken his revenge. Discharged from service at the Miskatonic Club after the incident of the wrong-color shoe polish, Soames had played the waiting game, living like a tramp with other darkly muttering hobos who brood sullenly beneath the bridges of the Miskatonic, until (as he later confessed at his trial) he noticed on the copy of the *Arkham Advertiser* he was using as a blanket a back-page report of his former master's removal to the madhouse. As the police led Soames away from the scene of the crime (and also later when prison officials strapped him into the electric chair), he was heard to repeat, "Azathoth . . . Azathoth . . . Azathoth . . ."

Before reporting for basic training, I had one last meeting with Wendy, at her request. Since she'd already given me her word that she would keep the Derby papers safe until my return, I was confident she had nothing alarming to say. Fortunately, their brief marriage had been no less combative than their earlier relationship, so I wasn't worried that she was planning to fulfill her late husband's greedy desire to sell off the manuscripts after all.

"There is something I want to tell you before you go, Vartan. Ed didn't marry me to get out of the draft, at least that wasn't his main reason. For all his vulgarity he was still a gentleman at heart. When I told him I was, well, you see . . . you see . . ." She struggled a bit longer, and then came the astonishing revelation: "I'm pregnant—with his child!"

I thought I had noticed some abdominal swelling recently, but had attributed it to excessive eating in the aftermath of her husband's breakdown and murder. I was speechless.

"It's a boy, I just know it is! And do you know what I'm going to name him? It was Ed's final request. That last night he made me promise in case anything happened to him that I'd name our son after somebody we'd both admired a whole lot in Innsmouth . . . Asenath's father."

Later that year on Guadalcanal, after some months delay, I received an announcement of the birth, on April 27, of Ephraim Waite Upton.

III. THE HOUSE OF AZATHOTH

I had known Edward Pickman Derby, together with Daniel Upton and his son, Edward Derby Upton, all their tragically foreshortened lives. Members of two of Arkham's most distinguished old families, these three blue bloods shared a similar terrible fate. Derby, the poet-prodigy, after marrying a socially suitable if rather peculiar girl from Innsmouth, declined into madness—only to be murdered for no sane reason by his best friend, Dan Upton. Upton, the respectable architect, was declared unfit to stand trial, dying years later in the very sanitarium where he had emptied all six chambers of his revolver into Derby's brain. Upton junior, never more than a dilettante, after a long period of acting "queer," suffered a sudden mental collapse. Removed to the Arkham Sanitarium (yes, the same asylum as the others), he was there strangled by his former butler.

In my view such sorry results from otherwise exemplary citizens stem from inbreeding amongst the Massachusetts Bay aristocracy, parallel to what one finds in certain remote rural communities farther inland. Ed Upton's decision to marry someone of utterly different background—a physically repulsive Innsmouth girl who was, fortunately, not of the gentry like Derby's wife, Asenath—was no doubt eugenically sound. I have real hope that their son, Ephraim Waite Upton, presently in his teens, will escape the mental illness or family "curse" or whatever you want to call it which struck down his male progenitors. His grandmother, Mrs. Upton, was none too stable either, I might add.

Upon returning to private practice after leaving the bench in 1945 (the rumors that I was forced to retire over charges of favoritism during the war are completely baseless), I immediately offered my legal services to Wendy Babson Upton, Edward Upton's widow and heiress to the combined Derby-Upton fortunes. Thanks to therapy, as well as wartime rationing, she had lost about fifty pounds and thus her self-esteem was such to dispose her to retain me as her counsel. As a longtime family friend, I was particularly concerned that young Ephraim be properly provided for. I was fond of the lad, whose uncanny knack for exciting animals and for predicting bad weather I found especially endearing. In due course I was appointed his trustee.

One of the first items of business was to deal with Edward Derby's literary estate, which Wendy Upton controlled. Before the war a scholarly undergraduate had catalogued the collection of Derby papers in her late husband's possession. Now this same student, re-enrolled at Miskatonic after his discharge from the service, was eager to go ahead with plans to start a publishing company to bring Edward Derby's every written word into print. Wendy had promised this individual, an Armenian fellow, that he could be the editor of Azathoth House (the provisional name of the company), though as she later admitted to me she personally didn't care for his essentially intellectual and aesthetic attitude toward life. Since their understanding was merely verbal, however, she was not obliged to honor it. On my advice she agreed to my interviewing the young man before officially signing him on.

In the event Mr. Vartan Bagdasarian, a veteran of every major Pacific campaign from Guadalcanal to Okinawa, where he fought in the ranks with the "raggedy ass" Marines (college boys too smart for Officer Candidate School), impressed me as being ideally qualified for the job. Three years of combat hell evidently hadn't shaken his emotional detachment a whit. For someone with his iron nerve, managing a small specialty press with all its attendant terrors would be a piece of cake. Furthermore, the kid was willing to work for peanuts. Should his performance prove satisfactory, I hinted, he could look forward to his salary being adjusted accordingly. Azathoth House would be financed with a grant from the Upton-Derby Foundation, of which I was the director. (Postwar changes in the tax laws made it imperative that Wendy protect her income through the establishment of a 501(c)(3) non-profit organization.)

By the end of the year Azathoth House was incorporated by the Commonwealth of Massachusetts. For all his industry and ambition, however, Vartan was still a full-time student, so the editorial program had necessarily to get off to a modest start. The first title on the Azathoth schedule, an obvious choice, was a reissue of Derby's *Azathoth and Other Horrors,* which had gone out of print following the demise of the original Cambridge publisher in the early days of the Depression. Besides expanding the book's contents, Vartan wished to rearrange the poems in a more logical order, but I had to caution him to keep the format of the "new, textually corrected" edition very close to the previous one in order not to leave Azathoth House open to claims from certain parties in Innsmouth. These parties, relatives of Asenath Waite, were considering appealing against the earlier court ruling in order to obtain what they regarded as their fair share of the Derby estate. Profits from the sale of any new Derby publication might just push them over the line to file suit. Given this threat, *Azathoth and Other Horrors* had to be reprinted essentially as it stood, while plans for an edition of the stories were put on the shelf.

In the event, when it appeared in the spring of '46, the Azathoth House edition of the noxious nightmare lyrics of the "Bard of Arkham," as he was billed, didn't garner much in the way of either notice or sales. While I'm no expert on contemporary poetry, Derby's lush verse struck me as decidedly old-fashioned and obscure, based on what little of it I could force myself to read. When I expressed this view to Vartan, he assured me that Derby's reputation would ultimately rest on his fiction, which revealed his genius to far better advantage. Privately, I suspected that this eccentric author would never be more than a sort of literary cove, appealing mainly to an adolescent sensibility.

During that summer I was in the habit of dropping into the offices of Azathoth House, which occupied a two-room suite in the Peaslee Building downtown, every other week or so—unannounced. Business being slow, Vartan didn't have a whole lot to do except fill the occasional order for *Azathoth and Other Horrors,* and I wanted to make sure the kid wasn't abusing his trust as editor. He was apt to be out doing "research" at the Miskatonic library, where the Derby collection now resided, though I suspected he was really at work on his own projects, such as his senior honors thesis. On this particular afternoon I found him in, his desk piled high with heaps of what appeared to be old letters.

"How do you do, sir," said the Azathoth House editor, setting down a handwritten sheet covered with a familiar scrawl.

"You look like the cat who swallowed the proverbial canary, Vartan. What's up?"

"In the mail today, from the doctor who attended Justin Geoffrey—"

"Justin who?"

"Justin Geoffrey. He was a close correspondent of Edward Derby."

"So?"

"Surely, Judge, you have heard of the notorious Baudelairian poet, author of *The People of the Monolith,* who died screaming in a madhouse in 1926 after a visit to a sinister, ill-regarded village in Hungary?"

"Sounds like Ed's type."

"As I was saying, in today's mail there was a large package, postmarked Budapest, containing hundreds of letters written by Derby to Geoffrey from 1920 on—together with carbons of Geoffrey's side of the correspondence, up until the day before his death!"

"You mean to tell me a screaming madman was able to keep up a regular correspondence?"

"Well, I'll admit some of the later letters aren't all that lucid. But I have to say, from what I've perused so far, the theories articulated by Haeckel, Russell, Santayana, and other philosophers of the early modern period are but childish babble compared to the breadth of argument of these two *fantaisistes.* Especially piquant is their dialogue, or debate if you will, on the nature of Azathoth."

"How about that."

Azathoth, incidentally, is the name of the principal god in Derby's mythological pantheon. It is not Derby's invention, being of Assyrian origin, per Miskatonic's then chief librarian, Dr. Henry Armitage, who so informed me at the reception honoring Wendy for donating her late husband's friend's papers to the library.

"I estimate both sides of the correspondence will come to about five hundred and fifty book pages," Vartan continued, "assuming we use nine-point type."

"Hold your horses, kid. Let's not jump the gun. Why don't you save this idea for our next editorial meeting."

"But that's not till September!"

"Which gives you the rest of the summer to work up your proposal."

I saw it as my duty to check Vartan's enthusiasm whenever it threatened to run away with him. While I was willing to concede that a collection of Derby's letters might present fewer legal problems than other potential

projects, I felt the matter could wait until Wendy and Ephraim returned in
the fall from their vacation in Maine. Wendy, as president of Azathoth
House, had final approval of all editorial decisions.

Shortly after Labor Day the three of us gathered at Wendy's, the former
home of the Derbys, to discuss the Azathoth House list. Vartan announced
he'd already prepared a 2,000-page transcript, fully annotated and foot-
noted, of a Derby-Geoffrey letters volume, while Wendy in her turn suggested we publish a tribute to Asenath Waite, by a former headmistress of
Kingsport's Hall School, who'd joined her as companion on their recent
Maine tour. I for my part had received a couple of unsolicited submissions,
one a critical study entitled *A Literary Ptolemy*, the other a personal memoir,
Edward Derby: Pampered Poseur. Associational stuff, in other words, of interest only to hardcore fans.

We had barely begun to discuss the merits of these various projects
when we heard the front door slam open. In the next second young Ephraim came racing into the drawing room where we were seated and threw
himself into his mother's lap.

"What's the matter, honey?" asked Wendy.

"Oh, Mommy, it was horrid, just horrid," wailed the child.

"What was horrid, my pet?"

"The doggies—the library man—he hurt himself!"

The three of us did our best to console the boy, wondering what on
earth could have given him such a fright. Then the butler announced that
one of Arkham's finest was at the door, and we soon learned the sequel.
The officer, a member of the special branch assigned to the Miskatonic
campus, had been on patrol in the vicinity of the library when he heard
loud barking from the direction of the kennel. For years, at the insistence of
Dr. Armitage, the library had maintained a pack of foxhounds for security
purposes—about as egregious a misuse of university funds as one could
imagine. (The old fool should have been forced to retire years ago, but such
is the power of entrenched bureaucrats.) Ephraim, taking a detour through
the campus after nursery school let out, had wandered past the kennel.
There's no evidence the youngster deliberately taunted the dogs, but their
frantic yapping soon brought out the white-bearded fossil himself. Just as
Armitage reached the kennel, the dumb brutes burst through the gate and
knocked him to the ground. The pack came to an abrupt halt, apparently
confused by the collapse of their master. As the elderly librarian remained
prone, they raised a lugubrious howl. A minute later a member of the medi-

cal faculty on the scene pronounced him dead of a heart attack.

On hearing this somber news, Wendy sent Ephraim up to his room. A heavy silence ensued, broken by the officer to inquire whether it was usual to allow a four-year-old to walk home from school alone. Wendy replied that her son was extremely clever for his age and could perfectly well watch out for himself, thank you very much. The man seemed to accept this at face value, before returning to campus to make his report.

Further editorial discussion was clearly out of the question, and for the next hour we talked about how best to cheer up Ephraim after this traumatic episode. In the end we agreed to permit him the trip to Innsmouth he had been pestering his mother for ever since he could mouth intelligible words. But who was to take him? Letting him walk home from school unattended was one thing, but to allow him to journey to another town by himself was quite another. Wendy was busy with garden club duties most weekends (for years she'd been avoiding her poor relations in Innsmouth anyway), while Vartan claimed pressing school work (his senior paper, all that stood between him and his degree, was due by the end of October), so I was the obvious volunteer. As I have said, I was fond of the lad, and though past my prime I have yet to reach the level of decrepitude of, say, the late Henry Armitage.

The following Saturday, as it happened, was the annual Innsmouth Regatta—the perfect occasion for an outing to the rumor-shadowed seaport. Ephraim's sniffles dried up instantly when I joined him in his room and proposed the idea. That morning we picked up a picnic lunch provided by Wendy's chef and set off in the old Packard, in which Edward and Asenath used to enjoy extended motor trips, along the Innsmouth road. The sky was sunny and clear, promising perfect weather for boaters and spectators alike.

In the course of the ride across Cape Ann, Ephraim questioned me closely about Innsmouth, or to be precise its recent history. It was a puzzle why the boy took an interest in such a rundown and decadent place, though he'd always been proud that his namesake, Ephraim Waite, hailed from there. He smiled when I told him the war had given the local economy a badly needed shot in the arm. Yes, Ephraim was a most remarkable little chap, and like any bright and sensitive child he understood, I sensed, much more of the adult conversation he overheard than he let on.

We parked in the lot of the Marsh refinery, the town's principal employer, and found a spot on a grassy bluff near a waterfall to spread out our picnic. The Army Corps of Engineers had dredged the harbor and rebuilt the lighthouse, as part of the coastal defense against U-boats, and we had a fine view, aided by binoculars, of all the activity out on the water. First came the swimming races to Devil's Reef, visible as a long, black line far out to sea, then the fleet of the Innsmouth Yacht Club began to prepare for their start off the ancient stone breakwater than enclosed the harbor. Dozens of pleasure craft were anchored in the vicinity of the committee boat, their gaily colored pennants streaming in a light but steady wind.

Then, so typical of the New England shore, fair weather suddenly gave way to foul. As the cracked bell from one of Innsmouth's several church towers chimed the noon hour, the sky darkened, despite the lack of clouds, and the breeze freshened. The formerly placid sea filled with white caps. A series of horn blasts from the committee boat alerted the sailors that the race was cancelled. Hurricane season was not yet passed, and in a moment of panic I thought of the terrible storm which devastated Rhode Island in '38. My little cohort, on the other hand, seemed almost elated, too young to appreciate the danger. I hurriedly packed up the picnic things, but as I started for the car Ephraim threw a tantrum and insisted on staying. To my horror I saw that huge waves were now battering boats onto the breakwater, to which small groups of sodden human figures were clinging as best they could. We were witness to a major marine disaster!

Through the binoculars I watched in morbid fascination as the situation worsened, until I remembered myself and seized the boy by the arm and hauled him, howling in protest, back to the parking lot. We made it home without incident, for the storm appeared to have been curiously localized and of short if intense duration. Exhausted, Ephraim went right up to his room for a nap without complaint. It was front-page news in the next day's *Arkham Advertiser,* which reported that more than thirty people were drowned or missing in the aftermath of the "killer squall." I couldn't help noticing that among the dead were the names of every member of Asenath Waite's clan who had threatened to bring suit. They'd been having a well-publicized family reunion aboard one of the first vessels to be smashed to pieces against the breakwater, an overloaded "stink-pot" with an inadequate supply of life-jackets.

Even the darkest tragedy can have its bright spots, and I realized that at last Azathoth House could proceed with issuing the fiction of Edward Derby. I so informed Vartan when next I dropped by the Peaslee Building.

"Good Lord!" exclaimed the Azathoth House editor. "This is a most welcome development, Judge, most welcome indeed—and so unexpected. What a fluke of fate!"

"I thought you'd be pleased, Vartan."

"Of course, one has to sympathize with the Waite family . . ."

"Save your tears, kid. They were nothing but degenerates—bug-eyed, powerboat-loving, litigious degenerates."

"I suppose this means we ought to put the Derby-Geoffrey letters on the back burner until we publish the first fiction volume."

"Sounds okay to me, kid."

Vartan had already outlined a tentative table of contents for a three-volume edition of Edward Derby's complete tales, and promised to get started on pulling together the manuscripts as soon as he finished his thesis.

Over the next month young Ephraim made increasingly frequent after-school visits to the Azathoth House offices, where he didn't hesitate to offer the editor his advice. Having been something of a child prodigy himself, Vartan had mixed feelings at best, I surmised, about interference from one so precocious. In particular, he resented having to take time away from his own projects to attend to Ephraim's whims, such as having a look at the *Necronomicon,* once more made available to qualified scholars on orders from Dr. Armitage's successor. Naturally, the boy couldn't consult the dreaded volume on his own, and afterwards Vartan grumbled to me in private about having to spend an entire afternoon in the library reading room translating the Latin text for the four-year-old's benefit. His choicer epithets put me in mind of W. C. Fields on Charlie McCarthy or Baby Leroy.

Since Wendy signed his paychecks, however, it behooved Vartan to humor her son. On his side Ephraim appeared to relish his special relationship with "Uncle Vart," whom he begged to take him on a camping trip to Chesuncook, Maine, in time for Halloween. In August he and his mother had stayed only at posh coastal resorts, and for a change he wanted "to really rough it" (or "weally wuff it," at this stage the youth having as much trouble with his r's as Elmer Fudd). Again, despite the débâcle in Innsmouth, Wendy and I agreed to let the lad indulge his travel lust. Vartan was less than enthusiastic at the prospect, but he had no excuse this time, having just turned in his honors paper, "Textual Variations in Edward Derby's 'Azathoth': The Narrative Poem, Not the Prose Fragment." To appease him, Wendy promised to hook up the pair with a distant Derby cousin, whose lakefront house could serve as a base or refuge in that remote forested region. In addition, she could allow Vartan to use the old Packard. In the end, with ill-concealed distaste, he acquiesced.

*   *   *

The day after Halloween the telegram came from Jacob Lamar Derby. After spending the night in the woods, Vartan had returned in a dazed and disoriented state. Ephraim was fine, but Vartan could scarcely talk and was in no shape to drive home. Would I mind traveling to Chesuncook to retrieve "the lost boys"? It took nearly a whole day for me and Wendy's chauffeur to get there by car. Since it was so late and we of the relief party had neglected in our haste to bring camping gear, we all bunked down for the night on Derby's living-room floor. (The spare bedrooms were loaded with equipment to do with a device he called a "Zann transonifier." Evidently, our host was some kind of crackpot inventor.) A series of whistling noises outdoors and a metallic banging in the cellar interrupted what was otherwise a good night's sleep only intermittently.

In the morning the chauffeur took the Packard, while the two erstwhile campers rode with me in my Studebaker. In response to questions about their stay in the woods, Vartan grunted in what struck me as a feeble attempt at human speech, while Ephraim said in his childish lisp that they had "weally, weally wuffed it." When I asked the boy what had happened to Uncle Vart, he began to giggle and couldn't stop giggling until we were past Augusta. At the risk of imposing an overly adult interpretation on his reaction, I gathered he extracted an almost obscene and zestful irony from his companion's present situation.

Back in Arkham, I immediately scheduled an appointment for Vartan with my personal physician. While a thorough examination turned up no physical abnormalities, a subsequent psychological test indicated that he might be suffering from some peculiar personality disorder. Perhaps the horrors of his war experiences, so long suppressed, were finally catching up with him. He soon regained full use of his tongue, though he spoke in a strange, halting accent, which he had never betrayed before despite his foreign birth. It was as if English were now his second language.

Vartan did not object when I recommended he take a couple of weeks off from his Azathoth House duties, at half pay. During this supposed rest period he engaged in intense study at the Miskatonic library, where Ephraim invariably joined him after school. The two became inseparable, like brothers, though oddly enough it was Vartan who acted out the adoring junior role. If he was trying to impress Wendy, this shift in attitude did not go unnoticed. By December he was living in the apartment over her four-car garage, which she was only too glad to rent to him below the market rate.

Vartan began to act less cerebrally, more on a primitive or instinctual level, as evidenced by his change of editorial direction. In contrast to his original conception, he now recommended that we collect Derby's fiction in a single omnibus volume. Wendy and I approved this new format, and in the fall of '47 Azathoth House duly published *Forever Azathoth,* a title deliberately chosen to evoke a steamy bestseller of the day. The following year there appeared *Son of Azathoth,* a dozen or so posthumous collaborations by Edward Derby and, in smaller type, Vartan Bagdasarian. Since he had merely fulfilled Derby's obvious intentions for fragmented or otherwise incomplete works, Vartan was content to accept second billing. He seemed especially gratified when one astute reviewer deemed this second story collection superior to the first.

In 1949 Azathoth House published *The Derby-Geoffrey Letters: 1920–1926,* edited by Vartan Bagdasarian, who without any prompting had cut their correspondence down to about a fifth of the total and jettisoned the scholarly apparatus. Later that same year the house issued Vartan's senior honors thesis, which he had extensively revised and augmented since submitting it for his degree. I recall at the time his saying he hoped the *Miskatonic Library Bulletin* would run it as an abridged serial, but he soon had loftier ambitions. I have nothing against "vanity" publishing per se—and neither did Vartan, who was perfectly willing to put aside a percentage of his salary in order to subsidize *Edward Derby and His "Azathoth."* (Happily, he was also willing to drop the pompous academic title.) By 1955 the book had earned back its costs. Other projects, including a series of poetry volumes in homage to the late Edward Derby, underwritten by Miskatonic's Dead Edward Derby Society, as well as the Asenath tribute Wendy had been pushing, by her friend the former headmistress of the Hall School (feminist hagiography, in my opinion, not that I said so to my client), helped fill up the warehouse, located in industrial Bolton.

If on the surface Azathoth House had managed to achieve a measure of stability in its first decade, that was more than you could say for the emotional lives of the people behind it. As a wealthy widow, Wendy mingled freely in Arkham society, despite a certain crudity of manner which no amount of etiquette training could efface. To her credit, she was able to maintain her slimmer, postwar figure and with makeup, judiciously applied, highlight her less unattractive features. As a result, she had no lack of male admirers. Little Ephraim kept careful track of the gentlemen callers who most evenings appeared at the door, laden with gladioli and Schrafft's chocolates. Wendy confided that she preferred to play the singles game, but this may have been sour grapes, for as soon as there was any hint of possible wedding bells, invariably a terrible accident, often fatal, would befall the unlucky suitor. For example, one fellow, a member of the Foxfield horsey set who'd presented her with a diamond ring only the night before, fell off his polo pony during a match, whereupon all the beasts of the field, as if suddenly maddened, raced back and forth uncontrollably over his body, trampling him to a pulp. Just yards away, among the horrified onlookers, were Wendy and young Ephraim.

Poor Ephraim! By the onset of adolescence he had witnessed enough human pain to last a lifetime. No doubt his sang-froid, as the French say, helped carry him through. In truth, the only time I can remember the boy becoming visibly agitated was during the period, around his fifteenth birthday, when of all people Vartan started to pay court to Wendy! In retrospect, this should have come as no surprise. Among males of suitable age, Vartan had been the one constant and unassuming presence. Too, in recent years he had developed a suavity, an ease with women, hitherto conspicuously lacking. Perhaps, like his hero Edward Derby, he was moved to affect the role of autumnal gallant. One day, apropos of nothing, he had the audacity to remark that what he liked best about living above Wendy's garage was the unobstructed view of her bedroom window. For her part, Wendy did not discourage his belated attentions. She even admitted to me, after a couple of drinks, that she found his accent sexy and that she didn't always bother to draw the curtains when she undressed at night.

Ephraim, on the other hand, was beside himself. For years he had been used to Uncle Vart going along with his every whim. Now, when he proposed that the two of them take a camping trip to Maine for old time's sake, Vartan merely laughed—or so I later heard from Wendy, to whom he had run in tears. (In many respects he was still quite immature, in spite of his ability to look after himself from a very early age.) In an effort to make it up to the boy, and indirectly to his mother, Vartan agreed to give him driving lessons. Ephraim had just gotten his learner's permit, and was eager to test his road skills in the old Packard. An instructional date was set for the last day of April.

The following morning the telegram arrived from Chesuncook. This time they were both all right and would return to Arkham by evening. Though Vartan had hurt his head, he was fully capable of making the long drive home. I phoned Wendy, who said she'd been at a party the night before and hadn't even noticed Ephraim's absence. Now that he was a teen-ager, she felt it important that he assert his independence even more boldly than before. She didn't want to go down in history as one of those over-bearing, overprotective mothers.

Ephraim's explanation that he had persuaded Vartan at the last minute to drive up to Maine after all wasn't entirely convincing. My suspicions were further aroused when I later received report that the Packard had been seen speeding north out of Arkham with a boyish figure at the wheel and no passenger. As for Vartan, he claimed to be afflicted by some sort of amne-sia, brought on by the bad fall he'd taken in the woods. According to Eph-raim, Uncle Vart had slipped and knocked his head against one of the Indian standing stones common to the region. He could remember prepara-tions for the trip, but when he tried to piece together subsequent events it became clear he was confusing things with their first Maine expedition more than ten years earlier. Not only that, he was once again speaking in the flat American tones of his adopted state of Indiana!

As before I sent Vartan to my personal physician, who confirmed that the editor and scholar's memory loss extended back to the fall of 1946. Did this mean he could no longer do his job at Azathoth House? Or would he be able to adapt despite his debility? At my suggestion Vartan agreed to pursue a course of psychoanalysis, four times a week, until his condition improved. Azathoth House would foot forty percent of the bills for the first month, but after that . . . Well, we'd just have to see whether it made any sense to keep him on the payroll. I informed Vartan he shouldn't feel obliged to visit the office during this period, but I can't say I was too sur-prised the next time I dropped by the Peaslee Building to find him at his desk, albeit moaning with his face in his hands.

"Good afternoon, Vartan. Feeling better?"

"Good Lord, Judge, you startled me!"

"Head still sore?"

"It's horrible, just horrible. I can't believe it. I must have been out of my mind."

Clearly the Azathoth House editor had a long way to go toward total recovery. In front of him was an open copy of *Forever Azathoth,* scored with ink markings.

"At the library this morning I was finally able to check the original manuscripts. Just as I suspected, there must be literally hundreds if not thousands of textual errors, most of them deliberately introduced. In those few cases where a story had seen print, the corrupt magazine version was favored in every instance!"

"Does it really matter?"

"The fiction of Edward Derby remains for all intents and purposes unpublished!"

"Simmer down, Vartan. It can't be that bad."

"But it is that bad, I tell you! *Forever Azathoth* is a disgrace, sir, but it is a proud paragon of the scholar's craft in comparison to, to—I can scarcely bear to name it—*Son of Azathoth*." He made the book sound like some repellent reptile.

"Come on. Didn't at least one reviewer say *Son of Azathoth* was even better than the first Derby volume?"

Vartan groaned. What had happened to that once supreme confidence (bordering on arrogance) in his editorial judgment?

"Then there's what purports to be a 'revision' of my honors thesis," he continued. "Complete rubbish! A close textual analysis has been transformed into a mishmash of amateur psychologizing and secondhand reminiscence. What could have possessed me?"

"You tell me, kid. You're the Derby expert."

"These editorial changes aren't even in my handwriting! Didn't anyone notice?"

"Vartan, you haven't been yourself. You shouldn't get overexcited."

"Worst of all is the volume of Derby-Geoffrey letters. They've been whittled down to a farrago of schoolboy maunderings. Every significant philosophical exchange has been deleted! The entire debate on the nature of Azathoth—"

Again Vartan hid his face in his hands. He was beyond speech.

"Maybe you'd better take the rest of the day off," I said.

"What have I done?" he muttered, as he stood up to leave. "What have I done?"

"Nothing that the science of psychotherapy can't help you put right," I answered, escorting him to the door.

The next day Vartan did not show up at his analyst's. He missed his appointment for the following day as well. On the third day I began to worry, when Wendy reported she'd noticed no light in the garage apartment for the previous two nights. (Needless to say, Vartan had exhibited no signs of amorousness since returning from Maine.) On the evening of the fourth day, accompanied by Ephraim, I tried the apartment door. It wasn't locked.

I had wanted to investigate alone, in case there was anything unpleasant to be uncovered, but as usual the boy had gotten his way.

The place was empty. A half-drunk cup of tea rested on the heating coil, as if its owner were expecting to return at any moment. It was Ephraim who found the note. The first statement, he was sure, derived from one of the Geoffrey letters to Derby: "As for the semi-stable shoggoth brain, these multi-cellular protoplasmic masses are not, like Azathoth, 'without mind' or 'mindless,' but can acquire a dangerous degree of accidental intelligence." The second part was just as cryptic, reminiscent of Edward Derby's wildest poetic flights, but at least suggestive that Vartan Bagdasarian had disappeared of his own free will: "Last night I dreamed. Doubt Dr. Zimmerman will understand. The pit of the shoggoths. The Hooded Thing. Iä! Shub-Niggurath! I shall seek the House of Azathoth."

IV. Azathoth in Analysis

As a psychoanalyst practicing in Arkham, Massachusetts, I get my share of odd cases—when I get any at all. New Englanders tend to be a dour, stoic lot, viewing modern therapy with suspicion if not outright hostility. Those few souls who do find their way to my couch usually find it difficult to talk about their traumas. Thus the patient capable of speaking freely is of more than especial interest. One such patient, let us call him "Aa" (for reasons I'll explain shortly), represents perhaps the oddest case in my experience. Though we met for only a handful of sessions before his abrupt disappearance, he opened up to me hitherto uncharted realms of the human psyche—inner worlds so strange and wonderful as to demand their disclosure beyond an audience of my professional peers.

The friend who made the original referral, a retired judge and fellow member of the Miskatonic Club, informed me of the bare biographical facts. Of foreign birth, Aa had moved to this country with his parents as a young child. A Miskatonic Univeristy graduate and World War II veteran, he was the editor of a local small press specializing in books by and about the poet Edward Derby (a name I haven't bothered to change, since Derby is all but unknown outside an adolescent cult—hence there's little risk of violating patient confidentiality). At our first meeting, when I asked Aa to tell me about his family background, he replied, "What is there to say?" Given this resistance, I decided to focus on the present, that is, the immediate circumstances which had prompted him to seek my help.

"I realize you're here on the advice of others," I said, "but that's no excuse for being evasive. What the heck's been bugging you, anyway?"

"Sorry, doc. I'm afraid I haven't been myself lately."

"You haven't been yourself, huh. Then who exactly have you been?"

"I don't know. Rip Van Winkle? It's as if I've just woken up from a long sleep. A decade-long sleep."

The patient went on to explain that he could remember nothing of what he had done from the time he took a camping trip to the Maine woods in the fall of '46 until his return from a second camping trip to the same spot ten and a half years later. Yet he had seemingly performed his usual editorial duties in the interim at "Azathoth House."

"Azathoth? Ha! That's a funny name."

"It is in fact a very ancient name, perhaps Hebraic, perhaps Egyptian, or even Assyrian in origin. The etymology is a matter of dispute among Edward Derby scholars."

"Derby's that obscure poet who's become an object of fan worship at Miskatonic, right?"

"Indeed, though I believe his place in the pantheon of American writers will ultimately rest on his prose fiction."

For the rest of the session the patient surveyed the bizarre life and violent death of his literary hero, as well as Derby's major works, notably the narrative poem "Azathoth," not to be confused with the prose fragment of the same name. He had catalogued the poet's every scrap of paper and wished to see the entire Derby oeuvre published in a uniform multi-volume edition. It was obvious that Aa identified with this pathetic father figure to a dangerously neurotic degree.

At the next session Azathoth became our focus—the godlike entity, that is, as opposed to Edward Derby's various writings with that title. Even a Jungian or an Adlerian would have had no trouble interpreting Azathoth as a stronger, more masculine father figure than Derby himself. Aa agreed that an important therapeutic goal would be to transfer his infantile obsession from the fallible human being to the boundless daemon-sultan which blasphemes and bubbles at the center of nethermost infinity.

"Boy, you've really gone bananas over this Azathoth character," I remarked. "Have you ever thought of yourself as his avatar?"

"You mean do I regard myself as Azathoth's incarnation after the Hindu manner?"

"No, the Freudian manner. Look, I know you're of Asian ancestry, but you have to remember you're undergoing psychoanalysis, not a course in Eastern mysticism. Okay?"

"Pardon me, doc. I keep forgetting."

"'Azathoth's avatar' . . . a phrase worthy of Ed Derby himself, don't you think? I trust you won't object if I refer to you as that in any written study I make of your case."

"Not at all."

"May I call you 'Aa' for short?"

"Whatever suits you is fine with me."

With this kind of cooperation it was no surprise to find Aa eager to share further revelations at our third session. He had dreamed the previous night—of traveling through a long underground tunnel that led to a deep pit containing a "shoggoth."

"What in tarnation is a shoggoth?" I asked.

"A multi-cellular protoplasmic mass generally used for menial labor. I might add that though technically all but brainless, a shoggoth is capable of accidental intelligence."

"How do you know that?"

"Uh, the shoggoth told me—via telepathic communication."

For the remainder of the hour we speculated on the epistemological issue of conversing with an oversized amoeba whose I.Q. in theory barely exceeded its hat size. Given the shoggoth's great plasticity this number could be widely variable. The next day Aa provided an important insight. In his latest dreams he had returned to the underground pit, where he now recognized not only that he was dealing with multiple individuals (en masse, shoggoths are hard to tell apart) but that in many instances their primitive brains had been supplanted by superior minds from outside.

"How can you be so sure?" I asked. "Couldn't it have been a clumsy attempt to impress you, to seem smarter than they really were?"

"I don't think so, doc. In this morning's final dream sequence, just before I woke up, I looked down and saw a shapeless congeries of viscous, faintly self-luminous globules . . . In that instant I realized I was one of those superior minds from outside—in a shoggoth body."

"Weren't you frightened?"

"Not particularly."

I had to assume that as a leatherneck who had fought in every major battle in the Pacific from Guadalcanal to Okinawa, and as an editor who had to contend daily with the tribulations of running a small press, Aa was hardened to such extremes of physical and mental dislocation. In fact, in what was to prove our final session, he confessed that in subsequent dreams he had looked forward to engaging other shoggoth-bound minds in telepathic dialogue, until he discovered that no one was really interested in listening. The captive consciousnesses with whom he came into contact cared only to boast about their respective intellectual achievements— scholarly publications, favorable reviews, library sales, and so forth. Disillusioned, Aa had to accept that the pit of the shoggoths was filled with the equivalent of academic bores. As a member of the Miskatonic Club, with its surfeit of professors from the university, I know this breed all too well!

"There was a hooded thing that bleated 'Kamog! Kamog!'" said Aa. "That was the name of the imprint that was publishing his monograph on secret covens."

When the patient did not show up for his next scheduled session, I rang his office and left a message with the youth covering the phone. I later spoke with the retired judge, who confirmed that the Azathoth House editor had not shown up for work that day. When he missed yet another session, I became concerned. Some important questions remained unanswered. How was mind exchange effected and by whom? What was Azathoth's relationship to the shoggoths? And most vitally, were Aa's dreams repressed memories?

At week's end my friend the judge called to say he had been to Aa's apartment, where he had discovered a note indicating that our boy had left town. The reference to seeking the "House of Azathoth" was especially suggestive. The two of us agreed to meet that evening for a drink at the Miskatonic Club to discuss the situation.

"We have two issues to consider, the way I see it," the judge said over our brandy snifters. "First, why did he run off, and second, where did he go?"

"Aa's efforts to transfer his identification from Edward Derby to Azathoth may have been premature, triggering a fugue state," I replied.

"At our last meeting the kid was upset about some trivial editorial business, nothing that in my view should've pushed him over the edge."

"We can only speculate on the answer to your first question until he turns up again. Any ideas where he could have gone?"

"I have a hunch he's returned to Maine, to his favorite campsite, though what the connection is with the 'House of Azathoth' is beyond me. Did he give any clue in his final therapy session?"

"His subconscious afforded many marvelous glimpses of a place he called 'the pit of the shoggoths,' but we had yet to resolve whether it was a metaphor of the imagination or had a counterpart in the objective world. 'House' may of course refer to the domain of the positive father figure Aa was moving toward accepting."

Over cigars we resolved to travel at our earliest mutual convenience to Chesuncook, Maine, in search of the fugitive. I confess that financial considerations as much as concern for Aa's welfare motivated me to take this active step. As I indicated earlier, while many Arkham residents are in dire need of my services, lamentably few are disposed to visit my consulting rooms.

As it turned out, we had to accommodate ourselves to the schedule of a third party, the teenager I had spoken to when I tried to reach Aa at Azathoth House. The judge explained that he had not wanted Eph to accompany us because the lad, a ninth-grader at Arkham High, needed to study for final exams. In the end, however, he had relented, persuaded by the boy's mother, who had pointed out how attached her son was to the vanished editor. When the judge mentioned this woman's name, I was reminded that I had treated her during the war for a self-esteem problem.

Early one Saturday morning in June, the judge and I rendezvoused at the lovely Georgian mansion near the Miskatonic campus that was home to Eph and his mother—and former home of Edward Derby. It had been agreed that we would take the family car, a vintage Packard, without the chauffeur. Having recently obtained his road license, Eph was more than happy to do the driving honors. I have to say the youth impressed me with his brash self-confidence, wholly uncharacteristic for someone in the awkward and unattractive phase of adolescence. The judge rode up front, next to Eph at the wheel, while I stretched out in the classic vehicle's capacious rear seat.

From this position, rather against my will, I found myself suddenly in the role of family counselor. We had driven north out of Arkham in silence, but as we passed through Newburyport Eph started to pester the judge to let him drop out of school and assume the editorship of Azathoth House, where he had been working part-time. In a friendly but firm manner the older man advised him at least to finish high school before taking such a precipitate step. There were higher callings in life than running a small press devoted to a weirdo poet, the judge added. Wouldn't Dr. Zimmerman agree?

Not wishing to appear as yet another hostile adult to the lad, I did not support the judge outright, but complimented them both on the sincerity of their respective points of view. I stressed the value of maintaining an open dialogue, and went so far as to offer to schedule an appointment for them both when they might continue to discuss the issue that divided them within a formal analytic setting. While I refrained from saying so, the two had clearly bonded in a parent-child relationship the development of which would be fascinating to follow as Eph increasingly asserted his independence.

The judge replied that, chances were, once we located Aa, he would want to resume his duties at Azathoth House, so the question was probably moot. Eph muttered something unintelligible and thereafter lapsed into a sulk. In the time it took to travel the distance from Portsmouth to Augusta, the judge held forth (none too subtly) on various gentlemen he knew from the Miskatonic Club who had prospered in their careers thanks to a high school diploma.

I think we were all relieved when, after a full day on the road, we reached our destination, the lakefront home of Jacob Lamar Derby, whom the judge had alerted to expect us. An eccentric inventor and distant cousin of the late poet, our host led us on a trail through the underbrush to a secluded clearing on his property where we could pitch our tent. (Before leaving us, he apologized that the house itself was too cluttered to permit our sleeping there.) We hurriedly set up camp in the lengthening shadows cast by the sun sinking below the tops of the surrounding pines. I am, to put it mildly, no nature buff, though I did not admit this to my companions, who were not shy in expressing their excitement at spending the night close to the wildest, deepest, and least explored forest belt in Maine. The judge felt confident that the woods held the key to Aa's disappearance, while Eph was eager to make an early start in the morning. Despite his having done all the driving that day, the youth betrayed no sign of tiredness.

After a supper of baked beans warmed in the can over an open fire, the judge told a number of ghost stories, which though quite conventional in concept and lacking in psychological complexity were received more warmly than his earlier tales of exemplary Miskatonic Club members who had made good through education. It was almost midnight before we finally doused the fire and in the darkness changed into our pajamas. Inside the tent I flopped down on what I hoped was my sleeping bag and in an instant was dead to the world. An instant later I felt a foot in my ribs and heard the judge yelling to me to roll over.

As one who likes to sleep late on weekends, I was not surprised to find myself alone in the tent when I awoke the next morning. I assumed my fellow campers were already up and brewing the coffee—but why did I smell nothing? Outside I saw no evidence of breakfast preparations or of the judge and Eph. The sun was well above tree level. The only sound was the cry of a distant raptor. At first I figured they were making a preliminary scouting expedition and would be returning at any moment, but after an hour I began to face the fact that they had abandoned me. A solid breakfast of leftover beans helped me cope with my feelings of rejection.

After another hour I was dealing with feelings of inadequacy, bordering on panic. I feared my comrades had gotten lost in the woods and I would have to raise the alarm. With only one or two false turns through the brush I found my way back to the inventor's house, where I was reassured to see the Packard parked out front. Then I remembered that Eph had the car keys. Escape from that desolate spot might not be so easy.

I considered knocking on Derby's door, through which I could hear a great deal of metallic clanging and banging, but decided on balance not to disturb the man in the midst of his labors. I walked back to the campsite, with the idea of searching Eph's belongings for the car keys.

To my immense relief when I emerged into the clearing I spotted the missing duo standing by the tent. But something was not quite right. The judge's jaw hung slack. As I drew closer I could see that his clothes were torn and stuck with burrs. Dried blood covered the side of his face. When I called out if he was all right, he made no answer.

"What the heck's going on here, Eph?" I asked. "What's the matter with the judge?"

"I'm afraid the judge has hurt himself. During our walk this morning he stumbled into an Indian standing stone and hit his head. Some of these stones are almost hidden in the undergrowth and the forest floor can be slippery."

I had the sense that Eph, like many guilt-ridden teenagers, was not telling the whole truth, but in the circumstances I decided it best not to challenge him. The judge required immediate medical attention, and while I am of course an M.D. it had been years since I had treated mere physical trauma. The judge retained consciousness, if not his powers of speech, and we were able to hustle him with little trouble out of the clearing in the direction of civilization.

This time I did not hesitate to pound on Jacob Lamar Derby's door—

loud enough to compete with the noise inside the house. Eventually, Derby did emerge. He took one look at the judge and offered to ring the town farm. Though the nearest hospital was a hundred miles to the south, he told us, Chesuncook did maintain a small lunatic asylum, capable of handling minor emergencies. As a matter of fact, his cousin had once been held there. At his request we waited on the porch while he returned inside to phone.

A minute later he came back to report that the staff at the farm would appreciate our transporting the patient. Their "ambulance" (actually a pickup truck, according to Derby) was still in the shop for repairs. Our host was glad to come along and show us the way. Since Eph insisted on staying close to the judge, the two of them rode in the back while I took the wheel of the old Packard with the backwoods eccentric beside me.

As I negotiated the car down the bumpy, rutted dirt road toward the town center, Derby shifted restlessly in his seat. I intuited that something concerned him other than the judge's accident or Chesuncook's modest public services. Being a typical Yankee, however, he was too inhibited to reveal the source of his pain. At the madhouse, a Victorian pile with a high tower and spiked fence out of a Charles Addams cartoon, we delivered the judge into the care of the on-duty physician. He allowed Eph to accompany the patient into the treatment room, while Derby and I waited in the reception area.

I was on the verge of picking up a year-old *Reader's Digest* when my companion seized my arm and said, "Doc, I gotta talk to ya."

"I suspected you were fretting over something, Derby. Speak right up. Repression is unhealthy."

"I promised I wouldn't tell anybody, but—"

"Who did you promise?"

"That foreign fella, who hitched up here from Awkum."

"You mean the editor of Azathoth House?" I repeated Aa's real name.

"Yeah, that's the one. We had quite a chat about his job at Aza-what's House, how they were publishin' or rather ruinin' cousin Ed's stories and all."

"When was this?"

"Just a couple of days ago, right before he left town. He was pretty sure you or the judge or somebody would come lookin' for him, but it was too late. He'd found what he'd come to the woods for."

"Which was?"

Before Derby could answer, the attending physician returned to announce some grim news—the judge appeared to have suffered brain damage and they wanted to keep him overnight for observation. If necessary they were prepared to commit him for the long run. I did not like the sound of this. While it may have been uncharitable of me, my guess was that patients of the judge's caliber (and means to pay) were few and far between, and the local farm was not about to surrender such a prize readily. When I recited my professional credentials and demanded to see the patient, my colleague had no choice but to show me and Derby into the treatment room, where we found the judge resting on a stool, fingering his now bandaged temple. Eph hovered over him.

"And just how do you know this individual has suffered brain damage, doctor?" I asked.

"Just listen," the man replied.

The judge, I noticed, was mumbling to himself. I had to ask Eph to step out of the way so I could get close enough to catch what he was saying. At first I thought it was nonsense, but then his words took coherent form, that of a by now familiar mantra: "Azathoth . . . the pit of the shoggoths . . . Azathoth . . . the pit of the shoggoths . . ."

Almost six months later I received a letter from Aa, postmarked Milwaukee. He apologized for breaking off analysis without warning, but I had to believe that he had excellent reasons for abruptly leaving Arkham. He was grateful for our few sessions since they had helped him realize where he needed to go, and whom he needed to consult, in order to gain a new purpose in life. The bulk of the letter was devoted to an enthusiastic account of one Robert Harrison Blake, a devotee of the weird apparently even more obscure than Edward Derby. Blake had perished in a freak accident in Providence, Rhode Island, two years after Derby's death, and his papers were in sore need of editing. In sum, Aa had fastened on yet another cult figure in his search for the perfect father.

I like to think the judge would have been pleased to learn that the former editor of Azathoth House was once again profitably employed. Unfortunately, the judge remains confined at the town farm in Chesuncook. The local Maine authorities have resisted my every effort to get him transferred to the Arkham Sanitarium, and at this point I have all but given up the fight. I am in theory welcome to visit the patient in his cell "downeast," but while I am curious to try to determine first-hand what drove him insane, I fear this is one case beyond the power of psychoanalysis to cure. Besides, Chesuncook is a long way to go, and of late I have had plenty to occupy me in Arkham.

In truth, I practice my profession rarely these days, as I have increasingly assumed the role of informal adviser to Eph's mother, filling the vacancy left by the judge. While I of course lack his great legal acumen, his amazing knack for reducing taxes for Arkham's more prosperous citizens, I believe at this stage I have more to offer Wendy—we have been on a first-name basis ever since she invited me to move into her garage apartment—than a dry New England bachelor. (It is gratifying to note how she has maintained the slimmer figure she achieved through the therapy she underwent with me during the war.) Out of loyalty Wendy took the initiative in the attempt to get the judge sprung from Chesuncook, but she eventually agreed to abandon the struggle, consoling herself with the thought that he was probably safer there, given the Arkham Sanitarium's high patient murder rate.

And what of young Eph through all this time of change? On the ride home from Maine in the aftermath of our fateful camping trip he said nothing, evidently shocked into silence by the cruel injury that had robbed the judge of his reason. I gently suggested that, in the light of his need to come to terms with the loss of his elderly mentor, he might consider a session or two of grief therapy back in Arkham, naturally with his mother's permission. As it turned out, Eph did not follow up on my offer, too traumatized perhaps to share as yet with anyone what had actually happened to the judge in the woods that morning. On a more positive note, he did immerse himself in his duties at Azathoth House, making of them a full-time summer job. In September I went along with Wendy when she honored his wish not to return to Arkham High. Having flunked most of his final exams shortly after our return from Maine, he would in any event have had to repeat the ninth grade.

By the fall, Eph was the de facto editor of Azathoth House—as approved by the unofficial board of directors, consisting of Wendy and myself. While this position has its diverting moments (at our first meeting the lad proposed reprinting the *Necronomicon* in an expurgated cloth edition, while at the second we had to calm him down after receipt of a letter from Jacob Lamar Derby threatening to sue as Edward Derby's rightful heir), I confess that I care more about joining Wendy in a loftier enterprise—riding to hounds at the exclusive Foxfield Hunt Club. I still patronize the Miskatonic Club, but its facilities and university-oriented crowd have their limits. If Wendy, with her working-class origins in shadowed Innsmouth, could be accepted by Foxfield, well, there has to be hope for me. In my ample free time I have been taking riding lessons at the stable where she keeps her horses.

Eph has also been taking lessons, on weekends, and I have promised that the two of us will go out for a ride soon, possibly this coming Saturday. He is sure we can borrow a foxhound or two to help us explore the trails through the woods west of Arkham. I am quite looking forward to cultivating our special one-on-one relationship, of finally giving the poor boy what he has been missing all his life, a role for which my professional experience well qualifies me, a father.

V. Bride of Azathoth

If there is anything worse in this world than growing old it is not growing old. By this I simply mean that many good people die too young. Such a one was the gifted Asenath Waite, my ward, who made a most unfortunate match which was to bring her to an early grave. Why she ever fell under the sway of Edward Derby, an overrated local poet not nearly her intellectual equal, I shall never understand, but then as a lifelong spinster now in my seventies what would I know of such things.

My family, the Kingsport Holdens, have always had a connection with the Innsmouth Waites, so I was not entirely surprised to learn that the late Ephraim Waite had appointed me in his will to be the guardian of his only child. At the time I was still comparatively young, full of energy and self-confidence in my new post as headmistress of the Hall School, and thus welcomed this additional challenge. I was aware that old Ephraim, who had neglected his daughter in favor of the study of certain arcane books, had expected my guardianship to be purely nominal, but I was determined to take an active role in the girl's upbringing.

When she arrived in Kingsport for her first day of school, I was reminded that I had not seen Asenath since she was a bashful fifth-grader. Over the intervening years she had blossomed into a striking young lady— dark, smallish, and very good-looking except for over-protuberant eyes, probably symptomatic of an untreated thyroid condition. I immediately decided that, rather than place her in the dormitory with the other boarders, she would have the spare bedroom in my personal suite. Such favoritism is of course unwise as a rule, but something in her expression convinced me that Asenath could more than hold her own against the other girls, who would have already targeted her for their taunts on account of her status as my ward. Her coming from Innsmouth would also be a liability, given that town's notoriety as the cesspool of the North Shore.

That first term my instincts were proved right. Where the typical Hall girl tended to push, pinch, and pull hair in a scrap, Asenath did not hesitate to fight like a man with both fists flying. Those snobs who disparaged Innsmouth in front of her deserved the trip to the infirmary with which she threatened them. When the school bully, who was twice her size, bumped her once too often on the hockey field during an away match against the Miskatonic University junior women's team, Asenath came back with a high-stick that knocked her nemesis cold. Asenath had to sit out the rest of the game, but the school bully left well enough alone after that. I should say that the Hall School has traditionally been tolerant of aggressive behavior, normal enough in adolescents, within a framework of strict discipline.

Asenath impressed her fellow students not only on the playing field. She quickly developed a reputation as a magician, amazing everyone with a variety of tricks—from making balls disappear inside three cups to turning a stack of nickels into a stack of pennies and back again. It was as a hypnotist, however, that she achieved her greatest popularity, regaling many an impromptu pajama party after lights-out with her ability to "cloud minds." For a time "out-of-body experiences" were all the rage among those lucky enough to be susceptible to her powers. While Asenath could well have lorded her natural superiority over her schoolmates, she was never less than one of the girls, preferring the communal dorm shower to her private bath within my suite.

Asenath, of course, was no angel. Once she and another pretty girl who was mature for her age forged a parental pass and went on a weekend frolic in Arkham. When the manager of the hotel where they had registered became suspicious and phoned, I dropped all business to go apprehend the miscreants personally. I fear I had to expel her companion on the spot, while in Asenath's case I did not spare the rod.

Suffice it to say that in the light of our unusual relationship I could not allow myself to be too easy on my ward when she disobeyed. My ministrations no doubt strengthened Asenath's character, helping her to become the first Hall girl ever to be elected senior class president by unanimous vote. She seemed destined to triumph in the larger life of the world. Alas, for all the benefits of a Hall School education it cannot adequately prepare its graduates for the dreadful creatures who dominate the larger life of the world, men. In her last year at Miskatonic, she succumbed to the boyish charms of Edward Derby, with whom she shared a special course in medieval metaphysics. Within months of their meeting, this putative poet had lured her Svengali-like into promising to honor and obey him before a justice of the peace. My poor little Asenath, blinded by passion!

I prefer not to dwell on their doomed marriage, whose tragic outcome I have already chronicled at painful length in my memoir, *The Asenath Mystique*. I could bring myself to write this account only years later, with the encouragement and support of my dear friend Wendy Babson Upton. Wendy's older sister, Eunice, had come from Innsmouth to work for Asenath in Arkham after she became Mrs. Derby, until dismissed over a trifle by her wretch of a husband, and it was this tie that led to my bond with Wendy. It is only fair to add that by this point, shortly after the war, Wendy herself had risen to the top of Arkham society as the widow of Edward Derby Upton, the late heir to the combined Derby-Upton fortunes. That her little boy happened to be the namesake of Ephraim Waite further cemented our friendship.

Wendy was fortunate at this period to have the counsel of a wily lawyer, who helped her to establish Azathoth House, the eventual publisher of my Asenath memoir. While I might have held both the man and his work in low regard, Edward Derby had in the years since his demise developed something of a cult following, and Wendy would have been a fool as the sole heir to his literary estate not to take advantage of this potential market. Wendy once told me that Azathoth was Edward Derby's name for a favorite boyhood kitten, from whose death he had never recovered. His cavalier treatment of Asenath in later life may well have stemmed from the unresolved anger over this loss.

Some people are just better at weathering their childhood traumas than others. For instance, from a tender age Eph Upton has been exposed to more than one violent death, starting with the drowning of dozens in a freak storm off the coast of Innsmouth. Many of the victims of this marine disaster were poor relations of Asenath's, a fact that must have been very disturbing to the boy once he was old enough to comprehend it. And yet Eph seems not to have suffered any lasting emotional damage. I know at first-hand whereof I speak, for as fate would have it I was to witness an accident involving the teenage Eph which, while not fatal, could well have left psychic scars.

One Saturday morning I was out for a walk in the woods west of Arkham when I heard a dog bark in the distance. I looked in the direction of the sound and spotted two figures approaching on horseback. The autumn leaves were still thick on the trees, and I didn't have much of a view. Not until they were quite near, evidently unaware of my presence, did I recognize the two—it was Eph and Dr. Zimmerman, the town shrink, who had treated Wendy for an esteem problem during the war and had lately been courting her, much to the dismay of those with her best interests at heart.

I was about to call out a greeting but I let out a scream instead, as Eph suddenly toppled off his saddle. Both horses began to rear and buck and neigh, while the doctor gripped his stead's mane for dear life. An inexperienced rider, he was in the next moment thrown from his mount. The unseen dog let out a lugubrious howl. I rushed through the undergrowth as fast I could to reach the scene of this calamity.

By the time I struggled onto the bridle path the two horses had bolted, their shrill whinnies vanishing in the direction of the Foxfield Hunt Club. Eph was crawling on all fours, his nose to the ground, while the dog—a foxhound—was pawing the chest of Dr. Zimmerman, who lay apparently stunned on his back. Then a truly alarming thing took place. Both man and dog were seized by terrible convulsions. I could only stand by helplessly. After about a minute these convulsions abruptly ceased and the doctor rose purposefully to his feet and strode over to Eph, who had been oddly rooting around the base of a large oak. The man leaned over the lad and the two of them again went into fits. As before I could only gape in terror, unable to move. In twenty years of running an all-girls school I had seen some pretty strange sights, but nothing to compare to this performance.

Then once more it was all over. Eph stood up, brushed himself off, and turned to me with a boyish smirk.

"Ah, Miss Holden, what a pleasant surprise. How kind of you to come to the rescue."

"Are you hurt, Eph?" I replied, though his nonchalant manner suggested he could not be too seriously injured.

"Only a bit shaken, I think. But I fear Dr. Zimmeran . . ."

Arkham's premier psychoanalyst was now rolling on his back in a patch of ivy, a look of dumb amazement on his face. Eph and I had to help him up, though it was clear he was going to have trouble walking unaided. We each took an arm and led him slowly back toward the stables. Once the doctor broke away to go after a rabbit that crossed our path, but he stumbled after only a few steps and we had to hoist him to his feet again. In response to our queries he could make only low gurgling noises. At other times his tongue lolled out of his mouth in a most disconcerting manner.

As for the fox dog, who Eph said was named Fearless, she had bounded off into the woods at some point while the other two were undergoing their queer tremblings. The teenager whistled for Fearless at intervals along the trail but got no response.

In the days that followed I called frequently on Wendy, who was in dire need of a sympathetic shoulder to cry on while her beau was kept under observation at the Arkham Sanitarium. There he lay on the floor of his room, showing a healthy appetite but not much else. Then one night about a week after his confinement a careless nurse forgot to lock the door and the patient escaped. The next morning everyone heard the tragic sequel. A motorist on the Foxfield road, driving in the small hours, had been unable to brake in time when a deer darted into his headlights. The motorist swerved and missed the deer but not the man who had been chasing the animal a short distance behind. At the emergency room of Arkham's St. Mary's Hospital Dr. Zimmerman was declared dead on arrival.

Eph and I did our best to console Wendy, who had had the darnedest luck with suitors over the years. I tried to suggest gently that maybe her remarrying just was not meant to be. To add to her woes, Azathoth House was under siege from a distant Derby cousin. From his home in Chesuncook, Maine, this troublemaker was writing her letters claiming that as Edward Derby's nearest living relative he ought to have control of the literary estate. The threat of legal action from this quarter especially infuriated Eph, who dismissed the man as an illiterate bumpkin. No doubt the faithful family lawyer could have been of assistance in this matter, but sad to say he was no longer in his right mind after suffering a severe blow to the head while on a camping trip with Eph to this same remote region of Maine earlier in the year. Life certainly has its funny coincidences!

Eph vowed to return to Maine to deal with Mr. Derby directly, man to man as it were, but his editorial duties—not to mention filling orders and otherwise taking care of all warehouse operations in Bolton—kept him tied to Azathoth House. He was too busy to do any riding, and only once to my knowledge visited the stables, to check to see that Fearless was all right, after some members of the Foxfield Hunt caught her wandering nearly starved in the woods and returned her to the kennel.

Wendy was still in mourning when, about a month after the accident, a telegram arrived from Mr. Derby stating that other business was bringing him to Arkham and maybe it made sense for the opposing parties to discuss their differences face to face. Wendy and I were having tea that afternoon in her drawing room, and she immediately phoned her son at the office to relay the gist of this message. From their brief exchange I gathered Eph refused to countenance any such meeting. After she hung up Wendy burst into tears.

"Oh, Miss Holden, what am I to do?" she sobbed. "Nothing seems to be going my way these days."

"There, there, my dear," I said. I set down my cup and moved over to join her on the settee.

"This legal wrangling is just too, too depressing."

Once more the tears flowed and I gave her a big hug.

"Eph, he's a good boy I know," Wendy continued, "but there are times when he can be so, I don't know . . . stubborn."

"There, there, honey. I realize Eph is every mother's dream, just as you're the perfect mother, but you mustn't forget that he's a man after all, a young man, and you can't always rely on his judgment."

"I just have no one to turn to—except for you, Miss Holden. You're my only friend!"

"My dear girl!" I squeezed her even tighter this time, then in the emotion of the moment offered some advice that I later came to regret:

"Wendy, what's to stop you from meeting this Mr. Derby yourself? Did Eph say you couldn't?"

"No, but—"

"Why don't you wire back and invite him for a social visit—here at the house."

"I'm not sure Eph—"

"Why tell Eph? At least not until after you've met with Mr. Derby. Perhaps by then you two will have reached some understanding and you can surprise Eph with the good news. We women with our common sense can usually get things done better than men with their big egos. You owe it to yourself—and to Azathoth House—at least to try."

"Well, okay, if you really think so."

"I do think so. And what's more I promise to be here with you when Mr. Derby comes to call. A friendly, non-confrontational atmosphere should do wonders!"

A week later I was back in Wendy's drawing room, helping her arrange the fresh flowers ordered for the occasion, when the maid came in to announce that Mr. Jacob Lamar Derby was on the doorstep. It was just four o'clock. Wendy and I rose from the settee when he entered, a heavyset man of about forty, dressed in a shabby corduroy suit and carrying a battered valise. He looked neither of us in the eye when we shook hands, and seemed on the whole uncomfortable in such elegant surroundings. At Wendy's direction he took a seat in the Sheraton wing chair opposite the settee.

"Nice place you got here, Mrs. Upton."

"Yes, this was originally Edward Derby's home. All the fine furnishings you see are eighteenth century. They once belonged to the Derby family."

"But they don't now?"

"Well, no. As a matter of fact my late husband was designated Edward Derby's heir, Mr. … Derby."

To break the ensuing silence I asked our guest if he cared for some tea. When the conversation resumed, it was on a safer topic, his career as an inventor. He said nothing specific about what he was working on, except that he had been at it a long time and felt he was on the verge of a breakthrough. All he needed now, he indicated, was enough money to allow him to complete the job. He had come to Arkham to see a banker somebody had referred him to about a loan, though this banker, with whom he had met that morning, had not been encouraging. What would really be the answer to his prayers at this point would be the backing of a private investor.

Mr. Derby blushed, and again I had to rescue the situation by asking him as politely as I could to state his position vis à vis Azathoth House.

"Well, ladies, I'll admit to you I don't have much formal education. But I do read some and I think I have an idea when something's fine literature and something else is garbage. See here for instance." From his valise he removed two Edward Derby books, *Forever Azathoth* and its sequel, *Son of Azathoth*. I had started both these story volumes, but frankly had not gotten very far in either one.

"Yes, those are two of our steadier sellers," said Wendy.

"Have you read them, Mrs. Upton?"

"To be perfectly honest with you, Mr. Derby, as president of Azathoth House I merely look at the sales figures. I have nothing to do with editorial matters."

"You mean your son, that young fella I met in Maine, he's in charge?"

"That's right. Eph has taken over as full-time editorial director of Azathoth House. I wish he hadn't dropped out of high school, but"—and here Wendy couldn't repress a smile—"a high school diploma isn't always essential to success in life, is it, Mr. Derby?"

"Yeah, well . . . It's just that *Forever Azathoth* here is full of mistakes. Take the word *shoggoth,* for example."

"Shoggoth? That's a silly-sounding name. Anything to do with Azathoth?" said Wendy, still in a teasing mood, I sensed.

"Maybe that's where the confusion is, Mrs. Upton. You see, *Azathoth* is a proper noun so it's capitalized. While shoggoths are smarter than some people, they're still kind of like generic animals. Thus *shoggoth* shouldn't be capitalized, yet it's spelled with a big 's' throughout the book."

"Do you think the average Edward Derby fan really cares about such distinctions, Mr. Derby?" I asked.

"Ma'am, I'm not your average fan. As a relative I've got an emotional stake in the integrity of the texts. Okay, maybe only a pedant would worry over the stuff not right in *Forever Azathoth.* But *Son of Azathoth* is another matter entirely. I have it on good authority cousin Ed didn't even write the contents."

"And whose authority is that?"

"Mr. Vartan Bagda-what's-his-name, that foreign fella who also came up to the campsite."

"Mr. Derby, do you know who the Azathoth House editor was when those books were published?"

"Uh, I'm not sure."

"Mr. Bagdasarian. So any so-called errors would be his responsibility."

"Well, that's just it, ma'am. He explained to me that somehow, I forget the details, the wrong texts were used. It wasn't his fault."

"I don't see that affixing editorial 'blame,' if that's what it is, serves any purpose at this late date," said Wendy.

"Couldn't you correct future editions, Mrs. Upton?"

"At the present rate of sales we don't expect to reprint either title in the near future, Mr. Derby. However, if you'd like to prepare a list of suggested changes, like lowercasing *shoggoth,* I promise you we'll consider them seriously."

"And could you put my name on the copyright page? It's not the money I care about, Mrs. Upton, it's the principle of the thing."

"I'm sure we can work out something to our mutual satisfaction, Mr. Derby."

One had to give Wendy credit for putting our potentially hostile visitor at his ease. Soon the two of them were chatting away about such inconsequentials as the fortunes of the Miskatonic football team and favorite television programs. Mr. Derby accepted a second cup of tea and then a third, seemingly unaware of the hour. When I casually asked Wendy when Eph usually came home from the office, she explained that he often worked late but could in fact return at any moment. Our guest finally took the hint and said his goodbyes. As Wendy escorted him out of the drawing room, I could hear her stress how important it was to keep their meeting a secret from her son for the time being.

As it turned out, Wendy had to tell the chef to put the food in the warming oven because Eph was so late. Wendy had invited me to join them for supper, and I was sure she was glad of my company given Eph's ill humor. He sat in sullen silence through most of the meal, until at his mother's prodding he revealed that a major publisher had just announced plans to bring out an unabridged paperback edition of the *Necronomicon*. This would not only compete with the expurgated cloth edition, which Azathoth House was to publish, but was potentially highly dangerous. In his view dimmer readers simply could not be trusted to handle some of the more esoteric spells and formulae in that forbidden tome.

I suspect young Eph must have been preoccupied with this and other problems to do with Azathoth House, because otherwise he would have surely noticed that his mother was up to something. I myself was out of town for the next week or so, attending a series of fund raisers for the Hall School in several New England states. A retired headmistress is always a popular draw among the old girls at such functions.

Not until I had returned home to Kingsport and picked up the Sunday *Arkham Advertiser* did I realize what mischief had gone on in my absence. There on the front page of the society section was a photograph taken at Saturday's Miskatonic football game showing Wendy and Jacob Lamar Derby in the bleachers, holding hands!

The caption below speculated whether, after so much bad luck with romance, Arkham's most eligible widow had at last found Mr. Right.

When I rang Wendy, the maid answered the phone. Her mistress, she informed me, was out—where she didn't know but with whom she could easily guess. With scarcely any prompting from me, she went on to say that Mr. Derby had returned to the house the day after he came to tea, clearly by pre-arrangement, and had been a constant visitor since. One afternoon he and Mrs. Upton went shopping, and the next day he appeared wearing a brand new corduroy suit. The night before the football game he moved from his hotel into the garage apartment, formerly tenanted by the late Dr. Zimmerman.

As for the young master, the maid confirmed that Eph had been spending nearly every waking hour at Azathoth House. When he was at home he was too self-absorbed to notice the obvious, and he never looked at the newspaper. In addition, no one on the staff had the guts to tell him what they all knew would be the last thing he wanted to hear.

I was hurt when Wendy did not return my phone calls. Was this any way to treat me, her "only friend"? I was too proud to act at first, but toward the end of the week with still no word from Wendy I decided I could wait no longer. Since Kingsport and Arkham are neighboring towns, I was able to drive to her house near the Miskatonic campus within minutes, despite the rush-hour traffic. When the maid opened the door, I insisted that she not announce me. I wished to surprise Mrs. Upton.

I could hear the sound of a television coming from the den, and there I found my friend and Mr. Derby, like two peas in a pod, sitting on the couch watching some insipid game show.

"Wendy, how could you!" I exclaimed.

"Oh, Miss Holden, forgive me. I was going to tell you, but Jake and I have been having so much fun together I plain forgot!"

"Wendy, I—"

I was very close to losing control. Luckily, before I could say more, Eph entered the room, evidently home early for a change. A clever lad, Eph I was certain could recognize a cozy scene when he saw one.

"Mother, what are you doing with this gentleman?"

"Eph, you remember Mr. Derby," said Wendy quietly, "from your camping trip to Maine."

"Good to see you again, son," said Mr. Derby, rising and extending his hand.

Eph did not shake the man's hand. His reply left no doubt how he felt toward this unexpected visitor:

"Leave this house at once, you ignorant crackpot!"

"Oh, Eph, please!" cried Wendy. "You don't understand. Jake and I have worked out all our differences. We're on the same side now."

"Mother, what do you mean? Has this clod bamboozled you into handing over control of the Edward Derby literary estate?"

"No, Eph, he—"

"He hasn't made you sign any papers, has he?"

"No, Eph, he hasn't."

"That's a relief," I chimed in.

"Jake hasn't *made* me sign anything. Of my own free will, though, I plan to, I plan to—"

"You plan to *what*, Mother?"

"Oh, Eph, Miss Holden, don't be angry. Jake and I were waiting for the right time to tell you. We want you to share our happiness."

Eph looked aghast. I too was speechless.

"The date is set for Saturday," said Wendy, "and we would like you to, to . . ."

"Poor sweetie, too overcome with emotion to speak," said her paramour. "Eph, ma'am, what Wendy is trying to say is, we want you to participate in our nuptials—as best man and old maid of honor!"

That Saturday morning I went over to Wendy's house to help her prepare, though in truth she gave me far more emotional support than I gave her. In a gesture toward tradition, Mr. Derby had retreated to the garage apartment, in order to avoid seeing his bride until the wedding ceremony. Between giggles, as she slipped on her best organdy gown, Wendy confessed that the two of them had spent their last unwedded night, as they had every other night that week, in her bedroom. I could scarcely hold back my tears.

I did not see Eph. Wendy assumed that her son had taken the old Packard to the service station for a last-minute check-up before the honeymoon—in Chesuncook, Maine. If it was any consolation, the joyful couple had insisted that I join them on the drive up, along with Eph, who would be acting as chauffeur. According to Wendy, Eph had wanted to have a "business" chat with his future stepfather in private before the wedding, but the groom had laughed off the idea. As far as he was concerned, Azathoth House affairs could wait until after the honeymoon.

At noon all the principals rendezvoused at the Arkham court house. There the justice of the peace—the same justice of the peace, as fate would have it, who had married Edward Derby and Asenath Waite some thirty years earlier—united Jacob Lamar Derby, who was attired in his new corduroy suit, and Wendy Babson Upton in secular matrimony. I sobbed at intervals. Eph, on the other hand, performed his duties in the charade calmly, seemingly having accepted the inevitable with more grace than I was displaying.

Back at Wendy's some dozen members of the Arkham social elite, all that were available given the short notice, gathered to partake of the reception luncheon the servants had hastily set up in the conservatory. Everyone drank a good deal, to dull the pain, I suppose, except for Eph, who of course had to stay sober for the long drive ahead.

At last Wendy and "Jake," as he insisted I call him in his new role, were ready to depart. The guests assembled on the front steps to shower the couple with rice as they ran the gauntlet to the waiting Packard, decorated with a "Just Married" sign on the trunk and trailing tin cans from the bumper. On the Foxfield road Eph pulled the car over and got out to remove the tin cans. Wendy and Jake insisted, however, that the sign remain.

While we no longer had to endure the grating noise of metal on asphalt, we could now hear another sound, a sort of low groaning or growling, which seemed to emanate from the back of the car somewhere. From my position next to Eph in the front seat, I hesitated to turn around for fear of discovering that the newlyweds were the source of this unsettling, animal-like sound. Sleepy from the champagne I had consumed at the reception, and with the taciturn Eph no company, I finally dozed off north of Augusta.

It was dark when we arrived at Jake's lakefront cabin, deep in the Maine forest. The rest of us waited in the Packard while our host got out and lighted the porch lamp. With the motor turned off I was again aware of the earlier groaning sound—which now was clearly coming from the trunk. Wendy, still mooning like a lovesick calf, claimed not to notice, but when I called it to Eph's attention he said he would investigate since he had to unload the suitcases anyway.

Seconds later, as I was climbing out of the car, I heard the trunk open—and then came that bloodcurdling howl! The open trunk blocked my view, but it sounded as if two demons were in a desperate life-and-death struggle. Then Eph rolled into sight in the dirt driveway—with a dog tearing and worrying at his throat! I shrieked—and so did Wendy, brought abruptly back to earth by this appalling scene. But most terrible of all was that Eph appeared to be pulling his punches, as if he were an actor in a grade-B western saloon brawl! His attacker I could see well enough was no mastiff, no gigantic Hound of the Baskervilles, but only a foxhound and not an especially large female at that.

If Wendy and I were shocked into inaction, not so her new husband. Jacob Lamar Derby ran into the cabin and shortly returned bearing a shotgun. It was easy for him to take a bead on the animal's head, for Eph had ceased resisting. I hid my face in my hands just before the blast.

When I opened my eyes Jake was bending over Eph. I avoided looking too closely at the now motionless form of the foxhound. Then, as if we had not already suffered enough trauma for one evening, the older man went into convulsions, queerly like those Eph and Dr. Zimmerman had gone through in the woods west of Arkham! I screamed, I admit it, like one of those brainless female victims in a cheap horror film.

A minute later, thank the Lord, Jake revived and took command. Eph was still alive, if barely. We had to get him to the hospital fast. No time to wait for an ambulance. Before either Wendy or I could protest that maybe it was better not to move him, Jake had scooped up his stepson and plopped him onto the backseat of the Packard. I rode in front with Jake at the wheel, while Wendy sat in the back staunching Eph's neck wounds as best she could with strips torn from her organdy gown.

Though he had spent most of his adult life in Chesuncook, Jake nonetheless had to stop and ask directions to the "hospital." In fact, we soon learned that the town had no hospital as such, just a lunatic asylum with an M.D. or two on staff. Wendy mumbled that she remembered this was where her former lawyer who had lost his marbles was at present incarcerated.

What happened next is all rather a blur, but the upshot was that Wendy elected to spend the night at the asylum, where Eph was in intensive care, or what passes for intensive care in a hick burg like Chesuncook. When Jake offered to drive me back to the cabin, I did not argue. I was reluctant to leave Wendy, but decided I definitely could use some rest. I was just too exhausted, both physically and emotionally, to be of any assistance to anyone.

"Poor Eph," said Jake once we were back in the car. "Guess he thought he was pulling another prank—like tying tin cans to the bumper. Kind of cruel to the animal, though. Probably he drugged Fearless when he picked her up at the kennel. Fearless must've really resented such treatment seeing how she went for the kill like that."

Did he say *Fearless*? How did Jake know the creature's name, I wondered.

"You know, Miss Holden, I get the feeling maybe Eph doesn't approve of me marrying his mom. But I trust he'll accept things in time, in the event he lives. I have to say those doctors at the asylum didn't strike me as especially on the ball."

Did this backwoods boob really care whether or not Eph survived? It was disturbing to think that he might not.

"Yeah, it's a shame our honeymoon's off to a bad start," Jake resumed, "but I'm sure Wendy and I are really going to like being married. I'd been a bachelor way too long. It's no fun to live alone. You've lived alone all your life, though, haven't you, Miss Holden? Except when Asenath was your ward all those years ago at the Hall School. Tell me, do you think she enjoyed those spankings with a metal ruler as much as you did?"

The impertinence of the man! I would have to have a word with Wendy after this immediate crisis was over about her speaking too freely of my private life. By this point, as we left the feeble outpost of civilization that constituted the town center, I was feeling decidedly uncomfortable in the company of Jacob Lamar Derby. It was a relief when after driving a few miles the porch light of the cabin came into view, a beacon amid the blackness of the surrounding forest. But the fiend next to me drove past the cabin down a narrow rutted road deeper into the woods. When I protested we had gone too far, he stopped the Packard. With the headlights off I could see nothing.

"How come you've never gotten hitched, Miss Holden? Hey, don't get upset! I bet I know the answer—no man was good enough for you in this world. But let me tell you, folks aren't the only folks hereabouts—folks that don't have much truck with the concept of gender. I know it's late and I promised Wendy I'd get back to the asylum as soon as I dropped you off, but the pit's nearby and I just know you, the two of you, will hit it off fine.

"So how about it, Miss Holden? Believe me, you're never too old to take the plunge!"

VI. Son of Azathoth

I am Vartan Bagdasarian, Jr., keeper of the Edward Derby flame that my father kept before me—though I must confess that there was a nineteen-year gap in between when Derby scholarship languished in ignorance and ineptitude. What drove my father to abandon his editorial post at Azathoth House, publisher of the poetical and fictional works of Edward Derby, I cannot say for sure. Perhaps his leaving had something to do with his conviction that for much of his tenure he hadn't been in his right mind. It was as if some imposter had possessed him and perversely produced such travesties as *Forever Azathoth,* a story collection derived from inferior texts, and *Son of Azathoth,* a collection of tales based on Derby notes or outlines fleshed out by himself. These inexplicable "posthumous collaborations," it must be said, were a particular embarrassment. A veteran of World War II, my father never tired of describing at bloody length how his Marine platoon beat the hell out of the Japs, but ask him about his experiences at Azathoth House and he would shudder and give you one of those "thousand yard" stares.

Most of what I knew of my father's painful past came second-hand, from my mother, in whom he'd confided in their early days together. It is a testament to my father's resilience that soon after relinquishing his Edward Derby studies he found a new writer worthy of his scholarly attentions—and a bride to boot. Miss Belinda Blake, niece of the fantasist Robert Blake, had been more than helpful when my father arrived in Milwaukee in the spring of '57 seeking access to her late uncle's papers. Indeed, the two got along so well that they were married that August. (I was born the following June.) On the strength of his pioneering bibliographic and critical work on the Blake papers, my father was able to establish himself within a few years as the leading authority on the "Shaggai Feaster."

As I child I grew up on Robert Blake's stories, poems, letters, and other writings, in a home decorated with his paintings of nameless, unhuman monsters and profoundly alien, non-terrestrial landscapes. It was only natural that I should rebel against this influence and develop an enthusiasm for the works of Edward Derby. I took immense delight in the annoyance this bookish preference caused my father, who forbade me from owning any Azathoth House editions but couldn't deny me the cheap Lancer reprints that were then proliferating as part of the general fantasy boom.

With the publication in 1975 of Ronald Horn's *Edward Pickman Derby: The Biography,* I was confirmed in my ambition to become the foremost Derby scholar of my generation, and applied for early admission to Miskatonic University. From Horn's bio I knew the Miskatonic library housed a major Derby manuscript collection. By this date my father had somewhat mellowed and didn't grumble when I received my official acceptance letter. He conceded that there was plenty of work to be done to put Derby scholarship back on track, and as his son I was of course uniquely qualified to do so. When I asked him if he had any final advice to offer before I set off for his alma mater, he hesitated a moment then said, with a weak laugh, that I should think twice before accepting any invitations to go camping.

On arrival in Arkham, Massachusetts, I decided to forego much of freshman orientation in favor of exploring the university's Edward Derby collection. Imagine my surprise when, on consulting the library's card catalogue, I discovered the drawer for my literary hero missing! Luckily, the catalogue room was nearly empty, and I soon located the culprit—a fellow who looked barely old enough to be a student.

"Excuse me, but I'm afraid you have my Edward Derby drawer," I said.

"Get lost. This is my Edward Derby drawer," the kid replied.

"I have some important research to do."

"That's funny. So do I."

Thus was born a partnership destined to have such far-reaching consequences for the field of Edward Derby studies. We quickly forgot our quarrel over who had the greater claim to the drawer, so engrossed did we become in discussing the occult cult poet and his conception of Azathoth. I argued that the boundless daemon-sultan fitted the Platonic notion of an ideal form, while my fresh-faced rival held the Aristotelian view that the noxious entity was merely a social construct. After about an hour we left the library for the student center across the street, where we continued our debate over glasses of root beer, Edward Derby's favorite beverage, according to his biographer.

My companion was also entering his freshman year at Miskatonic, I learned, and was a native of nearby Kingsport. He first became interested in Edward Derby after reading a memoir of Derby's wife, *The Asenath Mystique*.

"I've heard of that," I said.

"It was written by my great-aunt, though she died—or rather disappeared—before I was born."

"Her name was Holden, wasn't it?"

"Yes, Miss Holden. Apparently, no one ever called her by her first name. I'm George Holden, by the way." He set down his root beer and extended his hand.

"Vartan Bagdasarian, Jr.," I said, accepting his handshake.

"No! Are you by any chance related to the founder of the Dead Edward Derby Society?"

"Yes, I'm his son."

"Wow! He's a legend around here!"

"I take it the Dead Edward Derby Society's still going strong at Miskatonic."

"Uh, not exactly. The society had its last formal meeting in 1955. They broke up in a dispute over a volume of poetical tributes to Derby, I believe."

"Oh."

"Yes, when I say your father's a legend, I mean only among a very small, select circle."

George proceeded to outline the current, moribund state of Azathoth House. *Forever Azathoth* and *Son of Azathoth* were still in print, but the seminal poetry collection, *Azathoth and Other Horrors,* and the volume of correspondence, *The Derby-Geoffrey Letters: 1920–1926,* were not. Over the past couple of decades Azathoth House had issued no new Derby material. Instead they'd concentrated on publishing mediocre mysteries featuring a psychic detective from Innsmouth. The author was one "Ephraim Waite," which George guessed to be a pseudonym.

"Their latest release," he said, "is *Azathoth Redux.*"

"*Azathoth* what?"

"*Azathoth Redux.* It's a collection of Derby-inspired stories by this guy Ephraim Waite, whoever he is."

"Doesn't sound promising."

"One problem is Azathoth House has no proper in-house editor."

"Why not?"

"I gather the owners, in order to save money, do all the work themselves."

"Who are the owners?"

"A husband-wife team, Jake and Wendy Derby. He's a distant cousin."

"Right. I remember. Horn mentions them in his epilogue."

"They've been running the place for years. As it happens, they're the guests of honor at a party this Friday at the Gallows Hill Book Shop. The public's invited to come help celebrate thirty years of Azathoth House. Wanna go?"

Well, this was fortuitous! The opening seminar of a special course in oriental metaphysics presented a scheduling conflict, but in the end I realized I had no choice.

That Friday evening, on the walk over to the Gallows Hill Book Shop, which was located in the seedy neighborhood north of campus, George asked that I keep his identity as Miss Holden's great-nephew under my hat. It seems his great-aunt had been a close friend of Wendy Derby, or Upton as she then was, at the time of her marriage to Jake Derby; so close in fact that she'd accompanied the newlyweds on their ill-fated honeymoon. A prank involving a savage foxhound hidden in the trunk of the couple's car had gone horribly wrong, resulting in the near-fatal injury of their driver, the bride's teenage son by her previous marriage. This mishap had occurred late at night, soon after their arrival at the isolated Maine cabin where they were staying. The police later theorized that the old lady must have wandered off at some point in shock. At any rate, no body was ever found, and her case remains unsolved. George had no wish to remind the Derbys of this past trauma.

I in turn decided it best not to mention that I was the son of their one-time editor. Mr. and Mrs. Derby's memories of my father's years at Azathoth House might be just as emotionally fraught as his own.

The Gallows Hill Book Shop stood out amid a row of drab storefronts, thanks to an illuminated poster in the window proclaiming "Thirty Years of Azathoth House." This poster featured the famous "wedding day" photo of Edward Derby in which he looks either nervous or terrified. Inside we found a few hippies hovering around a table littered with salty snack foods and bottles of root beer. A long-haired freak with marijuana breath invited us to dig in. We helped ourselves to plastic cups of root beer before heading for the back of the shop where there was a table with books on display—mostly leatherette-bound copies of *Azathoth Redux,* along with the *Necronomicon,* in an expurgated paperback edition, and *The Asenath Mystique.* Sitting behind the table was a middle-aged couple, like an overweight version of Grant Wood's *American Gothic.*

"Step right up, young fellas," said Mr. Jacob Lamar Derby. "Get your limited numbered signed copies of *Azathoth Redux.* Only—" He cited a price that was well beyond my budget.

"Isn't that kinda steep," said George, "for a collection of what are, after all—"

"Look here, son," the man interrupted. "This is a deluxe edition, with marbled end papers, silk bookmark, and color plates." He opened the book to an especially garish illustration of a giant blob wrapping a tentacle around an old woman in front of what appeared to be an underground altar.

Both George and I leaned over for a better look, and in so doing I accidentally slopped half my root beer on the open page.

"Oh, dear," said Mrs. Derby, reaching with a handkerchief to mop up the mess.

"Heh, heh, guess that's your copy now," said her mate, with ill-concealed glee.

Between us George and I came up with enough cash to pay for the damaged volume. We said we were buying it jointly.

"Would you like me to inscribe it to you both?" asked Mr. Derby.

"Uh, gee, let me think," said George, who I assumed was as worried as I was about revealing who we were prematurely. "Say, hold on a sec, you aren't the author. Why should you sign?"

"Because I'm the publisher. The author's already signed."

"How come Ephraim Waite's not here?" I asked, in an effort to buy more time.

"He's from Innsmouth," he answered, as if that explained the author's absence.

"Won't the book be more valuable in the future," said George, "if it's not inscribed to a couple of, uh, nobodies like us?"

"Quit stalling. Tell me your names." Something in the man's tone suggested that it would be smarter to oblige him than not, so we did.

"George Holden," Mr. Derby muttered as he scribbled on the flyleaf, "and what was that second name?"

"Vartan Bagdasarian, Jr.," I mumbled.

"How do you sp— Hey, wait a minute! Don't tell me you're related to—"

"Yes, I'm the son of Vartan Bagdasarian, former editor of Azathoth House."

"I should've known when you spilled the root beer. Good Lord, boy, you're as clumsy as your old man! Did he ever tell you about the time he dropped Edward Derby's clock?"

"My father doesn't like to talk much about the past."

"My, my, I always wondered what happened to Vart," said Mrs. Derby. "We met through the Dead Edward Derby Society at Miskatonic ages ago. Never mind how long!" She giggled. "To be honest, at first I thought your dad was a total egghead, but later we became great pals. When he lived over the garage, why—"

"Please, Wendy," growled her husband.

"Oh, Jake, don't be so jealous," tittered Mrs. Derby, hiding her blushes behind her sodden handkerchief.

This perhaps wasn't the ideal introduction to the proprietors of Azathoth House, but at least the ice was broken. For the moment George and I had the Derbys pretty much to ourselves, since few other customers ventured over to buy *Azathoth Redux* or any of the other books on display. I tried to pump Mr. Derby for anecdotes about his cousin not included in the Horn bio, but he kept returning to the subject of Ephraim Waite and what a fantastic author he was. George was seemingly getting on better with Mrs. Derby, who interrupted her husband to tell him how excited she was to learn that George was related to her dear departed friend, Miss Holden.

I next tried to sound out Mr. Derby on Azathoth—did he take the Platonic or the Aristotelian point of view?—but instead of answering he abruptly leapt up from his chair and stalked over to the refreshment table. There he accosted the long-haired freak that originally greeted us, evidently the shop's owner, who was showing off an oversized tome to the assembled fans.

"What are doing with that book!" shouted Mr. Derby.

"Easy, man," the freak replied.

"You're not selling it, are you?"

"No, man, it's my personal copy."

"Don't you know that book's extremely dangerous?"

"Hey, don't get heavy. I don't even read Latin."

"That's why Azathoth House published an expurgated, abridged version—in English—so fools like you won't get burned by the real thing."

"Yeah, well, even if I don't understand it, it's still cool to own the real thing."

"Look, man, why don't you wise up and just sell it to me. Name your price."

By this point everyone in the store had stopped to watch this extraordinary scene. The place was silent. Then the freak said, "Okay, okay, if you're so hung up on material things I'll let you have it for the cost of the root beer and munchies. Okay?"

Mr. Derby pulled out his wallet. The freak handed over the book. It was the *Necronomicon.*

Later, walking back to campus, George and I discussed the *Necronomicon,* which I knew from reading Horn was an ancient book of esoteric magic that had had some obscure significance for Edward Derby. What we'd seen at the book shop appeared to have been some sort of modern reprint. Neither of us could fathom why Mr. Derby had been so offended by someone else possessing it—or so keen to acquire it for himself.

We were to learn more shortly. One night the following week, while I was busy catching up on my oriental metaphysics, the dean dropped by the dorm to give me a note which he said the sender had insisted on his delivering personally. It was on heavy cream stationery, embossed with a crest, and engraved with the name of Mrs. Jacob Lamar Derby. In a round, schoolgirlish hand, she invited me and George—"I so enjoyed our chat at the party for Azathoth House!!!"—to come over for tea sometime. Under the R.S.V.P. was a phone number.

We welcomed the invitation as an opportunity to propose new Derby books for the Azathoth House list. The initial focus of our researches was on those papers that could be classified as amateur journalism, in particular *The Reactionary*, the periodical Derby had produced for the Confederate Amateur Press Association. We both agreed that a compilation of all 183 issues would be as much of a revelation to the larger Derbyian public as it had been to us. (Horn had scarcely touched on his a.p.a. activity.) In critiquing the florid verses penned by certain C.A.P.A. members of the fair sex, the future author of "To Asenath" could be delightfully vicious.

I duly phoned Mrs. Derby, and on the appointed afternoon George and I wended our way into the lovely residential neighborhood west of campus, where we readily found the stately home of the Derbys on elm-free Endicott Street. A maid greeted us at the door and showed us into an elegantly furnished sitting room. We sat down on the settee in front of the coffee table, on which rested a silver tea service and a platter of thin, crustless sandwiches. We'd already tucked into these when Mrs. Derby entered.

"Just help yourselves, boys," she said with a smile. "I'm sure the food at Miskatonic hasn't improved any since I was a coed."

We expressed our thanks as best we could with our mouths full. Since the sandwiches were on the dry side, I waited until our hostess had served the tea before presenting the case for publishing *The Reactionary*. George supported me by quoting some of Derby's more sarcastic comments on the amateur writings of his intellectual inferiors. I admitted that this collection represented only the first step toward issuing the complete Derby canon, which would by me calculations fill twenty fat volumes. We of course couldn't expect to finish the entire project during our undergraduate years, but were prepared, if all went well, to stick with it for as long as necessary. Our brains and enthusiasm would more than make up for our youth and inexperience.

"My yes, that's very interesting," said Mrs. Derby. "I'm sure Jake will think so, too."

Though she didn't say so explicitly, I assumed she and Mr. Derby would have to confer on our initial proposal before giving it the green light.

"But enough about business," she continued. "You boys still look hungry. I'll ring for the maid to replenish the sandwich supply."

While we ate, Mrs. Derby reminisced about Miss Holden and those halcyon days when she and my father used to hang out at "Derby Manor," then the home of her first husband-to-be, Ed Upton, son of Dan Upton, the cold-blooded murderer of Edward Derby. She choked up a little when she mentioned her own son, Ephraim. Eph had never fully recovered from his "accident," having entirely lost his ambition to run Azathoth House. Happily, he'd developed instead an interest in tinkering like his stepfather and had, since getting out of the hospital, been living at the family's lakeside cabin in Maine. At the same time her new husband, strangely enough, had cheerfully given up his career as an inventor and assumed editorial control of Azathoth House.

"Speaking of odd behavior," said George, "we couldn't help wondering why Mr. Derby blew up at that Gallows Hill Book Shop guy just because he owned a copy of the *Necronomicon*."

"Oh, it's so silly," said Mrs. Derby. "Jake can lose his cool over the darnedest things, even a book like this rival edition of the *Necronomicon*. I try to tell him it's no competition really for Azathoth Hosue. It's been offset from the original text, and who but a few nerdy occultists who know Latin would bother to read the whole nine hundred pages anyway? Our abridged English version is much more reader friendly."

"Who's the publisher?" I asked.

"Bonanza Books. They specialize in cheap reprints of works in the public domain. Instant remainders Jake calls them. He's written Bonanza a number of letters since he first noticed their *Necronomicon* in a mail-order catalogue, but they've been too rude to reply."

It was a story like this that made me better appreciate the agonies my father must have gone through. The next month George and I were likewise to suffer some editorial disappointment. Once again the dean personally delivered an envelope, a business-size one with the return address of Azathoth House. Inside was a form letter. The editors thanked us for our submission, but unfortunately it didn't fit their present publishing needs. At the bottom, written in the girlish hand of our late hostess, was a P.S.: "Sorry, but I'm afraid Mr. Derby simply hated your idea! Tea with you was such fun! We must do it again soon!"

Well, this was too bad. I had just forced myself to the end of *Azathoth Redux,* and it irked me that Azathoth House should be publishing these pedestrian Derby imitations while turning down a compilation of the master's actual prose. George, a more astute observer than I, had in the meantime noticed that Mr. Derby's inscription to us on the flyleaf bore an uncanny resemblance to Ephraim Waite's signature on the title page. There was no escaping the sorry conclusion. Azathoth House was now for all intents and purposes a vanity press!

George and I did some rethinking and concluded we had to act boldly—we would publish *The Reactionary* ourselves! In short order we formed our own firm, Pickman Press, with George as president and myself as editor-in-chief. The real challenge was the financing. An estimate from a printer in Bolton confirmed that it was ludicrous even to imagine we could afford to do a professional job on the book. We would have to start modestly—by making multiple photocopies of all 183 issues of *The Reactionary.*

I took advantage of my entrée with the dean, and applied for and received a part-time clerical job in his office, where I knew I would have access to a Xerox machine. It was a slow process, but by the end of the first semester I had smuggled in and copied most of the original issues of *The Reactionary* from the university library, with no one in authority the wiser.

With the aid of members of the Dead Edward Derby Society, which George and I had successfully revived that first semester, we were able to begin the collating after the Christmas break. We had to punch holes in the pages before inserting them in the binders since the photocopies proved too thick in the aggregate to staple. By spring break we had a hundred finished copies of *The Reactionary: Writings in the Confederate Amateur Press Association, 1911–1930,* by Edward Derby, edited and with an introduction by Vartan Bagdasarian, Jr., published by Pickman Press, George Holden president. The retail price covered what our production costs would have been had we paid for the paper.

The next obstacle was distribution. Since all ten members of the Dead Edward Derby Society had helped out, they were entitled to complimentary copies. Where were we to find other Derby buffs to buy the book? The answer was obvious—the Azathoth House mailing list.

I should say that George and I continued to be the guests of Mrs. Derby at the manor. The routine never varied. We would come over for tea and fill up on tiny tasteless sandwiches while she talked about the past. It became clear that she wasn't that interested in the present Azathoth House program, which appeared to form her husband's primary occupation. We kept a tactful silence when she confessed that she thought some overzealous fans put Edward Derby on too lofty a pedestal. She evidently bore him a grudge for mistreating his wife. Absent from these tea parties was Mr. Derby, who we gathered spent his days at the Azathoth House office located in the Peaslee Building downtown.

I should say, too, that while we told Mrs. Derby about the doings of the Dead Edward Derby Society, we said nothing about founding Pickman Press or publishing *The Reactionary*. We concurred that it would be best to present the book to the owners of Azathoth House as a fait accompli.

The day after official publication day, George and I brought a copy of *The Reactionary* with us to Derby Manor. It was high time anyhow that we gave Mrs. Derby something in return for her hospitality.

"Thank you, Vart. Thank you, George," said Mrs. Derby on receiving our gift. "That's very sweet of you. Why you've even signed it!"

In our respective positions as editor and president of Pickman Press, we'd inscribed the book to both Mr. and Mrs. Derby.

"His amateur writings reveal an unsuspected side to the Bard of Arkham," said George. "He could be a real scream, even if he did tend to repeat his best gags."

"Do you think Mr. Derby would mind," I said, getting straight to the point, "if we borrowed the Azathoth House mailing list? Or if that's asking too much, do you think he'd let us run an ad in the next Azathoth House flyer or catalogue?"

"Gosh, I couldn't say," she said in a voice that suggested we shouldn't get our hopes too high. "But I'll be sure to ask him tonight."

Quite unexpectedly, we were to get Mr. Derby's reaction to *The Reactionary* a lot sooner than that. For once he returned home from the office early, while we were still enjoying our tea. He came barreling into the sitting room waving a letter and cursing Bonanza Books for daring to refuse his offer to buy their remaining stock of the *Necronomicon*. During a pause in his tirade, Mrs. Derby reintroduced George and me, reminding him of our meeting the previous fall at the Gallows Hill Book Shop.

"Excuse me," said Mr. Derby, mopping his brow with the offending letter. "It's been a bad day at the office."

"Here, dear, have some tea," said Mrs. Derby, offering her spouse a cup of the soothing beverage. He took a seat on the settee from which George and I had risen at his dramatic entrance.

"What's this?" asked Mr. Derby, peering at the copy of *The Reactionary* on the coffee table.

"The boys were nice enough to bring us a present," said Mrs. Derby. "It's their first book."

"You call this a book? Looks more like a bound manuscript to me."

"Actually, it's Edward Derby's amateur journal, *The Reactionary*," I said. "The complete run."

"What is this, another cheap, unauthorized reprint!?" Mr. Derby started to thumb through the volume.

"Edward Derby's amateur journalism is in the public domain, I can assure you," said George. "We of Pickman Press have a perfect right to publish it, especially after you, er, after you rejected it."

"Ah, and I see you've even had the gall to inscribe this . . . this outrage!" Mr. Derby was trembling so badly that he slopped tea over the inscription.

"Do you think you could let us have a copy of the Azathoth House mailing list?" I asked. "Or if you prefer, we'd settle for a plug in your catalogue."

"Mailing list! Catalogue! You must be nuts!" roared Mr. Derby. "Here's what I think of your pathetic excuse for a publication!"

So saying, Mr. Derby stood up and, like a circus strongman with a telephone book (which frankly our edition of *The Reactionary* resembled), proceeded to rip the text apart. Too stunned to protest, George and I didn't wait for the maid to show us the door.

A few days after this distressing episode, I received an urgent summons to the dean's office. There I was surprised to find Mr. Derby, looking penitent. The dean left us alone. Naturally, I was wary, but Mr. Derby immediately and profusely apologized for his inappropriate behavior the other afternoon. He had let his anger at Bonanza Books run away with him. It was inexcusable. To make amends, he insisted on taking me to the student center for a drink.

There Mr. Derby bought me a root beer and listened, nodding from time to time in apparent sympathy, while I outlined Pickman Press's mission. When I finished my spiel, he remarked that our complete works of Edward Derby project was essentially what my father had envisioned. Then he said:

"How would you and George like to come to northern Maine, say, at the end of the month?"

"I don't know. Would this involve camping?"

"Not necessarily. Our cabin in Chesuncook should be able to accommodate us all, unless my stepson has let his inventions fill every nook and cranny. It should be at least as comfortable as the Miskatonic freshman dorms."

"Mr. Derby, isn't it kind of cold in northern Maine this time of year?"

"Vart, did your old man ever tell you about his trips to Maine?"

"Not that I remember—but there are certain things he doesn't talk about."

"Just as well, I suppose."

It was hard to tell what the man was thinking, but it was clear when he next spoke that he was in no mood to take no for an answer.

"Let me remind you, Vart, that we at Azathoth House control the rights to Edward Derby's fiction and poetry. If we're to engage in any cooperative publishing ventures with Pickman Press, we need to work out an arrangement. Wouldn't you agree an informal country setting would be conducive to friendly negotiation?"

"All right, but I'll have to consult George first."

In the end George and I decided we had nothing to lose and a great deal to gain. Obtaining permission from the estate was after all pretty important.

The last day of April, soon after dawn, we rendezvoused at the manor. Mr. Derby was waiting for us in the circular driveway, at the wheel of an antique car that George recognized as a Packard. We were thrilled when Mr. Derby said it had once belonged to his celebrated cousin. Its capacity to do forty-five miles per hour tops accounted for our early departure.

During the drive George and I amused ourselves by asking each other Edward Derby trivia questions. Our chauffeur didn't participate as such, though he claimed to know certain things about Edward Derby's marriage to Asenath Waite that no one else, not even that snoop Ronald Horn, would even dare to imagine. These intimate revelations were titillating in the extreme and, I might add, an egregious violation of the legendary couple's privacy—if in fact there was any truth in them. One had to wonder whether Mr. Derby was pulling our leg.

North of Augusta he warned us that we could expect to find his stepson, whom he hadn't seen in years, not quite right in the head. At last report Eph was still an out-patient at the local farm, where he'd spent months recuperating from his canine-inflicted wounds. On the plus side, Mr. Derby asserted, the lad's mental disability had kept him out of Vietnam.

We reached the lakeside cabin in Chesuncook at sunset. It was a scenic spot, if a tad isolated at the end of a narrow dirt road or driveway. Eph Upton appeared at the door while we were unloading the Packard—a typical rustic, dressed in overalls and a red bandana that didn't quite conceal his neck scars. In a hoarse voice he mumbled a brief welcome. He struck me as being not so much slow-witted as shy.

"You look great, boy," said Mr. Derby, slapping his stepson on the back. "It's been too long, far too long. Oh, and happy birthday! Your thirty-fifth, isn't it?"

Inside the cabin Mr. Derby handed Eph a package wrapped in paper decorated with cute little doggies. Eph silently opened it. It was a copy of *Azathoth Redux*.

"Thanks," Eph whispered.

"You may not understand all the words," said Mr. Derby, "but I bet you'll get a big kick out of the pictures."

Our host dished out some Boston baked beans for dinner, which we ate around a weather-beaten picnic table in the living room. When Mr. Derby asked Eph how his inventions were coming along, he answered in monosyllables. George and I were too tired to contribute to the conversation. After dinner Mr. Derby suggested we all go to bed so as to be rested for a hike early the next morning. Eph disappeared upstairs, while the rest of us settled ourselves on blankets on the living-room floor. The other rooms were crammed to bursting with machinery, according to Mr. Derby.

It seemed as if I'd been asleep only a minute before I felt a hand shaking my shoulder. It was Mr. Derby urging me in a low voice to get up and dress. We had to keep quiet in order not to wake Eph. There was no time for breakfast. In the dark I could hear George inquiring why we had to take a hike at this crazy hour and Mr. Derby replying that the time was particularly propitious for glimpsing certain unusual kinds of wildlife.

Outside Mr. Derby switched on a flashlight, and we followed him along a barely discernible trail away from the lake into the woods. It was damnably cold, but given our rapid if stumbling pace we soon warmed up. We could hear birds and beasts in the surrounding forest, and once I sensed an animal lumbering behind us, but all we could see in the feeble flashlight beam were clouds of tiny insects. Finally we paused, huffing and puffing, within a circle of granite boulders. Our guide identified these as Indian standing stones, but insisted we not linger over this curious site.

We tramped another half-hour before Mr. Derby gave the signal to stop again. By this time there was enough natural light to see more than a few feet into the gloom. We'd come to the base of a steep hill or cliff, shrouded with underbrush, which Mr. Derby proceeded to probe with a hunting knife. Within a couple of minutes he was hacking away at the brush, until there was revealed what looked like a large burrow or cave entrance.

"All set for the final, underground part of our outing, kids?" said Mr. Derby. "I promise you won't be disappointed."

"Are you sure it's safe to go in there?" said George.

"Look, you boys are about to have the kind of experience that any professional zoologist would envy."

"Yeah, but—"

"You want to make a deal with Azathoth House, don't you?"

This reminder clinched it. With Mr. Derby in the lead we crawled into the cave, which after ten feet or so opened up into a tunnel tall enough to stand up in. The dirt and rocky debris which littered this natural passage suggested that no other human beings had passed along it in some time. At fleeting intervals on the granite walls, in the flickering flashlight glow, we could make out crude drawings evocative of monsters from classical mythology. Mr. Derby explained that these were the work of superstitious Indians, long vanished.

"Neat stuff, Mr. Derby," said George, "but isn't there a risk of the roof caving in on us?"

"Metaphorically speaking . . . but, hey, wait till you see what lies ahead—it's well worth the risk."

Like faithful sheep, we continued to follow our shepherd. A hundred feet on the tunnel took a sharp turn to the left then another one to the right, and all of a sudden we emerged on a ledge jutting into an immense cavern or grotto—suffused with a soft phosphorescent light that rose from below, as if from some infernal cauldron.

"Wow, this is spectacular!" exclaimed George. "You weren't kidding."

"Far out!" was all I could say as I shielded my eyes against the light that shimmered and seethed in the unknown depths.

Despite his having witnessed this wonder before, Mr. Derby seemed just as hypnotized as George and me. Then he began to chant, in a language that sounded at first as if it might be Latin, but then shifted key into a wholly unearthly tongue, which echoed eerily around that subterranean nether world. Was there some response from the boiling luminescence below? No, there was a noise behind us—as of some person or some thing scrambling down the tunnel we'd just passed through!

A moment later a familiar form charged out on the ledge, shocking the three of us out of our collective reverie. It was Eph Upton and he was brandishing a large, cheaply-bound book—the Bonanza *Necronomicon!*

"I want my body back, you fiend!" he croaked.

"What are you talking about, Eph?" asked Mr. Derby, in the calm voice of an adult addressing an unreasonable child.

"The name's Jake—Jacob Lamar Derby—and you stole my body and my bride!"

"Pay him no mind, boys. He hasn't been in his right senses since his accident."

"Oh, yeah? I may have gone off my rocker when I woke up at the Chesuncook farm with a humdinger of a sore throat in the wrong carcass—but I eventually figured out I wasn't the first to experience a 'change of mind' thanks to you. Asenath and Dan Upton and Ed Upton and Fearless the foxhound and who knows how many others."

"You're raving, Eph."

"Eph, huh? How ironic. You couldn't resist putting your real name on that collection of garbage you have the temerity on the jacket to call literature."

"How dare you insult—" Mr. Derby was starting to sound angry.

"I read most of the stories last night before I turned in. Their awfulness couldn't disguise the fact that as 'fiction' they confirmed your actual crimes. I knew I had to act immediately. You almost gave me the slip this morning, but I grew up in these woods."

"You grew up in Arkham, Eph," said Mr. Derby, fingering the handle of the hunting knife.

"While I was at the farm I compared notes with that lawyer who used to advise Wendy. You thought you'd taken care of him too, but he recovered enough of his wits to realize you were guilty of murder. But how to prove it? More to the point, how to get revenge? Killing you wouldn't keep you in the grave."

"This is complete madness!"

"Only magic could do that. Then we got lucky. We discovered we could mail-order a copy of the *Necronomicon*. The complete, unexpurgated *Necronomicon*." Eph opened the book to a page highlighted in pink marker.

"The old judge is still alive, if barely, in case you didn't know. He was able to translate the Latin for me. Just listen."

Eph began to read from the ancient text.

"You idiot, you'll destroy us all!" shrieked Mr. Derby. He unsheathed the knife and lunged. But Eph was quick enough to block the blow with the *Necronomicon*. Both the forbidden tome and the pointed weapon flew out of their respective owners' hands and over the edge of the ledge. In the next instant the two foes locked limbs. They staggered to the brink of the ledge—I closed my eyes—and when I next opened them stepfather and stepson were gone. George had already fled up the tunnel. I was alone, except for a mighty cackle that swelled from below and reverberated through the cavern with all the mocking fury of the daemon-sultan Azathoth himself.

Of George's and my escape and return to Arkham, little need be said. The Chesuncook police appeared to accept our story that Mr. Derby and Eph had failed to return from an impromptu, early-morning hike. We feared telling the "truth" wouldn't go over very well, indeed might even lead to doubts of our sanity and forced detention at the local farm. (When I caught up with him outside the cave, George said Mr. Derby and Eph hadn't fallen into the pit, they'd been *pulled* in—by what exactly he wouldn't say.) In due course the missing men were declared dead, and I was able officially to assume the editorship of Azathoth House, whereupon I immediately sold the leftover stock of *Azathoth Redux* and all other "Ephraim Waite" titles to Bonanza Books. Thereafter Pickman Press confined itself to publishing fan fiction and poetry inspired by Edward Derby. (Since our adventure in Chesuncook, George has lost some of his original drive.) In addition to the complete works of Edward Derby, co-edited with my father, I have undertaken a new biography to supersede Horn as well as a less than candid history of Azathoth House, in deference to the feelings of its owner. After a suitable period of mourning, it remains finally to be said, Mrs. Derby again found marital happiness, this time with the Miskatonic dean.

SCREAM FOR JEEVES

.

I. Cats, Rats, and Bertie Wooster

"I am afraid, Jeeves, that we shall have to go," I said, as I nipped into the eggs and b. late one bright summer morning.

"Go, sir? Pray may I ask where to, sir?"

"To Anchester—to Exham Priory."

The telegram that Jeeves had delivered with the breakfast tray had been a lulu, a *cri de coeur* from my old friend Captain Edward "Tubby" Norrys:

> I say Bertie old man help! I am stuck here in this newly restored medieval monstrosity trying to buck up this gloomy old American bird progenitor of my late comrade at arms Alf Melmoth Delapore. Pop Delapore or de la Poer as he now styles himself you know how these Americans like to affect ancestral spellings Bertie has been having dreams of the queerest sort. All the cats have been acting rum as well. Come here at once and bring Jeeves. Jeeves is the only one who can get to the bottom of this mystery Bertie.—TUBBY

"What do you make of it, Jeeves?"

"Most sinister, sir."

"I know, Jeeves. Americans with sackfuls of the greenstuff to roll in tend to the eccentric. Throw in a few over-excited cats and you've got a recipe for disaster." As a rule I'm fond of the feline tribe, but in the aftermath of a certain luncheon engagement—of which more later—cats were for the moment low on my list.

"I would advocate the utmost caution in any effort to assist Captain Norrys, sir."

"But dash it all, Jeeves. Tubby and I were at school together. I suppose there's nothing for it. Telegraph the chump we're on our way, then crank up the two-seater. We leave in half-an-hour."

"Very good, sir."

I don't know if you've travelled much in the remoter reaches of the Welsh border, but that is where Jeeves and I found ourselves at dusk that evening. First the deserted streets of a forgotten village, where Jeeves spoke of the Augustan legion and the clash of arms, and all the tremendous pomp that followed the eagles; then the broad river swimming to full tide, the wide meadows, the cornfields whitening, and the deep lane winding on the slope between the hills and the water. At last we began to ascend and could see the half-shaped outlines of the hills beyond, and in the distance the glare of the furnace fire on the precipice from whose brink Exham Priory overlooked a desolate valley three miles west of the village of Anchester.

"A lonely and curious country, Jeeves," I said, casting the eye at the great and ancient wood on either side of the road. It was not a sight to put one in the mood to pull over for a loaf of bread and a jug of wine, if you know what I mean.

"In the words of Machen, sir, 'A territory all strange and unvisited, and more unknown to Englishmen than the very heart of Africa.'"

"Machen?"

"Arthur Machen, sir."

The name was new to me. "Pal of yours?"

"Indeed, sir, the distinguished Welsh mystic and *fantaisiste* was a frequent visitor to my Aunt Purefoy's house in Caerleon-on-Usk."

A short time later we turned into a drive and the towers of the priory, formerly part of the estate of the Norrys family, hove into view. The light was dim but I could not help thinking of that morbid American poet—the chappie who went about sozzled with a raven on his shoulder, don't you know, the one who penned those immortal lines:

> *Tum tum tum-tum tum tum tum-tum*
> *By good angels tum-tum-tum*
> *Tum tum tum tum stately palace—*
> *Tum-tum-tum palace—reared its head.*

"Quite the stately palace, er stately home, Jeeves, what?"

"Exham Priory is known for its peculiarly composite architecture, sir. Gothic towers rest on a Saxon or Romanesque substructure, whose foundation in turn is of a still earlier order or blend of orders—Roman, and even Druidic or native Cymric, if legends speak truly. Furthermore, sir, the priory stands on the site of a prehistoric temple; a Druidical of ante-Druidical thing which must have been contemporary with Stonehenge."

"Thank you, Jeeves." It beats me where Jeeves picks up this stuff, but the man is forever improving the mind by reading books of the highest brow.

* * *

We were greeted in the front hall by Tubby, who as he waddled across the marble more than ever resembled one of those Japanese Sumo wrestlers after an especially satisfying twelve-course meal—except in this case, of course, dinner had been held up pending our arrival.

"I'm so glad you and Jeeves are finally here, Bertie. I'm afraid Pop de la Poer has been suffering from increasingly severe delusions."

"Off his onion, is he?"

"You must jolly along the old boy as best you can, Bertie. Humour him in his every whim, until Jeeves can figure out what the devil is going on."

"You can count on Bertram to rally round and display the cheerful countenance," I assured the amiable fathead, who shook in gratitude like a jelly—or more precisely a pantry full of jellies.

A servant showed me to my room, a circular chamber in the east tower, where by the light of electric bulbs which rather clumsily counterfeited candles, I changed into evening clothes. Jeeves shimmered in as invisibly as the sheeted figure of ghostly lore and, as usual, assisted with the knotting of the tie.

"Mr. de la Poer's valet has just informed me of restlessness among all the cats in the house last night, sir."

"*All* the cats? Tell me, Jeeves, just how many of the bally creatures do you suppose infest this infernal shack?"

"Nine, sir. They were seen to rove from room to room, restless and disturbed, and to sniff constantly about the walls which form part of the old Gothic structure."

The subject of cats reminded me of the recent occasion on which Sir Roderick Glossup, the nerve specialist, came to lunch at my flat. Jeeves had fixed it so the young master had appeared an absolute loony, one of his fruitier wheezes having been to stick an overripe salmon in the bedroom by an open window. No sooner had Sir Roderick and I slipped on the nosebags than a frightful shindy started from the next room, sounding as though all the cats in London, assisted by delegates from outlying suburbs, had got together to settle their differences once and for all. You can see why the prospect of a chorus of cats at Exham Priory did not appeal.

"When he reported the incident to his master, sir," continued Jeeves, "the man suggested that there must be some singular odour or emanation from the old stonework, imperceptible to human senses, but affecting the delicate organs of cats even through the new woodwork."

"Something smells fishy here, Jeeves," I said, still quaking from the memory of the remains I had found on the bedroom carpet after about a hundred and fifteen cats had finished their picnic.

"I suspect the source of this odour or emanation is a bird of an altogether feather, sir, if you will pardon my saying so. In my estimation, the evidence indicates intramural murine activity."

"Rats in the walls, eh? Well, I'll give you odds on, Jeeves, that nine cats will make short work of any vermin that dares poke its whiskers into the cheese *chez* de la Poer."

"I would not wish to hazard a wager on the outcome, sir, until we have ascertained the exact nature of this rodent manifestation."

"Speaking of the Stilton, Jeeves, it's time I legged it for the trough."

"*À bon chat, bon rat,* sir."

I went down to the dining room, where seated at the head of the table was a cove of about sixty-five, an austere New England type about whom there still seemed to cling the greyness of Massachusetts business life.

"What ho, what ho, what ho!" I said, trying to strike the genial note.

My host, who had been sipping at the soup like some small animal, suspended the spoon just long enough to murmur a reply, as if to say the arrival of a Wooster at the watering-hole was to him a matter of little concern. As I took my place at his elbow, I surmised that the old buzzard was going to prove about as garrulous as "Silent" Cal Coolidge, soon to become the American president after that other bloke would so unexpectedly cash in the poker chips. Tubby was clearly too busy shovelling the feed down the pit to hold up his end of the bright and sparkling. So, after a few crisp remarks on the weather, I turned the conversation round to ancestors. You know how Americans like to burble on about their ancestors, especially when they have any worth the price of eggs, and Pop de la Poer did not disappoint.

"Do you realise, Mr. Wooster, that the fireside tales represent the de la Poers as a race of hereditary daemons besides whom Gilles de Retz and the Marquis de Sade would seem the veriest tyros?"

"Retz and Sade," I replied with a knowing nod of the lemon. "Weren't they those two French johnnies who went sixteen rounds with no decision in '03?"

"Some of the worst characters married into the family. Lady Margaret Trevor from Cornwall, wife of Godfrey, the second son of the fifth baron, became a favourite bane of children all over the countryside, and the heroine of a particularly horrible old ballad not yet extinct near the Welsh border."

"A ballad? Not the one by chance that starts, 'There was a young lady from Dorset / Who couldn't unfasten her corset'? I forget the middle part, but it ends something like 'Whatever you do, my good man, don't force it.'"

"Preserved in balladry, too, though not illustrating the same point is the hideous tale of Mary de la Poer, who shortly after her marriage to the Earl of Shrewsfield was killed by him and his mother, both of the slayers being absolved and blessed by the priest to whom they confessed what they dared not repeat to the world."

"Frightful dragon, was she? Sounds a bit like my Aunt Agatha."

When the geezer had exhausted the subject of his ancestors—and a rum lot they were too, all cultists and murderers and health-food fanatics, if you could credit the old legends—he filled me in on present family circs.

"Mr. Wooster, I am a retired manufacturer no longer young. Three years ago I lost my only son, Alfred, my motherless boy."

"But surely your son must have had aunts?"

"When he returned from the Great War a maimed invalid, I thought of nothing but his care, even placing my business under the direction of partners."

"Great War? Cavaliers and Roundheads, what?"

He went on to describe the restoration of the priory—it had been a stupendous task, for the deserted pile had rather resembled the ruins of one's breakfast egg—until finally, after wiping the remnants of an indifferent pear *soufflé* from the chin, the last of the de la Poers announced that he was sleepy and we packed it in for the night.

I wish I could report that the chat over the breakfast table the next morning was all sunshine and mirth, but it was not.

"I trust you slept well, Mr. Wooster," said my host, as he pushed the kippers about the plate in a morose, devil-take-the-hindmost sort of way.

"Like a top, old sport. Like a top."

"I was harassed by dreams of the most horrible sort. First there was a vision of a Roman feast like that of Trimalchio, with a horror in a covered platter."

"Could it have been something you ate?" I said, sounding the solicitous note. I didn't want to hurt the old fellow's feelings, of course, so I refrained from saying that the fish sauce the night before had been somewhat below par. In truth, the cook at Exham Priory was not even in the running with Anatole, my Aunt Dahlia's French chef and God's gift to the gastric juices.

"Next I seemed to be looking down from an immense height upon a twilit grotto, knee-deep in filth, where a white-bearded daemon swineherd drove about with his staff a flock of fungous, flabby beasts whose appearance filled me with unutterable loathing."

"Could it have been something you read before retiring? 'Mary Had a Little Lamb' perhaps? Mind you, that one's about a shepherdess, not a swineherd, but it's the same sort of thing, don't you know."

"Then, as the swineherd paused and nodded over his task, a mighty swarm of rats rained down on the stinking abyss and fell to devouring beasts and man alike."

"Rats! By Jove, this is getting a bit thick. My man Jeeves thinks rats may have been the party to blame for your cats carrying on the other day like they had broken into the catnip."

Well, this emulsion of cats and rats would soon get even thicker. Tubby and I spent an uneventful afternoon messing about the priory's extensive gardens, filled with coarse vegetables, which were to turn up at the evening meal as a sodden *mélange*. That night the pumpkin had barely hit the pillow of the four-poster before there arose a veritable nightmare of feline yelling and clawing from somewhere below. I put on the dressing gown and went out to investigate, finding a pyjama-clad Pop de la Poer in the midst of an army of cats running excitedly around the oak-panelled walls of the study.

"The walls are alive with nauseous sound—the verminous slithering of ravenous, gigantic rats!" exclaimed the master of the manse.

"You don't say. As a child I think I read something about a giant rat of Sumatra—or at any rate, a passing reference."

"You imbecile, can't you hear them stampeding in the walls?"

Before I could reply in the negative, the entire four-footed crew plunged precipitously out the door, down several flights of stairs, beating us in the biped class by several lengths to the closed door of the sub-cellar. There the gang proceeded to squat, yowling. Shortly we were joined at the portal by Tubby, Jeeves, and a host of household servants, and after some floor debate the committee resolved to explore the sub-cellar while the trail was still hot, so to speak. As we descended, lantern in hand and the cats in the vanguard, we could not repress a thrill at the knowledge that the vault was built by Roman mittens.

"Every low arch and massive pillar is Roman, sir," observed Jeeves. "Not the debased Romanesque of the bungling Saxons, but the severe and harmonious classicism of the age of the Caesars."

"I say, Jeeves, take a gander at these inscriptions: P. GETAE . . . TEMP . . . L. PRAEC . . . VS . . . PONTIFI . . . ATYS . . . Atys? Isn't he one of those chaps one reads in third-year Latin?"

"Atys is not an author, sir, but I have read Catullus and know something of the hideous rites of the Eastern god, whose worship was so mixed with that of Cybele."

"Catullus." The name had an ominous ring. "No connection with cats, I hope?"

"None, sir."

"Ah, that's a relief."

The dumb chums, if that's the term I want, had in fact ceased their howls and were licking their fur and otherwise behaving in a peaceful, law-abiding manner near a group of brown-stained blocks—or altars, according to Jeeves—except for one alabaster old gentleman, who was pawing frantically around the bottom of the large stone altar in the centre of the room.

"Hullo, what is it, Snow-Man?" asked Tubby. Like the proverbial mountain that toddled off to Mahomet, my friend rolled over to the altar in question and set down the lantern the better to scrape among the lichens clustered at the base. He did not find anything, and was about to abandon his efforts, when Jeeves coughed in that unobtrusive way of his, like a sheep clearing its throat in the mist.

"Pardon me, sir, but I think the company should note that the lantern is slightly but certainly flickering from a draught of air which it had not before received, and which comes indubitably from the crevice between floor and altar where Captain Norrys was scraping away the lichens."

"How right you are, Jeeves." We Woosters are renowned for our fighting ancestors—the grand old Sieur de Wocestre displayed a great deal of vim at the Battle of Agincourt—but there are times when it is prudent to blow the horn of alarm and execute a tactical withdrawal.

We spent the rest of the night in the brilliantly lighted study, wagging the chin over what we should do next. The discovery that some vault deeper than the deepest known masonry of the Romans underlay the sub-cellar had given us a nasty jar. Should we try to move the altar stone and risk landing in the soup below—or throw in the towel and wash our hands of it for good?

"Well, Jeeves," I said at last, after the rest of us had exercised the brain cells to no avail. "Do you have any ideas?"

"I would recommend that you compromise, sir, and return to London to gather a group of archaeologists and scientific men fit to cope with the mystery."

"I say, that's a capital idea!" exclaimed Tubby. Even de la Poer *père* grumbled his assent, and everyone agreed that this was a masterly course of action, one that Napoleon would have been proud to hit upon in his prime.

"You stand alone, Jeeves," I said.

"I endeavour to give satisfaction, sir."

"Er . . . any chance you might like to have a go at braving the unknown depths by yourself, Jeeves?"

"I would prefer not to, sir. *Nolle prosequi*."

"As you please, Jeeves."

"Thank you, sir."

Less than a fortnight later I was still congratulating myself upon my narrow escape from Castle de la Poer and its pestilential pets—I had begged off the subsequent recruitment drive and been lying low ever since—when Jeeves floated in and announced a visitor on the doorstep.

"Captain Norrys to see you, sir."

"Tubby, eh? Did he say what he wanted, Jeeves?"

"He did not confide his mission to me, sir."

"Very well, Jeeves," I said, hoping against hope that the poor sap wished to see me on some neutral affair, like our going partners in the forthcoming annual Drones Darts Tournament. "Show him in."

For a moment I thought a gelatin dessert of a size to gag an elephant had come to pay its respects—and spoil the sitting-room rug with its viscous trail—but it was, of course, only my roly-poly pal.

"Bertie, how are you?"

"Couldn't be better—now that I've returned to the metrop." I meant to sound cool and distant, but it did no good. The human pudding continued to wax enthusiastic.

"Bertie, you must come back to Exham Priory to explore the sub-sub-cellar with us. It'll be such a lark."

"Tubby, I'd sooner saunter down the aisle with Honoria Glossup than go back to that dungeon." In case I didn't mention it, la Glossup is Sir R.'s daughter, a dreadful girl who forced me to read Nietzsche during the brief period of our engagement. Or am I confusing her with Florence Craye, another horror who once viewed Betram as ripe for reform through matrimony?

"Please, Bertie. We've rounded up some prize scientific chaps, five real corkers, including Sir William Brinton."

"Sir William who?"

"As I recall, sir," said Jeeves from the sideboard, "Sir William's excavations in the Troad excited most of the world in their day."

"Thank you, Jeeves, but this egghead's credentials are not—what's the word I want, Jeeves?"

"Germane, sir?"

"Yes—they are not germane to the issue. For another thing, I have the distinct feeling I've worn out the welcome mat in this de la Poer's baleful eyes. For all my lending of the sympathetic ear and shoulder, ours was hardly a teary farewell."

"I'm not asking much, Bertie."

"What would you have me do next, Tubby, pinch the old blister's favourite cat?"

Well, what could I do? In the final appeal a Wooster always rallies round his old schoolmates. One must obey the Code.

"All right then, I'll go."

"Stout fellow, Bertie. Oh, and be sure you bring Jeeves. While these scientific chappies may be brainy enough in their own fields, no one beats Jeeves in the overall grey-matter department."

It may in fact have been a sign of his high intelligence that Jeeves was not particularly keen on the idea of a return engagement at Exham Priory, but in the end he dutifully accompanied the young master for an encore performance. All was tranquil late that August morning when we gathered in the sub-cellar. The cast included nine members of the human species and one of the feline, for the investigators were anxious that Snow-Man be present in case any rats, living or spectral, tried to give us the raspberry. While Sir William Brinton, discreetly assisted by Jeeves, directed the raising of the central altar stone, I chatted with one of the assembled savants, a fellow named Thornton, devoted to the psychic.

"Any notions what might lie in store below?" I asked, thinking he might have more insight than those with a more materialist bent.

"Matter is as really awful and unknown as spirit," the man explained in a tone that suggested it all should be perfectly plain to a child. "Science itself but dallies on the threshold, scarcely gaining more than a glimpse of the wonders of the inner place."

"Yes, quite. I see what you mean," I replied, though frankly I didn't.

Within an hour the altar stone was tilting backwards, counterbalanced by Tubby, and there lay revealed— But how shall I describe it? I don't know if you've ridden much through the tunnel-of-horrors featured at the better amusement parks, but the scene before us reminded me strongly of same. Through a nearly square opening in the tiled floor, sprawling on a flight of stone steps, was a ghastly array of human or semi-human bones. Not a pretty sight, you understand, but at least there was a cool breeze with something of freshness in it blowing up the arched passage. I mean to say, it could have been a noxious rush as from a closed vault. We did not pause long, but shiveringly began to cut a swath through the ancestral debris down the steps. It was then that Jeeves noticed something odd.

"You will observe, sir, that the hewn walls of the passage, according to the direction of the strokes, must have been chiselled from beneath."

"*From beneath*, you say, Jeeves?"

"Yes, sir."

"But in that case—"

"For the sake of your sanity, sir, I would advise you not to ruminate on the implications."

I wonder that any man among us wasn't sticking straws in his hair ere long, for at the foot of the steps we stumbled into a twilit grotto of enormous height that in atmosphere rivalled the scalier London nightclubs in the wee hours.

"Great Scott!" I cried.

"My God!" croaked another throat.

Tubby in his inarticulate way merely gargled, while Jeeves raised his left eyebrow a quarter of an inch, a sure sign of emotional distress.

There were low buildings that I imagine even Noah would have considered shabby with age—and bones heaped about everywhere, as if someone intent on emptying the closet of the family skeleton had instead uprooted the entire family tree. After recovering from the initial shock, the others set about examining the dump, a fascinating process if you were an anthropologist or an architect—but not so to Bertram, whose nerve endings by this time were standing an inch out from the skin. I had just lit up a calming gasper, when that fiend Snow-Man, taking offence perhaps at the sudden flare of the match, pounced out of the shadows toward the trouser leg. My nerves shot out another inch, and for the nonce panic overthrew sweet reason in the old bean. I fled headlong into the midnight cavern, with the hell-cat in hot pursuit.

We did not pause long, but shiveringly began

I gave the blasted animal the slip in the dark, but dash it, I eventually realised I'd lost the human herd.

"I say there, Tubby, where are you?" I hollered. "Jeeves, I say, hall-o, hall-o, hall-o!"

Well, I kept wandering about and calling, don't you know, and thinking how tiresome it was to play blind-man's-bluff for one. Then something bumped into me—something hard and lean. I knew it wasn't rats—though in a manner of speaking, I imagine you could say it was one big rat. I instantly recognised the American accent: "Shall a Wooster hold the hand of a de la Poer? . . . He's cuckoo, I tell you . . . that spineless worm . . . Curse you, Wooster, I'll teach you to goggle at what my family do!" Further aspersions on the Wooster name followed, some in Latin, a language I rather enjoy hearing, especially from Jeeves, but not in present circs. When the blighter began to growl like a pagan lion in search of its next Christian, I decided it was high time to hoof it. It wasn't a graceful exit. I scampered off and was cruising at about forty m.p.h. when I rammed the coco-nut against an object even harder on Mohs' scale than Pop de la Poer—or so it felt in that final moment before everything went black.

After what seemed like aeons, I awoke to find myself home in bed, the melon throbbing. I was just about to ring for Jeeves, when the faithful servitor drifted in with the tissue-restorer on the salver.

"Good Lord! Was it Boat-Race Night last night?" Then I quaffed the soothing brew, and our underground adventure all came back to me like a pulp thriller.

"What happened, Jeeves?" I groaned.

"After three hours we discovered you in the blackness, sir. It appears that you collided with a low-hanging rock. You will be relieved to learn that the physicians anticipate a full recovery."

"Venture far into that grisly Tartarus, did you?"

"We shall never know what sightless Stygian worlds yawn beyond the little distance we went, sir, for it was decided that such secrets are not good for mankind."

"Quite the wisest course, Jeeves, if you ask me. Man has done jolly well to date without shining the spotlight at the dirt under the carpet at Exham Priory, and I daresay if he keeps a lid on it for the future he'll be all right."

"*Dulce est ignorantia,* sir."

Despite his assurances, however, I could see by a faint twitching of the lip that Jeeves was troubled.

"Do you have something unpleasant to tell me, Jeeves?"

"Yes, sir. Unfortunately, I have some extremely disturbing news to impart."

"Out with it then, my man. Don't brood."

"I regret that it is my mournful duty to inform you, sir, that certain members of our subterranean expedition suffered grave harm." The lip again wavered. "Mr. de la Poer . . ."

"Gone totally potty, has he?"

"It is my understanding of his case that his aberration has grown from a mere eccentricity to a dark mania, involving a profound and peculiar personality change. Reversion to type, I believe, is the term employed by the professional psychologists. Mr. de la Poer is presently ensconced at Hanwell Hospital, under the direct supervision of Sir Roderick Glossup."

"Takes a loony to cure a loony, I always say."

"As for Captain Norrys, sir . . ." Jeeves coughed, like a sheep choking on a haggis. "An accident befell him that resulted in massive and irreversible physical trauma."

"You mean to say, Jeeves, he's handed in the dinner-pail?"

"Yes, sir. If I may say so, the manner of his passing was exceedingly gruesome."

"Spare me the details, Jeeves." I laughed. One of those short bitter ones.

"It would seem that Providence doesn't always look after the chumps of this world," I said, after some sober reflection.

"Indeed not, sir."

"And now I'm faced with having to scare up a new partner for the Drones Darts Tournament, what?"

"Yes, sir."

"Any ideas?"

"As the matter does not require immediate attention, sir, I suggest you devote yourself to gaining further repose."

"Right then, Jeeves. I'll catch a spot more of the dreamless."

"Most sensible, sir. So soon after your ordeal you should take care to avoid passing beyond the Gate of Deeper Slumber into dreamland."

II. Something Foetid

You ask me to explain why I don't go in for locking self in meat lockers overnight or joining expeditions to the South Pole. As those who know Bertram best will tell you, we Woosters prefer sunny skies and balmy breezes to blinding blizzards, hot water to ice in the bedroom. More fond of fair weather than of foul, of the cup of tea than of the flask of liquid nitrogen, I rarely catch cold. A nasty case, however, did keep me in bed during the two days of my betrothal to Pauline Stoker. What I will do is to relate the circs., and leave it to you to judge whether or not the young master acted like an absolute ass.

Soon after recovering from the rummy affair of the cats and rats and atavistic urges run amok which my late chum Captain Edward "Tubby" Norrys got me mixed up in, I decided it would be a sound scheme to settle down for a spell of exile in the city of New York. I know some chaps think that New York is not a sentient perpetuation of Old New York as the metrop. is of Old London and Gay Paree of Old Paris; that it is in fact dead as a dormouse and its denizens all mad as hatters. But, dash it, I'm bound to say New York's a most sprightly place to be exiled in. Everybody was awfully good to me; blokes introduced me to other blokes, and it wasn't long before I knew squads of the right sort—artists and writers and so forth.

Randy, the bird I am about to treat of, was one of the writers. He told me at our first meeting that he had once been an author of popular novels: "They were graceful novels, in which I mirthlessly and urbanely laughed at the dreams I lightly sketched; but I saw that their sophistication had sapped all their life away. Ironic humour dragged down all the twilight minarets I reared, and the earthly fear of improbability blasted all the delicate and amazing flowers in the faery gardens."

"Fairies in the garden, you say. Have you by chance been to Cottingley? Conan Doyle in that recent book of his reports that the place is swarming with the tiny wingèd creatures. He's got the snapshots to prove it, too."

Over the past couple of years Randy had turned his quill to another literary form, the short story. One of his efforts, he said with some pride, had had an unexpected effect upon the public: "When my tale, 'The Attic Window,' appeared in the January 1922 issue of *Whispers,* in a good many places it was taken off the stands at the complaints of silly milksops."

"I had a piece, 'What the Well-dressed Young Man is Wearing,' in *Milady's Boudoir,* my Aunt Dahlia's magazine," I replied, not to be outdone. "Though I must say it didn't create the same kind of frenzy among the milque-toasts."

Whatever the aesthetic rewards of this market, the financial ones had been nothing to write home about. In the spring of 1923 Randy had to secure some dreary and unprofitable magazine work; and being unable to pay any substantial rent, began drifting from one cheap boarding establishment to another until coming upon a house in West Fourteenth Street which gave him the pip rather less than the others he had sampled. The floors were clean, the linen tolerably regular, the hot water not too often cold or turned off; and although the inhabitants were mostly Spaniards of the wrong sort, there was one inmate that you wouldn't be ashamed to take to your club, a doctor by the name of Muñoz. This Muñoz, unfortunately, couldn't even accept an invitation out to the corner chemist, as he suffered from some queer ailment that confined him to his flat.

For my friend this invalid's welfare had of late become an *idée fixe,* if that's the term I want, so when Randy trickled into my apartment one forenoon, I knew his visit had to concern his fellow lodger. The very first words I spoke were: "Randy, how is Doc Muñoz?"

The poor chap gave one of those mirthless and urbane laughs. He was looking anxious and worried, like a fairy who has flitted too long amidst twilight minarets and amazing flowers.

"I'm so scared, Bertie," said Randy. "Hector's too sick to look after himself—he's sicker and sicker all the time. He relies on the landlady's son to bring him food and laundry and medicines and chemicals. Not only that, he does all his own housework."

"Does all his own housework! Great Scott, the queasy blighter must be at the end of his bally tether. Is there nothing to be done?"

"Bertie, that's why I stopped by today. Though Hector refuses to consult a doctor, I'm sure he'd welcome a visit from someone with a mind as keen and analytical as a physician's, someone who understands the psychology of the individual, someone—"

"My blushes, Randy," I murmured in a deprecating voice.

"—someone, in short, like your man Jeeves."

About my man Jeeves, I mean to say, what? I'll be the first to admit that from the collar upward he stands alone. But, dash it, he's not the only member of the Wooster household who can lend the glad hand in time of need. I was just about to issue a snappy rejoinder, when the man himself shimmered in, his map as blank as a night-gaunt's. Stifling my pique, I put the facts of the case before him and asked if he would delve into the matter.

"I have nothing to suggest at present, sir."

"Nothing, Jeeves?"

"Nothing, sir."

From a certain frostiness in Jeeves's tone, I deduced that something was amiss. Then it struck me: the fellow was still sulking over the patterned suit I had picked up for a mere twenty dollars the other day in Brooklyn and was even now sporting on the person.

"Jeeves objects to my new suit, Randy, but I tell you, a chappie can't go wrong at Franklin Clothes."

"An headquarters of prize-fight hangers-on and race-track touts, if you will pardon my saying so, sir."

"It's a pity, Jeeves, that you fail to appreciate the fizziest and freshest in American men's fashion. Wouldn't you agree, Randy?"

"Well, Bertie, let me put it this way. If I were you I'd steer clear of Italian restaurants. In those duds you might be mistaken for a tablecloth."

In the end I ventured downtown alone that evening to Randy's place on West Fourteenth Street, a four-storey mansion of brownstone, oldish by American standards, and fitted with woodwork and marble that looked as if they had been salvaged from the Augean stables—before Hercules applied the mop and broom. I was met in the hall by the landlady, Mrs. Herrero, whose whiskered mug would have qualified her as the star attraction of any circus sideshow.

"Ah, Mistair Jeeves. I so glad you come."

"Wooster's the name, my good man . . . er, woman."

"Is just in time. Doctair Muñoz, he have speel his chemicals."

"Well, I shouldn't worry if he spilled his chemicals on the woodwork or marble. I daresay no one will notice."

"All day he take funnee-smelling baths."

"Oh, really? Perhaps he got soap in his eyes and grabbed the jar of hydrogen sulphide instead of the bubble bath."

"He cannot get excite."

"He can't get outside? Yes, I know, Randy, told me, but—"

"And the sal-ammoniac—"

"Sal who?"

"Qué?"

I was prepared to play Pat to Mrs. Herrero's Mike as long as I had to, but at that moment Randy arrived and put the kibosh on the cross-talk. "Don't mind her," he explained, as he clouted his landlady affectionately on the occiput, "she's from Barcelona."

"He great once," Mrs. Herrero cried after us, as we tripped up the stairs. "My faither in Barcelona have hear of heem."

Doc Muñoz lived on the top floor, directly above Randy, in a bedsitter suite complete with laboratory. Our knock on the door was answered by a pint-sized bloke who looked about as lifelike as one of those waxworks at Madame Tussaud's. A puss as livid as a plum pie was adorned with a short iron-grey beard, somewhat less full than the chin-fungus on Mrs. Herrero.

"I've brought someone to see you, Hector," said my companion.

"I told you no visitors, Randy," the man—or mannikin—replied in a voice that sounded like a gramophone record after about the two thousandth play. It was hard to believe that this gargoyle had once impressed the lower orders of Barcelona with his greatness.

"Mr. Wooster here's no ordinary visitor, Hector. He's, uh . . . he's uh, had a heart attack and in need of medical attention," my pal improvised. The doc remained unmoved—and unmoving—like a stuffed baboon. "Please, Hector, let us in. Last week you fixed the arm of that mechanic—O'Reilly, wasn't it?—who got hurt all of a sudden."

"Very well, enter," he rasped.

"How kind of you. It's nothing really—just a wee twinge of the aortic valve," I said, warming to my rôle, though it didn't stay warm for long. As we crossed the threshold, we were struck by a blast of chill air that would have staggered Scott of the Antarctic. Refrigerating machinery resembling some futurist's nightmare and rumbling like a locomotive filled up about half the room—which smelled like a perfume emporium of the sort patronised by the cheaper class of shopgirl.

"I have a fondness for exotic spices and Egyptian incense," our host confided.

You might not have trusted Doc Muñoz to judge the roses at your garden-club flower show, but in another department he displayed superior blood and breeding.

"I greatly admire your suit, Mr. Wooster," he said, as I removed the collar and shirt studs. "The cut and fit are perfect."

"Would that everyone were as discriminating," I replied, throwing Randy a meaningful glance.

In the course of the examination, the doc explained his methods: "I am the bitterest of sworn enemies to death, Mr. Wooster, and have sunk my fortune and lost all my friends in a lifetime of bizarre experiments devoted to its bafflement and extirpation."

"Oh, yes?"

"I do not scorn the incantations of the mediaevalists, since I believe these cryptic formulae to contain rare psychological stimuli which might conceivably have singular effects on the substance of a nervous system from which all organic pulsations have fled."

"Ah."

"Will and consciousness are stronger than organic life itself, so that if a bodily frame be but originally healthy and carefully preserved, it may through a scientific enhancement of these qualities retain a kind of nervous animation despite the most serious impairments, defects, or even absences in the battery of specific organs."

"!?"

No doubt Jeeves could have put a finger on the nub of this bedside banter, but it was all Greek to Bertram, who by this juncture was quivering like an aspen, what with frost forming on the exposed anatomy and *eau de shopgirl* running riot through the nasal passages.

After pronouncing the core of the Wooster corpus brim full of organic pulsations, the doc proceeded to gas about an aged sawbones of his acquaintance, one Torres of Valencia, who had shared his earlier experiments and nursed him through a great illness some eighteen years before: "No sooner had the venerable practitioner saved me than he himself succumbed to the grim enemy he had fought. Perhaps the strain had been too great, for the methods of healing had been most extraordinary, involving scenes and processes not welcomed by elderly and conservative Galens."

"I say, old top," I replied. "Sounds as if this Torres would have been better off shoving his scenes and processes at the more youthful and liberal natives of Galencia."

After some further cheery chit-chat about the good old days back in Iberia, Randy and I made our exit. Our departure came none too soon for Wooster, B. It's one thing to brave the hazardous elements and odours of a stranger's apartment but quite another to have to hold up your end of the bright and sparkling with a being who oozes the kind of charm and vitality one usually associates with a ventriloquist's dummy.

At the front door my friend expressed his disappointment that our party had been short one member: "I'm sorry you couldn't persuade Jeeves to join us, Bertie. However, maybe Jeeves can figure out how to help Hector when you report to him."

"*If* I report to him," I shot back. And I meant it to sting.

Back home, after a hot bath free of all funny smells, I of course felt much chirpier. When Jeeves drifted in with the nightcap on the salver, I gave him the lowdown on the evening's adventure with a blithe spirit: "So there you have it, Jeeves. Doc Muñoz has an excellent eye for fashion, but over the years these queer medical experiments have left him a spent force."

"Most eldritch, sir."

"Quite, Jeeves."

"If I may be permitted to say so, sir, Dr. Muñoz's ideas appear to be as fundamentally unsound as those of Nietzsche."

"You're entitled to your opinion, Jeeves, though Randy assures me otherwise." My literary chum had once shown me a piece in one of those obscure journals he contributes to—"Nietzcheism [*sic*] and Idealism" I think was the title—which suggested that the ideas of this self-styled superman were as sound as a bell.

"I would not rely on Mr. Carter's judgement, sir."

"Why not, Jeeves?" I replied a trifle testily. "Why shouldn't I put complete faith in the judgement of one who has sacrifice all for Art?"

"I have made inquiries in your absence, sir. Despite his assertions to the contrary, Mr. Carter does not depend solely on story sales to the pulp magazines for his livelihood."

"Oh, no?"

"No, sir. In truth, the gentleman is a millionaire of extremely eccentric tastes and habits. His slumming in New York City, sir, is but his latest fancy."

"Who fed you this folderol, Jeeves?"

"His man Parks, sir. He was kind enough to supply the essential background information."

"His man Parks?"

"Yes, sir. Parks looks after a second residence that Mr. Carter clandestinely maintains in a far more suitable neighborhood of the city than the one he ostensibly calls home."

One does not as a rule enjoy one's valet accusing one's friends of playing false, and now was no exception. "Randy comes of an ancient line, Jeeves, composed of delicate and sensitive men with strange visions," I said hotly.

"Indeed, sir."

"A flame-eyed Crusader learnt wild secrets of the Saracens that held him captive."

"Very good, sir."

"The first Sir Randolph Carter studied magic when Elizabeth was queen."

"Yes, sir."

"And Edmund Carter just escaped hanging in the Salem witchcraft."

"*Quod erat demonstratum,* sir. I fear Mr. Carter has inherited the family predilection for the *outré*. Parks informs me that Mr. Carter once lived with a man in the south and shared his studies for seven years, till horror overtook them one midnight in an unknown and archaic graveyard, and only one emerged where two had entered."

"Sheer rot, Jeeves."

"Parks for years has born patiently with his master's vagaries, sir."

"What utter tripe."

"I would advise you, sir, not to allow Mr. Carter to draw you any deeper into this matter concerning Dr. Muñoz. It is apparent that Dr. Muñoz is beyond all earthly assistance. As the lesser of two evils, sir, I recommend you accept the invitation which Miss Pauline Stoker issued over the 'phone this evening. Miss Stoker desires you to visit her at her father's Long Island estate at your earliest convenience."

I paused, taking a pensive sip from the beaker. I was dashed if I would humble myself before the man, yet perhaps Jeeves did smell a genuine stinker. There was something foetid about this Muñoz business. Although Pauline Stoker is one of those hearty girls who insists on playing five sets of tennis before breakfast, her taste in perfume is above reproach.

"Right you are, Jeeves. A spot of fresh country air would do wonders for the old aortic valve."

"Very good, sir."

"Oh, and Jeeves," I said, as if the idea were merely a careless afterthought. "When you pack my bag, please be sure to include my new suit, the one from Franklin Clothes."

"Surely not, sir," said Jeeves in a low, cold voice, as if he had been bitten on the leg by a zoog. I could see that I was in for yet another round in that colossal contest of wills which from time to time darkens our relationship. But, fortified by the soothing beverage, I stood my ground. After a good deal of give-and-take we reached a split decision: the garment in question would travel with me to the country—but not Jeeves.

"I do not wish to be placed in a position, sir," the man protested, "where persons of refinement might misapprehend that I condone your wearing in public such Byzantine refuse."

As things turned out, I had no occasion to show off my new suit, as I spent most of my time *chez* Stoker recovering from a cold which no doubt had originated within the polar precincts of Doc Muñoz's bedsitter. Of course, the thirty-six holes of golf Pauline dragged me through the day I arrived—one of those crisp autumn days where the wind sweeps down the fairway in frore gusts as if from interstellar space—may have further weakened the Wooster constitution. Or then again it may have been the proposal of marriage I let slip in a moment of madness after sinking a fifteen-footer on the seventeenth. Whatever the source of my affliction, I stayed in bed for forty-eight hours, dosed with three different nostrums. The third night I had just begun to descend the seven-hundred steps to the Gate of Deeper Slumber, when a servant awoke me with an urgent summons to the 'phone.

"Bertie!" gasped a familiar voice over the line. "Thanks heavens I've reached you. The pump on Hector's refrigerating machine has broken down. Within three hours the process of ammonia cooling will become impossible. You must return to the city at once."

"But I say, Randy, it's past eleven o'clock and I'm feeling far from perky."

"I've checked the train schedule, Bertie. You'll have plenty of time to catch the 12:03 back to town."

"Why don't you ring up Jeeves?"

"Jeeves was over earlier this evening—he gave me your number in the country—but damn the luck, he seems to have gone off for the night. I get no answer at your apartment. Not only that, I can't reach my man Parks."

"You never told me you employed a man, Randy."

"No, Bertie, I guess I never did."

"You know, Randy, Jeeves has told me some rum stories about your past."

For a few seconds all I could hear in the receiver was a kind of guttural coughing, like a ghast choking on a gug.

"Sorry, Bertie. I know at times I haven't been totally on the level," my friend conceded. "Still, I have always tried to live as befits a man of keen thought and good heritage."

"Would you say, Randy, that deserting a pal in an unknown and archaic graveyard at midnight befits a man of keen thought and good heritage?"

"I can explain, Bertie—"

"You shared a study with the chap for seven years!"

"Only five years—"

"I bet you were prefects together, too."

"Bertie, listen, uh . . . That night in the graveyard was, uh . . . was, uh, a prank. Harley Warren came back from below. He was no fool. . . . And this is no prank! This is an emergency, a matter of life and death!"

Well, what was a fellow to do in the face of such a piteous plea? I could not leave my chum in the lurch. Even on his bed of pain, a Wooster rallies round.

"Oh, very well then, Randy. I'll be there in a jiffy."

What with the train halting at every milk stop en route, and the dearth of cabs at the terminal in the wee hours, it was rather longer than a jiffy before I alighted at Randy's boarding-house. A sleepy and unshaven Mrs. Herrero greeted me at the door with a few choice epithets in her native tongue. Upstairs in the doc's flat I found Randy and the moribund hermit, the melon tightly bandaged, looking like a refugee from King Tut's tomb. The place no longer sounded like a locomotive at full throttle, and the pervading scent was now that of ammonia, redolent of the detergent Mrs. Herrero should have been using to swab down the woodwork and marble.

"Bertie! At last!" exclaimed my pal. A low rattle—one of those short hollow ones—issued from the throat of the mummy impersonator at his side.

"Were you by chance able to fix the fridge on your own, Randy?" I asked hopefully.

"I brought in O'Reilly from the neighbouring all-night garage, but he said nothing could be done till morning, when we'll have to get our hands on a new piston."

"Anything I can do?"

"Yes, as a matter of fact there is, Bertie. While I look after Hector here, please go out and get all the ice you can from every all-night drug store and cafeteria you can find. Okay?"

The prospect of traipsing about lower Manhattan before dawn, further risking the organic pulsations, did not appeal. Nonetheless, I spent the next couple of hours at the task, laying the spoils in front of the closed bathroom door, behind which the doc retired at about 5 A.M. "More—more!" the blister kept croaking, like a brat whose appetite for frozen treats knows no bounds.

At length a warmish day broke, and the shops opened one by one. It was then that Randy insisted I try to enlist the services of Mrs. Herrero's offspring, Esteban.

"Now see here, laddie," I said, holding up the defective part. "This pump piston."

"*Sí.*"

"This ice." I gestured at the miniature igloo that now blocked the bathroom door.

"*Sí.*"

"It's very simple. Either you go fetch the ice—or you order a new piston."

"How I order piston?"

"All right then, I'll order the piston and you fetch ice."

"*Qué?*"

A bop on the bean with the pump piston did not raise the level of the fathead's wits, though it did succeed in provoking the ire of Herrero *mère*, who was hovering in the vicinity like a mother hydra: "Mistair Woostair, I sorry. Esteban he can no help. No way, nossir."

Herrero and son slipped out through the puddles that for the nonce gave Doc Muñoz's bedsitter the appearance of an Arctic lagoon.

"That settles it," said Randy, raging violently. "Our only hope is to get ahold of Jeeves. You've got to give him another ring, Bertie."

We had been trying in vain every half-hour or so to telephone Jeeves and Parks at their respective digs, but only now, with the sun already high in the heavens, did I get through to the man.

"Jeeves, where have you been all night?" I said sharply.

"After looking in on Mr. Carter and Dr. Muñoz, sir, I joined Parks at his club, the New York branch of the Junior Ganymede. The amenities of that estimable institution proved so agreeable that we remained on the premises until eight o'clock this morning."

"Jeeves, I have been back in the burg since 3 A.M. and require your aid instanter."

"I apologise, sir. In view of the worrisome state of your health, I did not anticipate your returning quite so soon from the country. How may I be of assistance?"

I proceeded to outline the present crisis, drawing his attention to the crucial role of the pump piston.

"I had the opportunity to inspect the mechanism of which you speak last night, sir. I believe I know of a suitable supply house far downtown where one might obtain a replacement. If you, sir, will perform this errand of mercy, Parks and I will meet you at Mr. Carter's West Fourteenth Street address with the appropriate tools for repair."

"Very good, Jeeves. We'll save the old doc yet!"

Well, what with discovering that Jeeves was wrong about the supply house he named and having to run hither and thither by subway and surface car to a number of other pump-piston purveyors, I did not return with the necessary part until approximately 1:30 P.M. By this time Bertram was a spent force and could barely drag self upstairs. In the hall outside the doc's apartment stood Jeeves, Randy, and a brisk little Cockney who could only have been Parks. Parks was busily chiding his master for allowing Doc Muñoz to shut them out: "Oy, guv'nor, so you leaves 'ome for ice and 'e in there sneaks out the bath and locks the bloomin' door, wot?" Jeeves was fiddling with some wire device at the door, behind which came no sound save a nameless sort of slow, thick dripping.

"Oh, Bertie," moaned my friend. "What kept you?"

"Dash it all, Randy, I did all I could!"

"I am afraid, sir, that you are not in time," said Jeeves solemnly.

"Not in time! You mean to say that my superhuman exertions over the past fourteen hours have been for naught? I spend half the night in a breathless, foodless search for ice and the whole morning in a hectic quest for pistons, and you tell me, Jeeves, you tell me I'm not in time?"

"It is most unfortunate, sir, but yes, that is the case."

I was sorely tempted to start smacking the lemon with the object of my wasted efforts, when Jeeves raised a restraining hand.

"I have just now managed to turn the key, sir," the man said coolly. "In your over-excited condition, sir, I would advise you to wait in the hall. Anyone else who chooses to enter should take the precaution of holding a pocket handkerchief to his nose."

Jeeves was referring to the nauseous odour that was seeping in waves from beneath the closed door, a fragrance rather reminiscent of the over-ripe salmon he once stuck in the bedroom while I lunched with my nemesis, the nerve specialist Sir Roderick Glossup. As the door swung open, revealing a south room blazing with the warm sun of early afternoon, the fishy smell swelled a thousandfold. The stomach churned, the knees buckled. The autumn heat lingered fearsomely. Then everything went black.

By the end of the week, after a programme featuring a thirty-six-hour snooze followed by a steady diet of Jeeves's tissue-restorers, I had regained my pep. Randy, on the other hand, when he came by, looked rather the worse for wear—like a fairy who has flitted so long amidst twilight minarets and amazing flowers that he has decided to call it a day and throw in the towel.

"I'm terribly sorry about Doc Muñoz, Randy," I said, offering my condolences. "But at least we gave it the old school try, what?"

"I guess so," the chump replied mournfully.

"Tut-tut, old stick. This Muñoz was scarcely the last word in loony old scholars. You'll soon find yourself another."

"I doubt it," sighed my friend. "By the way, Bertie, speaking of old scholars, I dreamed of my grandfather last night. He reminded me of a key. . . ." Randy went on to describe a great silver key handed down from the Carters who consorted with wild-eyed Saracens and witches and what not. Housed in a carved oak box of archaic wonder, this key lay forgotten in the attic of the ancestral homestead in Arkham, Mass., whither the dreamer intended shortly to return.

"Hunting up old keys," I replied warmly. "Now there's a hobby not likely to land a chap in the soup, Randy."

After some final reflections on the occasionally titanic significance of dreams, my chum announced his departure: "So, Bertie, this is good-bye. Parks and I leave New York tomorrow."

Before I could return the farewell, Jeeves wafted in, smiling faintly, like an obliging ghoul.

"Good-bye, Jeeves," said Randy, turning to the man. "And thanks again for your gift. Hector would have approved."

"Thank you, sir."

"I say, Randy, what—" But the chap had already biffed off.

"Forgive me for interrupting, sir, but while you were entertaining Mr. Carter, Miss Pauline Stoker 'phoned."

"Oh?" I quavered. In all the recent excitement the bally girl had totally slipped my mind, and I dreaded hearing the sequel.

"Miss Stoker asked me to inform you, sir, that you may consider your engagement off as of the moment you sneaked out of her father's house."

"She's handing me the mitten, you say, Jeeves?"

"Your precipitous midnight flight did not impress her favourably—nor did your subsequent lack of communication, sir."

"You didn't explain I was busy helping a pal?"

"No, sir. I thought it best not to correct her negative view of your behaviour. Indeed, she was almost inclined to forgive you, except that—"

"Except what, Jeeves?"

"Except that Sir Roderick Glossup happened to have a word with her father, J. Washburn Stoker, about your past, sir."

Ever since the episode of the cats and the fish in the bedroom alluded to elsewhere in these memoirs of mine, R. Glossup has regarded Bertram as barmy to the core. While I wasn't privy to their colloquy, of course, I've no doubt the old pot of poison convinced Pop Stoker to be wary of any prospective son-in-law who keeps a hundred and fifteen cats in the home.

"Well, Jeeves, if Randy can endure the demise of the doc," I said after musing awhile, "I suppose I can bear the loss of a fiancée." In all honesty it was a relief to realise I didn't have to order the new sponge-bag trousers and gardenia, because my nomination had been cancelled. Pauline's beauty had maddened me like wine, but even the finest vintages can leave a chap feeling fried.

"I am pleased to hear you express such a philosophical view of the situation, sir. If I might make a small confession—" Jeeves coughed.

"Yes, Jeeves?"

"I believe you would agree, sir, that Mr. Carter's concern for his upstairs neighbour had its peculiar aspects."

"Now that you mention it, Jeeves, Randy did overdo it a bit."

"Although Dr. Muñoz was headed for a certain and familiar doom, sir, Parks and I resolved during your absence from the city to tip Nature's own sweet and cunning hand."

"What are you driving at, Jeeves?"

"I devised a stratagem, sir, whereby I made an appointment to meet Dr. Muñoz. Parks and Mr. Carter were also present. At one point in the evening, while Parks distracted our hosts with an amusing imitation of their landlady, I took the opportunity to tinker with the pumping action of the refrigerating equipment."

"You mean to say, Jeeves, you bunged a monkey wrench into the machinery?"

"In effect, sir. Thereafter it was a simple matter, as you know—" Jeeves coughed again. "It was a simple matter to ensure that the pump was not repaired in time."

"Jeeves! Have you no shame?" I cried. It is one thing to admit to adding insult to injury, quite another to engage in conduct to which even a Machiavelli or a Borgia would hesitate to stoop.

"I can assure you, sir, that Parks and I acted in the best interest of his master. As for Dr. Muñoz—"

"I say, Jeeves, what about Doc Muñoz? What-in-the-devil did you find in the old bird's flat after my collapse?"

"Are you by chance familiar, sir, with Arthur Machen's 'Novel of the White Powder'?"

"Really, Jeeves. You should know the only novels I read are mysteries and thrillers. Cosmetics aren't in my line. . . . Machen. Say, isn't he that pal of yours?"

"Yes, sir. The Welsh mystic used often to visit my Aunt Purefoy—"

"Oh, right, now I remember—you told me before. But I'm still in the dark about the doc."

"Very well, sir, do you recall the story by Edgar Allan Poe entitled 'Facts in the Case of M. Valdemar'?"

"That dimly rings a bell, Jeeves. Something about a little Frenchman who wears his arm in a sling, what?"

"Not exactly, sir."

"Oh, well, never mind then. . . . Oh, one last thing, Jeeves. That gift Randy was thanking you for. Dare I ask—"

"The gentleman was thanking me for your suit, sir."

"You don't mean my suit from Franklin Clothes, do you?"

"Yes, sir, I do. When I unpacked your bag after your return from Long Island, I took the liberty of notifying Mr. Carter of its availability."

"I can't imagine why Randy would want my suit, Jeeves."

"If I may explain, sir, the suit was not for the gentleman himself but was to be delivered to the funeral parlour in possession of Dr. Muñoz's remains. It was my understanding that the late physician's own wardrobe included no suitable burial attire, and as he had voiced his admiration—"

"But I say, Jeeves. The doc and I were hardly the same size." I am on the tall and willowy side, while the stiff barely scraped my coat-tails.

"In the circumstances, sir, a precise fit was not deemed essential."

"Jeeves, I say—"

"In the meantime, sir, if you desire a replacement, I recommend you patronise Howards Men's and Young Men's Clothes. A courteous salesman of my acquaintance there would be glad to show you their plain blue serge."

III. The Rummy Affair of Young Charlie

Life is a hideous thingummy. Take the case of Arthur "Pongo" Jermyn, for instance. Art was not like any other Egg, Bean, or Crumpet, for he was a poet and a dreamer, the sort of chappie who after a few quick ones would declare that the stars are God's daisy-chain, that every time a fairy hiccoughs a wee baby is born, and that we humans are not a separate species. This poetic lunacy fitted right in with his *outré* personal appearance. It is easy to say just what the poor chimp—sorry, chump—resembled. To swing across the Drones swimming-bath by the ropes and rings was with him the work of a moment, if you know what I mean. Even Tuppy Glossup's looping back the last ring did not cause Sir Arthur to drop into the fluid and ruin his specially tailored dress-clothes with the fifty-inch sleeves.

A sensitive bird, Art. Later that same night, after St. John speculated rather too freely on the unknown origins of his music-hall mother, he went out on the moor and set fire to his clothing. Spared the frying pan of the soup, his entire outfit, extra-long arms and all, was like the "mad truth" in the sonnet, "devoured by a flame." Unfortunately, so was my late pal, as the ass hadn't bothered to disrobe. I can assure you that those rumours about his first seeing a boxed *object* which had come from Africa are only so much rot. It was his looking like a supporting player out of an Edgar Rice Burroughs jungle thriller, not this *object* (which was merely the mummy of one of his white-ape ancestors), that led to his awful doom.

Yes, life can be a rummy thing—downright scaly, don't you know, as also shown by the case of Charles "Dexter" Ward. I had never heard of this Ward till the fateful day—one of those juicy late spring ones, with a seething, impenetrable sky of bluish coruscations—that my Aunt Agatha unexpectedly appeared on the doorstep.

"Mrs. Spenser Gregson to see you, sir," announced Jeeves.

"Oh, gosh!" I said, shaken to the core. I had recently arisen from the abyss of sleep, and a surprise visit from Aunt Agatha was about as welcome as a midnight call from a reanimated corpse.

"Bertie!" exclaimed Aunt Agatha, following hot on the faithful servitor's heels. I noticed that she was looking somewhat pale and peaked, rather like Art Jermyn's great-great-great-grandmother.

"Oh hullo, old ancestor," I chirped. "Topping weather we've been having, what?"

"It is celibate bachelors like you, Bertie, who make a person realise why the human race will have to give way to the hardy coleopterous species. Instead of lolling about indoors this lovely morning you should be out chasing some charming girl in the Park."

"No, really, I say, please!" I said, blushing richly. Aunt Agatha owns two or three of these gent's magazines, and she keeps forgetting she isn't in an editorial meeting.

"Bertie, I didn't come here to lecture you on your lack of a sex life."

"Oh, no?"

"No. I had to see you immediately on a much graver matter. In today's post I received a most distressing letter from some dear American friends of mine, Mr. and Mrs. Theodore Howland Ward, of Providence, in New England. They are extremely worried about their son, Charles."

"Oh, yes?"

"Yes. A year ago, the senior Wards report, Charles determined after coming of age to take the European trip they had hitherto denied him. Before sailing for Liverpool, he promised to write to them fully and faithfully. Letters soon told of his safe arrival, and of his securing good quarters in Great Russell Street, London; where he proposed to stay till he had exhausted the resources of the British Museum in a certain direction."

"Sounds like a bookish cove."

"The alarming thing is, he has shunned all family friends."

"A shy bookish cove." While I didn't say so, with family friends like Aunt Agatha, the chap had probably avoided a lot of hell-and-high-water by cheesing the trans-Atlantic introductions.

"Of his daily life he wrote but little. Study and experiment consumed all his time, and he mentioned a laboratory which he had established in one of his rooms."

"I say, not a well-cooled laboratory!" I yipped, chilled to the marrow. The previous autumn in New York I'd run afoul of a blighter who enjoyed doing experiments in the home, and I was still reeling from the experience. Could this American chappie be a chip off the same iceberg?

"His last communication was a brief note telling of his departure for Paris."

"Flown the metrop., has he?" I said in some relief, for the conversation seemed to have been drifting towards Bertram's being called upon to roll out the welcome wagon—show the young blister the best and brightest night spots, lunch him at one's club, all that sort of thing. "Well, I'm sure that after a year of messing about museums in all directions, even a shy bookish cove would be ready to stampede to Paris like a ghoul to a grave-yard."

"Bertie, it is imperative that you and Jeeves go to Paris right away. You must check up on the boy and do everything you can to keep him out of mischief."

"Yes, but I say . . ."

"Bertie!"

"But, dash it all . . ."

"I am counting on you, Bertie, not to let the Wards down. In my reply I shall tell them you are already en route to Paris."

Further resistance was clearly useless, so once again in the face of supe-rior force I hoisted the white flag and cried uncle—or in this case, aunt. Af-ter the triumphant withdrawal of the aged relative, I case a mournful eye at Jeeves, who had been fooling with some silver in the background.

"I had better be packing, sir?"

"I suppose so."

I could see from the way he absent-mindedly slipped a spoon into his pocket that the man was not altogether satisfied with this turn in our affairs.

"Forgive me for saying so, sir," said Jeeves, "but it is my impression from Mrs. Gregson's remarks—"

"I know, Jeeves," I said, raising a restraining hand. "You're going to advise me not to throw caution to the wind and lope in on all-fours, but you can take it from me, one does not lightly or carelessly defy Aunt Agatha."

My experience is that when Aunt Agatha wants you to do a thing you do it, or else you find yourself wondering why the Old Ones made such a fuss when they had trouble with their shoggoths.

Paris, which we reached early the next day after a blasphemously choppy crossing and a noisome night in a train, fairly drips with gaiety and *joie de vivre* in the late spring, so I can't say that I was feeling too put out by the time we were settled at our hotel, a mere black-stone's away from Ward's own address in the Rue St. Jacques. Since I had no desire to venture over to his lodgings, where he might already be splashing the chemicals about the laboratory, I duly invited the lad to come round for tea *chez* Wooster. From his reply I could tell he was not keen on the prospect of accepting cucumber sandwiches from a stranger stooging for his people in Providence, but on the appointed afternoon he did pull in on schedule.

While an impartial observer would no doubt have considered the tall, slim bird that Jeeves ushered in a finer physical specimen than, say, Art Jermyn, there was about our visitor something quite (I hate to say this) bland. The handshake limp as a fish, the eye that resolutely refused to meet one's own, as well as the tendency to guzzle the tea and gobble the sandwiches like schoolboy home on holiday, were but the more salient signs—or so this same impartial observer would be forced to conclude—that here was a fellow sorely out of practice in the social graces department.

"Well, well, well, Ward," I said, taking the avuncular approach. "Must be rather jolly, your first time in Paris, what?"

"Actually, it's not my first time in Paris."

"It's not?"

"Nope. From London I made one or two flying trips for material in the Bibliothèque Nationale."

"Oh, ah, yes, of course. Our English material's never good enough for you Americans, so you pop over to Paris for French material in the Biblio-what's-it . . . Er, just what sort of material?"

"Nothing much really, just some stuff to do with my research."

"Research?"

"Yup, research."

"May I ask what kind of research?"

"Um, let me see now. I guess you could call it antiquarian research."

"You mean you're one of these collector blokes like my Uncle Tom who covets things like eighteenth-century silver cow-creamers?"

"Well, um, not exactly. I am pretty interested in old books and stuff like that, though. Right now I'm doing a special search among rare manuscripts of a private collector."

"A private collector? Maybe he knows my Uncle Tom. Mind my asking his name?"

"Well, I don't want to sound rude or anything, but I think it's better if I, um, just keep the guy's name to myself. Okay?"

I have always found that given half a chance most Americans on first acquaintance will spill their life stories and then some. Such, however, was not the case with Charlie Ward. Only when I touched on the home-town topic of Providence, Rhode Island, did he drop the mask and bare the soul a bit—though it did strike me as rum that a non-university man should wax rhapsodic over a place called College Hill.

"See here, Ward," I said, as our guest swabbed the last drops of tea out of his saucer with the last crust of sandwich bread. "You can take this shy bookish pose only so far. Instead of palling around with unnamed private collectors, you should be out stalking pretty girls in the Bois de Boulogne. At least that's what you can bet my Aunt Agatha would recommend."

"Gosh, Mr. Wooster, it's sure nice of you to give me all this free advice. I'll consider it real carefully. Okay? In the meantime, thanks *mucho* for the grub. *Adiós.*"

After our visitor tottered off, I turned to Jeeves for his assessment.

"Well, Jeeves, what do you make of the lad?"

"In my opinion, sir, the gentleman's studious eyes and slight stoop, together with his somewhat careless dress, give a dominant impression of harmless awkwardness rather than attractiveness."

"Short on attractiveness and long on awkwardness, yes, that's our boy in a nutshell, Jeeves. But harmless? Ha!" I laughed. One of those short ironic ones. "If you ask me, unless he cleans up his act, young Charlie could do more harm than a resurrected wizard left alone in a sandbox of essential saltes."

Over the fortnight that followed, I set about with the zeal of a missionary among the heathen to reveal to the reclusive New Englander the error of his unwholesome ways. Dining at fine restaurants was a wash-out, as the chap had an unholy suspicion of any and all unfamiliar food. Unlike the cucumber sandwiches which proved so boffo, the *ris de Dhole à la Financière* and the *velouté aux fleurs de Tcho-Tcho* went untasted on the platter. Wines were wasted as well, as he confessed to being a confirmed teetotaler. Similarly, outings to the Auteuil race course and to the Roville-sur-mer casinos only served to show that my Puritanical companion possessed not a drop of sporting blood. In short, he displayed none of the youthful ebullience which, for example, inflamed my cousins, Claude and Eustace, that time they descended on the metrop. from Oxford to pinch cats and policemen's helmets.

Only once, when he persuaded Jeeves and myself to play a parlour game called "Shoes and Socks," did my charge betray a spark of *esprit*. But even this was a bust, as the proceedings came to a screeching halt when he discovered I had travelled to the C., *sans* Bible. Assurances that I had won the prize for Scripture Knowledge at my private school did not appease. In the end Jeeves and I suffered no little embarrassment retrieving our footwear from the *gamin* on whom they had fallen when Ward dropped them out the hotel window in a sack.

"Jeeves, we're up against it this time," I declared in the aftermath of the shoes and socks episode. "If only Aunt Agatha weren't so bally set on saving the silly sap's soul, I'd chuck the case as fast as Charlie tossed the spats and garters *dans la rue*." On Aunt Agatha's orders, which arrived almost daily, I had been despatching regular progress reports. I knew that today's news from the French front would get a cool reception at GHQ London.

"Speaking of Mrs. Gregson, sir, she enclosed in her morning *communiqué* a missive from the Ward family physician, a Dr. Marinus Bicknell Willett. I have taken the liberty of perusing the contents. You may find, sir, that it sheds some light on the psychology of the individual."

"Why don't you just give me the gist, Jeeves."

"Very good, sir," the man replied, his usual solemn tone shading into the sepulchral. "Dr. Willett discloses that the youth underwent a three-year period of intensive occult study and graveyard searching before leaving for England."

"Hm, if I'm not mistaken, Jeeves, didn't that New York chum of mine also have a thing about graveyards?"

"Yes, sir. As you may recall, sir, Mr. Carter reportedly had a most unpleasant encounter in an unknown and archaic—"

"Yes, yes, never mind the sordid details. Pray continue, Jeeves. What other tit-bits does this Doc Willett have to offer about the patient?"

"Once, sir," intoned Jeeves, "he went south to talk with a strange old mulatto who dwelt in a swamp."

"I say, not the same chap with whom Randy used to share a study, do you suppose?"

"Dr. Willett does not make the association, sir."

"Quite suggestive, though, Jeeves, what?"

"Indeed, sir."

"Anything else, Jeeves?"

"Yes, sir. In addition, the young gentleman sought a small village in the Adirondacks whence reports of certain odd ceremonial practices had come."

"These are deep waters, Jeeves," I said, tenting the fingertips. "Or rather, high hills. Have you any clue to their meaning?"

"Arthur Machen, sir, has written of odd ceremonial practices among the natives of the Welsh hill country. I can well imagine villagers in the remote mountain areas of the United States of America also engaging in such practices."

"Well, Jeeves," I said, after brooding a bit on the ceremonial concept, "at this stage of the investigation only one thing is certain."

"And what may that be, sir?"

"That young Ward would be warmly received at any private hospital for the insane."

"The latest evidence, sir, would seem to support the notion that Mr. Ward is an exceedingly singular person."

"If it weren't for that cats-and-rats, or, cats-and-fish-in-the-bedroom business, I would immediately wire Sir Roderick Glossup: 'Loony American loose in Paris. Please reserve next available padded cell.'"

"I daresay, sir, we may yet require professional assistance."

The next development in the rummy affair of young Charlie seemed to augur the light before the dawn. The blighter disappeared, leaving behind no forwarding address. I was all set to throw in the towel and call it a day, when Aunt Agatha herself blew in for a surprise inspection. The old flesh and blood promised that she would have up "ye Legions from Underneath" and sic them on B. Wooster, unless he hopped to and resumed the chase. "All civilisation, all natural law, perhaps even the fate of the solar system and the universe depend on your following through, you miserable worm." Never one to mince words, Aunt Agatha, even if she did rather overstate the case.

So there was nothing for it but to give Jeeves his head and see if he could run our elusive scholar to ground. And by Jove, within the week he had sniffed out the lad's new lair, at a rooming-house in the Rue d'Auseil.

"Yoicks, Jeeves!" I ejaculated when the man announced that the quarry was at bay. "I mean to say, excellent!"

"I endeavour to give satisfaction, sir."

"So, Jeeves, our boy's holed up in the Rue d'Auseil. Is that by chance anywhere near the Auteuil race course?"

"No, sir. If you must know, sir, I experienced no small difficulty discovering Mr. Ward's present whereabouts."

"Oh, yes?"

"The Rue d'Auseil is not down in any map, sir."

"Oh, no?"

"No, sir. As Melville says, sir, true places never are."

"Like that lost city in Africa Art Jermyn was always gassing about, I suppose. But I say, Jeeves, let's stick to the *res*. What other data did you dig up?"

"Mr. Ward has ceased to affiliate with the private collector whose name he refused to divulge, sir. On the other hand, sir, it appears that his removal to the Rue d'Auseil was prompted by the desire to associate with yet another unusual individual."

"Were you able to scare up a name for this chap?"

"Yes, sir. The gentleman in question signs his name as Erich Zann. He is an old German viol-player, sir, a strange dumb man who plays each evening in a cheap theatre orchestra."

"Really, Jeeves, is this Zann's playing so vile that he has to settle for music-halls featuring the likes of Art Jermyn's mother?"

Nothing against Mrs. Jermyn personally, of course, despite all those frightful rumours St. John used to spread about the Drones, but you know the kind of chorus girl I mean.

"You misapprehend me, sir. A viol is a bowed stringed instrument with deep body, flat back, sloping shoulders, six strings, fretted fingerboard, low-arched bridge—"

"Please, Jeeves," I said, lifting a warning hand. "Your musical knowledge may be *nonpareil,* but we're once again wandering far afield. What in the dickens do you suppose Ward sees in this clammed-up codger?"

"I could not say, sir, as I have not spoken with the young gentleman. My informant, however, is not sanguine about Herr Zann's influence."

"Your informant?"

"Yes, sir. A third tenant of the house in the Rue d'Auseil, an elderly American and vigilant observer of the domestic scene, has been kind enough to supply the essential background information."

"One of these Nosey Parkers, eh?"

"You might say so, sir, although I believe his motives to be above reproach. Once I explained our situation *vis-à-vis* Mr. Ward, he proposed that we combine forces."

"Very good, Jeeves. But, I say, do you think we can trust this American buster? Can he deliver the goods?"

"He impressed me as a person on whom we can confidently rely in matters of the utmost delicacy, sir. Indeed, sir, I have taken the liberty of arranging a meeting to discuss how best to coordinate our efforts."

"Hasn't been reticent about revealing his name, has he?"

"Pardon me, sir, I should have mentioned it earlier." Jeeves gave one of those discreet coughs of his, like a sheep clearing its throat in the spray from an Alpine waterfall. "The gentleman introduces himself as Mr. Altamont, of Chicago."

The following forenoon Jeeves ushered into the presence a tall, gaunt chappie of seventy, sporting a tuft of chin-fuzz which gave him a general resemblance to the mug shots of Uncle Sam. Not my Uncle Sam, mind you, whose phiz I used to render in crayon at the risk of a thrashing as a tot, but the American imitation of our own John Bull.

"Howdy, mister," said the man, slapping the shoulder with a rough familiarity from which I shied like a startled faun. One can be mistaken in these things, of course, but this Altamont didn't strike me off-hand as the sort of johnny on whose utmost delicacy one could confidently rely.

"Oh, ah. The pleasure is all mine, old bean," I said, betraying no horror as the gargoyle poured his longish limbs into an armchair with not so much as a by-your-leave and relit a half-smoked, sodden cigar.

"It's Mr. Wooster, ain't it?" exclaimed the Irish-American. "Mr. Jeeves said you were pretty regular for a swell, the kind of fella you can count on to help bring home the bacon."

"As Jeeves will attest," I retorted, "I am extremely fond of the eggs and b. But you should understand, my dear chap, that it is my man who does all the grocery shopping for the household."

"Hey, no offence, mister. I just meant to say you're a dude who sticks to his guns, a guy who when the chips are down will walk the last mile for a pal."

"Well, we Woosters do have our Code, don't you know," I murmured, all very dignified and feudal.

"I'm not one to brag much, mister, but I've cracked a few codes in my day, too—a hundred and sixty all told. There was this one cipher that this gang in Chicago—"

"Chicago!" I cried. "Your native burg, is it not?"

"You bet, mister."

"The city that many of the *cognoscenti* consider the crime capital of the Western Hemisphere," I continued. "Home of speakeasies, bootleg liquor,

Tommy guns, *Weird Tales* magazine, what?"

"Gosh, I won't deny—"

"Al Capone wouldn't by chance be a pal of yours, would he?"

"Ha, ha," the man laughed, the stogie bobbing above the chin-fungus. "You implyin' I hang out with crooks? Believe me, friend, every now and then I act independent of the coppers, but I always land feet first on the right side of the law."

"I can assure you I sail a pretty straight course myself," I responded, "except on Boat-Race Night. I usually go for a swim in the Trafalgar Square fountain, which offence rates a five pound fine from the Bosher Street beak."

"Glad to hear you ain't above cutting a caper on occasion, mister."

Having hit on a common interest in the criminal impulse, I have to admit I found myself warming to the bloke, with his bluff, easy manner. Not that I was about to bet my little all on his utmost delicacy with any confidence, but I decided he at least deserved a hearing.

"See here, Altamont," I said at last. "Jeeves tells me you've got the dope on young Ward in his new digs. Just what's the posish and what do you propose we do?"

"Well, mister, here's the lowdown," the man replied, laying the remains of his cigar to rest in his breastpocket. "It so happens Charlie and I'd both like to sink our hooks into a certain manuscript belonging to this Zann fella."

"Right, the deaf, dumb, blind bird Jeeves was giving me the scoop on."

"It'd be a gol-darned shame if Zann's manuscript was to fall into the wrong hands—"

"I say, you're not another one of these collector types, are you?"

"No, sirree—though I used to do quite a business in my heyday tracking down stolen documents. Putting the finger on missing top-secret government papers was a specialty of mine."

"Are you going to suggest we pinch the thing? If so, I have to say I've got some experience in this line of larceny." I proceeded to relate how I once tried to intercept the manuscript of my Uncle Willoughby's reminiscences, which were full of stories about people who are the essence of propriety today being chucked out of music halls and such like back in the 'eighties. The anecdote about Art Jermyn's father, the itinerant American circus, and the huge bull gorilla of lighter than average colour was one of the fruitiest.

"Should be a piece of cake to slip into the gimp's room and filch the foolscap," I added. "Like taking fish from a Deep One, I should think."

"It ain't that simple, mister," said Altamont. "The catch is, the manuscript ain't down on paper yet—the swag's upstairs, stashed inside Herr Zann's noggin."

"I say, that does make for somewhat more of a challenge, doesn't it?"

"This is how I figure it. To get the guy to play ball, you have to play him the way an Indian snake charmer does a deadly swamp adder."

"Oh, ah, of course," I answered, though I hadn't the foggiest what he was driving at.

"'Music hath charm to soothe the savage beast' I recollect is the old saw," said Altamont in explanation.

"Excuse me, sir," said Jeeves, who shimmered in at that moment, "but I believe that the line from Congreve is 'Music has charms to soothe a savage breast.'"

"Thank you, Jeeves," I said, "but as you can see—"

"Say, your man here's one sharp cookie, mister," Altamont interjected. "I knew it when we met—he had to be the brains behind your operation."

Jeeves may be the Napoleon of valets, but we Woosters have our pride, don't you know, so I let the remark pass.

"Anyhow," continued the American, "I've tried all by my lonesome on my fiddle to coax Zann to ante up, but no dice. Charlie, on the other hand, hasn't had any better luck tooting on that zobo of his."

"I say, but where do I come in?" I was still as much in the dark as that chap Washington after the lights went out, but I was beginning to get a glimmer that a plum role awaited Bertram in this affair.

"Mr. Jeeves says you can belt out a tune with the best of 'em."

"I took the liberty of informing Mr. Altamont that you have a pleasant, light baritone, sir."

"What'll turn the trick, I reckon, is if we spring a little jam session on Zann some night, all impromptu like. I'll wager my wad that if we serenade the old duffer with a medley of music-hall melodies, he'll be ready by dawn to deliver the goods. So how about it, mister? Can I count you in?"

Well, I mean to say, this was a bit thick. After performing "Sonny Boy" at Beefy Bingham's clean, bright entertainment in the East End, I had sworn off singing outside the privacy of my own bath. Now I was being called upon to lead a chorus in a scheme as hare-brained as any I had heard in a goodish while. Then I thought of Aunt Agatha and what she would say and do if she found out I had funked this latest gag to fish young Ward out of the soup, and at that instant I resolved to take the plunge and seize the rising tide across the Rubicon, so to speak.

"All right, then," I declared. "Why not?"

An evening or two later, by the light of a gibbous moon, Jeeves and I were crossing not the Rubicon but a dark, ripe-smelling river spanned by a low-arched bridge as ponderous as Jeeves's definition of the word *viol*. *Vile,* too, was the word that sprang to the lips when we entered the neighbour-hood that lay beyond. An antiquarian's paradise I know some would call it, but plague spot would be more the *mot juste.* In my view the whole tangle of narrow cobbled streets and crazily leaning houses was in dire need of the wrecker's ball. Moreover, the Rue d'Auseil itself was aswarm with dodder-ing greybeards who looked as if they'd been pensioned off from Napo-leon's Grande Armée. No wonder the place wasn't down on any map.

We stopped at the third tottering house from the top of the street, an edifice that in tallishness rivalled the Eiffel Tower. At the door we were greeted by the chap who kept the joint, an ancient bird with bum legs named Blandot. As he directed us *en haut*, he wishes us *bonne chance*. I had assumed that this was to be a strictly private concert, but the landlord made it clear that Monsieur Altamont's musical soirée was the talk of the house and we could expect an avid audience.

Like an obedient bloodhound, Jeeves took the lead upstairs, pausing on the third floor to point towards Ward's apartment. As we trotted higher, the long sob of a violin pierced our hearts and ears, and when we gained the fifth floor we found waiting on the landing our American confederate, stringèd instrument clasped to the bosom.

"Howdy, folks!" the geezer wheezed, slapping us each on the back as best he could with bow in one hand and violin in the other. "Come on in!"

Our new friend steered us inside his room, where our noses were in-stantly assaulted by the reek of stale cigar smoke, not to mention other evil stenches which I have never smelled elsewhere (with the possible exception of Doc Muñoz's Fourteenth Street bedsitter) but which seemed to emanate from the test tubes and retorts that filled every nook and cranny of the oth-erwise Spartanly furnished premises.

"I say, you're not one of these chaps who, who like to . . ." I stam-mered, gripped by a nameless fear.

"Well, mister, I guess you could say experimentin's kind of a hobby of mine, just as it is Charlie's, by the way. He and I have even swapped a few recipes, er, formulas . . ."

Most disturbing, as Jeeves would say, was the fact that there was no source of running water within eyeballing distance. Running water, as any Etonian will tell you, is as much of the essence to the chemistry lab as fresh blood is to the vampire.

Jeeves, no doubt sensing the young master's distress, had some soothing words at the ready. "Observe, sir," said the man in a low, buzzing whisper, "that Mr. Altamont at least does not maintain a well-chilled laboratory."

Rather the opposite, one might add. In truth, Altamont's quarters were about as warmly oppressive as a sealed tomb on a summer's day. When I suggested, however, that an open window might be just the ticket, our host said no, an open window wasn't a smart idea on the Rue d'Auseil. So I resigned self to the fact that our rehearsal—we had a few hours to practice before Zann's return—would be a sticky business in more ways than one.

While I was fiddling with the sheet music which I'd purchased for the occasion—and a dashed lot of bother it was too, hunting up English lyrics at short notice in a foreign capital—Altamont asked: "You play an instrument, mister?"

"No, never have, my dear fellow, though now that you mention it," I said, casting Jeeves a meaningful glance, "I've always wanted to have a go at learning the banjolele." At this revelation Jeeves's left eyebrow may have flickered a quarter of an inch.

"Well, well, that's fine," replied Altamont. "Now what would you like to let your lungs loose on first? 'Old Man River' or 'The Yeoman's Wedding Song'?"

Barely had I cleared the throat and Altamont given a final twist to the G-string, when suddenly there came a tapping, a tentative, gentle sort of rapping, as the poet says, at the chamber door. At a nod from our host, Jeeves flew as swiftly and silently as a raven to see who was there.

"Hey, you guys weren't going to start without me, were you?" whined a peevish—if that's the word I want—Ward on the threshold. "I am a star zobo soloist, you know." In one hand he brandished a zobo, not an especially impressive weapon, mind you, but by the authoritative way he flourished the thing I could tell that he didn't care to be left out of the proceedings.

"Now, now, Charlie, simmer down," said Altamont. "Say, why don't you come on in?"

"Thanks. Um, don't mind if I do," said Ward, sounding as if he were merely accepting his due as a paid-up member in good standing of our little club.

Well, the long and short of it was, after a hasty huddle between Jeeves and Altamont, we opened our ranks and expanded from a duo into a trio. As it turned out, the mellow fruitiness of Charlie's zobo playing enriched the ensemble beyond measure, and I for one was not sorry to have him aboard. At one point, while Altamont was performing a solo, Jeeves whispered out of Ward's earshot that the elderly American had half-expected this contingency, indeed was prepared to grab "the bacon" and execute an "end run" under the younger American's very nose if he had to. His solo, incidentally, had that quality which I have noticed in all violin solos, of seeming to last much longer than it actually did.

By eleven o'clock, while we were far from fit to make our debut at the Albert Hall, we had our act well enough together to transfer it to Zann's garret, which was strategically located one floor directly above.

"For your information," said Altamont, as we mounted the rickety attic stairs, "a college kid who lived here a few years back almost got the old boy to cough up, but the bonehead blew it . . ."

"It is my understanding that the young gentleman was an impoverished student of metaphysics at the university, sir," said Jeeves.

A pass-key provided courtesy of Blandot allowed us to slip without fuss into Zann's room. Its size was very great, and seemed the greater because of its extraordinary barrenness and neglect. I mean to say, the abundance of dust and cobwebs would have embarrassed even Mrs. Herrero, Doc Muñoz's last landlady and housekeeper *manqué*. The fans soon began to trickle in, first the lame landlord then a pair of chaps from the third floor, an aged money-lender and a respectable upholsterer. The performers clustered round an iron music-stand, while the audience settled in three old-fashioned chairs and on the narrow iron bedstead. Despite a complaint or two about the lack of a programme, the mood of the crowd was on the whole relaxed and cheery. Finally, near midnight, the estimated kick-off time, Altamont gave Jeeves the signal to douse the lights, saying, "Now we must be silent and wait, gents."

After what seemed like fifteen minutes but from comparing notes afterwards was but forty-five seconds, we heard a clumping on the stairs, the grating of a key in the lock, and the creak of the swinging door. When the light flashed on it was all we could do to restrain ourselves from shouting surprise at the old maestro, who stood gaping in astonishment like a crook caught red-handed (or is it red-headed?) breaking into a bank vault *from beneath.*

He was a small, lean, bent person, with the shabby clothes of a vaude-ville comedian and a nearly bald head like the dome of St. Paul's or, if my Providence pal were telling this tale, like the dome of the Christian Science Church on College Hill. The silent way he started to get worked up, making funny faces and shaking the sinister black viol case he was carrying, rather reminded me of Harpo Marx, minus the fright wig. One couldn't help won-dering whether he'd ever considered billing himself as "Violo" Zann.

"Come on, Herr Zann," said Altamont, dragging the German by the el-bow to a free spot on the bedstead, "be a sport. Tonight we're entertaining you."

Over the old man's mute protests, Altamont rejoined Ward and me at the music-stand and raised his bow. On the downbeat we launched into "The Wedding of the Painted Doll," which drew appreciative applause at the finish from all hands except Zann's. Thus encouraged, we proceeded with growing confidence to perform "Singin' in the Rain," "Three Little Words," "Goodnight, Sweetheart," "My Love Parade," "Spring is Here," "Whose Baby Are You?" and part of "I Want an Automobile with a Horn That Goes Toot-Toot," in the order named.

It was as we were approaching the end of the last number that Zann sud-denly rose, seized his viol, and commenced to rend the night with the wildest playing I had ever heard outside the amateur musical evenings at the Drones. It would be useless to describe the playing of Erich Zann further, so I won't. In any case, the bloke shortly dropped the viol and stumbled over to the room's lone table, where he picked up a pencil and began to write like a compulsive epistolarian. (For a poor musician, he fortuitously kept reams of writing paper in the home.) We resumed our playing, which accompaniment seemed to drive the eccentric genius to pile up the feverishly written sheets at an ever faster clip. As the wee hours wore on, Ward and Altamont watched his progress with an increasingly lean and hungry eye.

I had just hit the opening quaver of "Sonny Boy" when young Charlie missed his cue. Out of the gate like a shot, he bounded to the table and was shovelling the manuscript pages into a bag before you could say John Clay. Zann, who was beginning to look a trifle glassy-eyed, seemed scarcely to no-tice the intrusion. Altamont, himself no spring chicken, was slow to blow the whistle. "Whoa, Bill!" he cried after a tick or two. "Up and at him, lads!"

Zann suddenly rose, seized his viol

The audience rose as one, though not with any appreciable alacrity. Both the money-lender and the upholsterer were past their prime, while a tortoise could have given bum-legged Blandot a run for his money. Nonetheless, the team—all presumably Altamont's accomplices—succeeded in tackling Ward and bringing him down short of his goal, the door, which Jeeves, who had moved like a phantom, was now tending. The contestants soon formed a scrum, with Charlie taking on all comers, a sort of Samson among the Philistines, if you will. Altamont, like archaic Nodens, bellowed his guidance from the sidelines.

And where, you might ask, was Bertram in the crisis? I had posted self by the room's one window, waiting in reserve as the good old ancestor did during the early phase of the Battle of Crécy. As the atmosphere grew foul with the dust and cobwebs kicked up in the struggle for the ms., I decided it would be a sound scheme to open the window, despite Altamont's previous admonitions against same. So I drew back the curtains, unlatched the shutter, and raised the sash of that highest of all gable windows.

Before I could admire the view, however, Fate socked me with the stuffed eelskin. That is to say, something soft and loose struck the old occiput. I turned to see that Ward had scattered most of the opposition about the floor like nine pins. Zann in particular was looking poorly, eyes springing out of the sockets and richocheting off the ceiling. Then I noticed the object of everyone's quest—which must have flown free in the fray—lying at the feet.

My course of action was clear. Charlie had just broken out of a clinch with Altamont and was now advancing menacingly in my direction. It was the work of a moment to sweep up the prize and drop it out the window, just as Ward did that time with the bag full of Jeeves's and my footwear. Except in this case, there was something rum about the outside view. It was very dark, but instead of the lights of the city outspread below, I saw— But how shall I describe it? I don't know if you've ever stared long and hard into one of those swirling thingummies which hypnotists like to poke in people's faces, but such was the image registering on the Wooster retina. Entrancing, you might say. Dashed entrancing. So entrancing I—

"Well, Jeeves," I was saying in the aftermath of our little adventure, back at the clean and comfortable hotel suite, "all's well that end's well, I suppose."

"Yes, sir. I would agree that Mr. Ward's precipitous departure for Prague absolves you of any further responsibility for his welfare.”

“I can’t help feeling a pang for old Altamont, though. A pity that Zann’s confessions, as well as the venerable musician himself, have passed beyond the gulf beyond the gulf beyond . . .”

“In my opinion, sir, Mr. Altamont will in time not be wholly sorry for the loss in undreamable abysses of Herr Zann’s closely written manuscript.”

“I say, Jeeves, what do you imagine Zann poured out on the page and why were Ward and Altamont so keen on seizing the contents? Any clue?”

“None, sir. Like the book cited by Poe’s German authority, sir, ‘es lasst sich nicht lesen—it does not permit itself to be read.’ ”

PARODIES AND PASTICHES

Tender Is the Night-Gaunt

Already with thee! tender is the night-
Gaunt, faceless flutterer, in cold damp flight.
"Ode to a night-Gaunt"

I.

Three times Rosemary Hoyt dreamed of Dick Diver at the large, proud, rose-colored hotel on the French Riviera, about halfway between Marseilles and the Italian border, and three times was she picked up on suspicion of unlawful loitering while still she paused on the pleasant shore below it. All reddish and rugose he blazed in her memory, with his soft, dull brown eyes and his somewhat probosidian nose. There was never any doubt where to find its nearest rival—at the circus or the zoo. His voice, with some faint Irish melody running through a fanfare of supernal trumpets and a clash of immortal cymbals, wowed the world-weary. Mystery hung over erudite Richard Diver (A.M. Yale, M.D. Johns Hopkins, degree in neuropathology Zurich) like poor children around a Christmas tree; and as Rosemary stood sunburned and shivering on the beach at sunset there swept up to her the poignancy and suspense of an almost-empty bank account, the pain of lost virginity, and the maddening need to locate the ladies'.

At length, sick with longing for that marvelous psychiatrist, nor able sleeping or waking to drive him from her mind, she asked the concierge at Gausse's Hôtel des Étrangers whether or not he had checked out.

"I am afraid so, Mademoiselle. He and Madame left nearly a month ago."

"For Paris?"

"No, Mademoiselle, for dreamland."

"Where's that?"

"I am not sure, Mademoiselle. Maybe I forget."

Although she could ill afford it, Rosemary fished a five hundred franc note out of her purse.

"Merci, Mademoiselle. Now I remember. You must descend the seven hundred steps to the Gate of Deeper Slumber."

"Is that near here?"

"About five miles away, on the road to Cannes."

II.

As she stood in the green-litten vegetable garden, feeling lousy from the moon-wine at lunch, Nicole contemplated the less than marvelous guest list; then she went on through a cabbage patch to a little menagerie where cats and zoogs were making a medley of spitting and caterwauling noises. From there she descended to a balustraded parapet and looked down seven hundred feet to the river Skai. Through a telescope she could see Dick waterskiing in his transparent black lace drawers lined with flesh-colored cloth, a curious garment which had provoked complaints from silly milksops in Provençal.

So they had left Provençal and rented a villa above hilly Ulthar, where according to an ancient and significant law no man may kill a cat but a cat may kill a zoog even in the off-season. The villa and its grounds, made out of a row of little green cottages and neatly fenced farms, encompassed a circular tower of ivied stone, once the modest Synagogue of the Reformed Ones, which afforded a splendid view of the quaint town itself, with its old peaked-roofed bars and overhanging upper story casinos and numberless brothels and narrow cobbled streets slippery with zoog blood.

Presently, Dick tumbled over the balustraded parapet, slippery with sweat from the well-nigh vertical climb from the river below.

"Nicole," he gasped, "I forgot to tell you that I invited King Kuranes, the Lord of Ooth-Nargai and the Sky around Serennian."

"Okey-dokey."

"I'm going to invite some ghouls, too. I want to give a really hideous, noxious, detestable party. I mean it. I want to give a party where there's baying at the moon and grave-robbing and babies snatched from cradles and replaced with changelings. You wait and see."

"I'll tell governess to lock the nursery door."

At seven o'clock that evening he came out to greet his first guests: the patriarch Atal, who had been up the forbidden peak Hatheg-Kla in the stony desert and had come down again alive but was still in therapy; and the perfumed and powdered priests Nasht and Kaman-Thah, whose cavern-temple with its flaming pink décor was the most popular dive in the Six Kingdoms.

"This had better be good, Richard dear," said Nasht.

"Yes, Saturday's our biggest night at the club," added Kaman-Thah.

"You boys make yourselves at home," said Dick. "You'll find gourds of moon-wine on the ivory dais in the circular tower."

"Moon-wine?" said Atal, mumbling in his beard. "Don't know about moon-wine. Had my share and more already today. How about a cup of water?"

To resume Rosemary's point of view it should be said that, by the time she reached the villa after getting lost in Ulthar, the guests were gathered on benches around a long diorite picnic table on the high terrace. Stout black men of Parg in maids' uniforms were serving the meat course. Dick smiled from his golden throne at the table's head, then pointed his nose decisively at Rosemary, saying with a lightness seeming to reveal a grandfatherly interest: "I'm going to save your virtue—I'm going to seat you between Atal, who's three hundred and one, and Old Kranon, the burgomaster." Nith, the lean notary, Shang, the blacksmith, Thul, the cutter of stone, and Zath, the coroner, all looked disappointed. Rosemary noticed she was the only woman present.

"Thank you, Dick, I know you're a gentleman of the old school," she said. "Not like those pushy zoogs. While I was walking through the enchanted wood one of them nipped loathsomely at my— Well, talk about fresh!"

"As I was saying earlier," said Atal, sipping his Oukranos river water, "I was trying to discourage this young fella from his quest, you see. I told him I was under a lot of pressure and didn't have time to answer all his questions even if I wanted to. Then he did a terrible thing. He plied me with moon-wine until I spilled the beans, hinting that the stone face carved on Mount Ngranek may be a likeness which earth's gods wrought of their own features in the days when they danced the Black Bottom. In disguise the younger among the Great Ones often espouse the comely peasant maidens, you see—"

"Espouse?" said Kaman-Thah. "*Please*, Atal. When did the gods ever *espouse* those sluts?"

"Don't use such language!" cried the venerable patriarch.

"Those gods can come off their mountain and *espouse* me all they want," said Nasht.

"You laugh now," muttered Atal into his cup, slopping water down his wispy white beard, "but it could mean big trouble for everyone in dreamland if this young fella—Randall Porter I think he said his name was—gets to Kadath in the cold waste and finds the Other Gods. As deities go they're all right, I suppose, but you have to remember that their soul and messenger is the crawling chaos Nyarlathotep."

"Tell me, has anyone heard the latest about poor Menes?" asked Dick. The ease with which he changed the subject, Rosemary thought, was astonishing.

"It is said that he has been appointed honorary president of this new quarantine program for cats who want to enter Ooth-Nargai," said Old Kranon.

"King Kuranes himself insisted," said Nith, the lean notary. "Cats can be detained even if they fly through the Sky around Serannian."

"I suspected it. It's an outrage," said Shang, the blacksmith.

"It's a scam to line the vets' pockets," said Thul, the cutter of stone.

"Six months is absurd," said Zath, the coroner.

"Are zoogs exempt?" inquired Dick, waving his nose politely around the table.

Rosemary admired how he showed an interest in what each of his guests had to say about this controversial if ultimately boring topic. In turn she talked shop with Old Kranon, or rather she listened while he talked shop, explaining that Menes had never really recovered from the traumatic loss of his favorite kitten as a boy. Her mind soon wandered elsewhere, as did her gaze, which strayed towards her other dinner partner, aged Atal, who was now dozing face down in his untasted plate of meat.

"Where *is* Her Royal Highness, anyway, Richard?" asked Nasht. "I thought you said she was invited."

Where was Nicole for that matter? wondered Rosemary. At that point Kaman-Thah, who had excused himself earlier, rushed back to the terrace and announced:

"Hey, girls, you aren't going to believe what I just saw in the bathroom!"

III.

Before Kaman-Thah could savor the impact of this show-stopper, he was upstaged by the entrance of two more guests. The entire company rose as one, with the exception of Rosemary, who lagged a second behind—but as she did so she realized who one of the new arrivals must be.

"Awfully sorry, dear boy," said King Kuranes to Dick, motioning for everybody to resume their seats. "I would've been here sooner, but on the road to Ulthar I met this American chappie, an old friend I used often to visit in waking days. Trust you don't mind my bringing him along. Allow me to introduce Mr. Randolph Carter, of Boston."

"I sure appreciate your letting me join your party, Dr. Diver," said the newcomer, pumping his host's rough and ruddy hand. "According to Ole Kuranie here, to be included in your world for a while is a remarkable experience."

"I certainly look back in awe, dear boy, at that carnival of affection you gave when you and your wife first came to dreamland," said the Lord of Ooth-Nargai.

"The happiness of my friends is my preoccupation," said Dick. "One has only to recognize the proud uniqueness of their destinies."

"Speaking of which, Doc," said Randolph Carter, squatting on the armrest of the golden throne, "I was wondering if you could help me realize my unique personal destiny."

"So long as you subscribe to my extraordinary virtuosity completely."

While he could have taken the vacant silver throne at the foot of the table, King Kuranes elected instead to squeeze in between Rosemary and Atal. This disturbance provoked the aged patriarch to lift his head from his plate and gape at the rising moon. Since Rosemary had no hope of getting Dick to herself that evening, she was content to settle for the attention of royalty.

Intermittently, she caught the gist of the general conversation, concerning whether or not Carter should seek Kadath in the cold waste, wherever that was, for her new dinner companion insisted on hearing in detail her initial impressions of dreamland. At last she succeeded in asking him what he, as an old friend, would advise Carter to do.

"My dear, I've been out beyond the stars in the ultimate void," said the king, "and I'm the only one ever to return sane from such a voyage—though I admit at times I suffer from post-cosmic stress syndrome. I told Randy earlier he ought to go back to Boston and forget this silly dream-quest, but you know how it is with you enterprising Yanks. For the sake of an aesthetic thrill you'll blithely risk all your marbles."

"I'm just a simple American girl, but the inhabitants of dreamland do seem to have more than their fair share of mental problems."

"Yes, there's a desperate need for qualified physicians to treat all the cases. That's why we're so lucky Dick has agreed to join our staff."

Kuranes went on to explain that he was director of the Dylath-Leen clinic, which he visited whenever he wasn't reigning in the rose-crystal Palace of the Seventy Delights at Celephaïs or in the turreted cloud-castle of sky-floating Serannian. In his spare time he liked to escape to his gray Gothic manor-house, near an ersatz Cornish fishing village and a Norman abbey he had reared to remind him of England. His latest fancy was to set up his own judiciary to enforce English law.

"Can't have all those disease-ridden cats infecting your green and pleasant land, can we?" teased Rosemary.

In the meantime, Kaman-Than, evidently blotto after another gourd of moon-wine, kept hinting to Shang, the blacksmith, and Thul, the cutter of stone, that the nasty thing he had seen in the bathroom concerned their absent hostess.

"I say, old man," said King Kuranes, "please don't talk that way about Mrs. Diver."

"I wasn't talking to you, your Highness."

"You weren't? My apologies."

"You bully!" screeched the priest.

"Steady, old man."

"You're stronger muscularly than I am, you brute!"

The Lord of Ooth-Nargai turned to Nasht and calmly recommended that he take his partner home—or better yet to their cavern-temple where such behavior was more acceptable. Kaman-Thah declared in shrill tones that he was not about to leave for any man while the night was young and did his lordship wish to step out on the balustraded parapet to discuss it further. This performance had the incidental effect of rousing Atal from his stupor. After rubbing the dried gravy from his eyes, the sage peered at Randolph Carter—and suddenly it was as if some fool had accidentally set off a cheap alarm clock.

"Don't go!" he shrieked. "It's not allowed, I tell you! Don't go, unless you want to end up like Barzai the Wise, who was drawn screaming into the sky for merely climbing the known peak of Hatheg-Kla. With unknown Kadath, if ever found, matters would be worse, much worse, I tell you. We're all doomed!"

While Dick had drunk about a zoogshead worth of moon-wine himself, he still had the presence of mind to signal to the black men of Parg to remove the party-poopers with the meat course. Aged Atal was going quietly enough, and Kaman-Thah appeared to be actually enjoying the manhandling, when a flock of ghouls, all naked and rubbery, vaulted onto the terrace. The subsequent cavalry charge scattered the pair and their ebony escorts like nine pins. At last, thought Rosemary, they were about to have some real fun.

IV.

Dick led the survivors of the previous night's party through a trench towards the rugged gray headlands. He was full of excitement that he was eager to communicate, though actually the ghoul who was once the Boston artist Richard Upton Pickman—dressed for the occasion in beret and paint-spattered smock—had seen battle service and he had not.

"These rocky headlands here cost one quarter of the ghoul army two weeks ago," he said to Rosemary. She looked out obediently at the blasted landscape, littered with broken javelins and hellish flutes. The ghoul that was Pickman and his entourage of dog-like lopers stopped glibbering in respect for their fallen comrades.

"See that cliff," continued Dick. "As the night-gaunt flies you could soar there in two minutes. The frightful detachments of moon-beasts and almost-humans spent half the day lumbering up to the top. It took the ghouls half-an-hour to annihilate those toad-like lunar blasphemies and their sardonic, wide-mouthed allies on the western headland. On the east cliff, however, where the leader of the moon-beasts was present, the ghouls didn't fare so well."

Pickman, who still remembered a little English, grunted a few monosyllables in protest.

"Okay, okay," said Dick. "I'm getting to that part. After the western battle was over, the surviving ghouls hastened across to the aid of their hard-pressed fellows and forced the invaders back along the narrow ridge of the east headland, thus turning the tide. In the end it was a total victory for the good guys."

The erstwhile Pickman meeped with approval, while one ghoul attempted to pinch Rosemary and several others eyed her full figure speculatively.

"Any chance I can see a battle while I'm here in dreamland?" she asked, slapping away a mold-caked paw.

"Why, the gugs and ghasts haven't quitted in the vaults of Zin, dear girl," said King Kuranes. "And in the vale of Pnath—"

"That's different," said Dick. "Gugs hunt ghasts underground—it's too dark for tourists. The moon-beast and almost-human business won't happen again soon, not for another few months anyway, but when it does you can be sure—"

"Maybe next time the gugs and ghasts will fight the moon-beasts and almost-humans above ground," said Rosemary.

"No, the gugs and ghasts would never be any good in the open air. Ghasts cannot live in real light, and gugs tend to drowse on sentry duty."

They dropped behind the others. Suddenly a shower of broken javelins and hellish flutes came down on them, and they ran into the next transverse, where they found Nasht and Kaman-Thah collecting battlefield souvenirs.

"Oops, my mistake," said Kaman-Thah, on the verge of hefting another load of debris over the top. "I thought you were the Lord of Ooth-Nargai." The high priest had challenged Kuranes to a duel—leather handbags at twenty paces—and was still smarting from the king's refusal to take him seriously. Rosemary burst out laughing.

"That Kaman-Thah, what a kidder," Dick said when they came out of the trench and faced a partly consumed refuse heap left by the ghoul army two weeks before.

"I fell in love with you the first time I saw you," she said quietly.

"My dear, I cannot tell you how much I appreciate you."

"I know you don't love me—I don't expect it."

"At my age a wholesome replacement process begins to operate, and love attains calm, cool depths based on tender association beside which the erotic infatuation of youth takes on a certain shade of cheapness or degradation. Mature tranquilized love—"

"Take me!"

"Take you where?"

Embarrassment moved him to confess that his mother had described him as "hideous" as a boy and unfit for the draft as a young man, even though her nose was nearly as prehensile as his own. To compensate he had married Nicole, who suffered from an insufficiency complex. The reason she had missed the party was because she was having a nervous breakdown in the bathroom. This time Nicole would have to cure herself. He was hoping a long trip would do the trick. Then rather bashfully he said:

"What I am coming to is this—Nicole and I are going with Randolph Carter to try to find Kadath in the cold waste—I wonder if you'd like to go with us."

"Oh, *would* I!"

V.

In the event their journey included a few unexpected detours. First, Dick and Randolph Carter got drunk on moon-wine with a wide-mouthed merchant in Dylath-Leen, and the next thing they knew they were all shanghaied to the dark side of the moon in one of the reeking galleys of the moon-beasts. Luckily, friendly cats flew to their rescue. Back in Dylath-Leen, they caught a boat to the port of Baharna on the isle of Oriab. There the whole party hiked up the hidden side of Ngranek, only to be seized by night-gaunts. Soon they were dodging gugs and ghasts in the vale of Pnath, and only narrowly escaped with the help of a few ghouls through the tower of Koth. Sensing that Dick was playing the hero in order to impress Rosemary, Nicole seized the helm of their galleon as they cruised into the harbor at Celephaïs, their next destination, and crashed into a wharf.

By this time everyone was ready for a rest at King Kuranes' rose-crystal Palace of the Seventy Delights, where the Lord of Ooth-Nargai proved an especially courteous host. Dick, though, after one too many gourds of moon-wine at a local tavern, felt the king was being a bit too attentive to Rosemary and picked a fight that ended up involving a waiter, a cab driver, and a bhole. Kuranes considered himself a benevolent monarch, but disturbing the peace was a very serious matter. He had lately constructed a quarantine station for cats in his gray gothic manor-house's dungeon, as yet unoccupied, and there Dick and the enormous viscous bhole were placed in a cell to dry out until their case could come to trial. In the circumstances the king deemed it best as well to suspend Dick from his position at the Dylath-Leen clinic.

Meanwhile, Nicole, eager to show she was well on the road to recovery, agreed to accompany Carter on the last leg of his journey. Rosemary elected to stay behind in Celephaïs and assist the king with his various projects to expand "Little England." In truth, she was coming to appreciate that Kuranes was quite the catch, being not only rich and nobly born but single and available. Never mind that he was dead in the waking world; she was happy to remain indefinitely in dreamland, where her lord and master would protect her from the unwanted advances of its less attractive entities.

To speed along this story further, it should be said that Nicole and Randolph Carter—after several more adventures, each more sanity threatening than the last—did finally reach their goal: the dazzling neon-litten castle atop unknown Kadath. They had to wait only a minute or two before they were led past the velvet rope.

Inside they followed the maddening beat of vile drums and the ecstatic blasts of tenor saxophones into a cocktail lounge, where a combo was performing an uptempo version of "Yes, We Have No Bananas"; to which were dancing slowly, awkwardly, and with frequent stepping on toes, the gauche and ultra-nouveau Other Gods.

"Not exactly the scene you were expecting, is it?" said Nicole.

"Gosh, no," said Randolph Carter, making no effort to hide his disappointment. "Atal didn't prepare me for this. Maybe we came on the wrong night."

Then the band took a break and the leader strode across the dance floor; a tall, slim figure in evening clothes with the mature face of an Egyptian gigolo. Close up to Randolph Carter and Nicole strode that dapper figure, who was not quite light enough to travel in a Pullman south of Mason-Dixon. He spoke, and in his suave tones there vibrated the syncopated rhythms of the jazz age.

"Nicole Diver," said the band leader, "you have had a long and tiresome voyage. First, you have had to put up with that drunken and philandering husband of yours. What a waste of talent! Second, you have had since your husband's unfortunate run-in with the law only this proper and provincial New Englander for company. What a waste of beauty! You deserve better."

"Hey, what about me?" interrupted Carter. "What about my quest?"

"You could have saved yourself a lot of trouble if you had just stayed in Boston—which is where I suggest you return a.s.a.p. As we speak a shantak is waiting to fly you express to Dylath-Leen. I have it from the highest authority that by the time you get there a certain American psychiatrist will have received his sentence—transportation to the waking world. You can do everyone a big favor and see him safely home to New England."

"I don't mean to sound rude," said Randolph Carter, "but who the heck are you to give me orders? Nyarlathotep?"

"No, I am Nodens," the elegant figure replied, "and that is my group, Nodens and the Night-Gaunts. The Crawling Chaos and the Bubbling Blasphemers won't start their gig at the castle for another three weeks."

Before Randolph Carter could respond to this surprising news, a pair of bouncers showed him outside to the waiting shantak. Nodens gave the band the nod to resume playing.

"Shall we dance?" he said to Nicole.

"Do you like what you see?" she murmured. "You know I was once white-Saxon-blonde."

"Baby, you are more beautiful now that your hair has darkened. When you were a kid it must have been like King Kuranes' turreted cloud-castle of sky-floating Serannian and more beautiful than you."

VI.

Nicole kept in touch with Dick after her commitment ceremony to Nodens; there were handwritten letters dozens of pages long on political and socio-economic matters, and about the children, who were now taking figure drawing from the ghoul who had once been Richard Upton Pickman.

In the last letter she had from him he told her that he was practicing in Arkham, Mass., and she got the impression that he had settled down with one of his aunts to keep house for him. She looked up Arkham in an atlas and couldn't find it. Perhaps, she liked to think, he was waiting to get going aesthetically again, like Napoleon at St. Helena—or was it Elba? His latest picture postcard was postmarked from Dunwich, Mass., which is some distance inland from Arkham and ridiculously old, older by far than any of the communities within thirty miles of it; in any case he is almost certainly in that section of New England, in one imaginary town or another. And vast infinities away, past the Gate of Deeper Slumber and the enchanted wood, Nicole and Nodens danced cheek to cheek at the exclusive neon-litten castle atop unknown Kadath.

The Sound and the Fungi

I.

Through the fence, between the abnormally curling and bizarre flower spaces, we could see the men playing golf. I may be an idiot, but if I can communicate in the first person I'm not going to pretend I cant tell a golf course from a pasture.

"Hello, caddie," said one of the men.

"He calling me?" Caddy said.

"No, he's talking to the boy carrying his golf clubs," Jason said.

"Hey, that's funny," Quentin said. "You've got the same name."

I started to cry. I didn't think it was funny.

"Hush," Caddy said. But I didn't hush and she came and put her arms around me and started to talk about the fresh "footprint" in the dirt by the garden. So we went along the fence and came to the garden fence, where we could see it. It was more like a "claw-print." From a central pad, pairs of saw-toothed nippers projected in opposite directions. I started to cry. I wasn't crying, and I tried to stop, looking at that hideously crab-like print which seemed to have some ambiguity of direction. I wasn't crying.

"Don't be a 'fraid cat," Quentin said.

"Benjy's scared," Caddy said.

"That print wont hurt you," Jason said. "But whatever made it might."

They came on—in the surging flood waters of the river where Caddy fell in and got her drawers wet. I was trying to say when I overheard a buzzing voice in imitation of human speech and I was trying to say and trying and the pinkish things were floating in the water and I tried to get away, but they kept coming on. They were flying over the hill to where I could see their great flapping wings silhouetted against the full moon and I tried to cry. I tried to keep from falling off the hill and I fell off the hill into a certain steep-sided gorge that even the black goat of the woods shunned.

"You cant take their picture no how," Quentin said.

"That so," Jason said.

148

"Not using ordinary camera films," Quentin said. "They're composed of a form of matter totally alien to our part of space."

Caddy took my hand and we went on past the barn and through the gate. There was a frog on the brick wall, squatting in the middle of it. Its body seemed altered in some queer, indescribable way, while its face had an expression the like of which no one ever saw in a frog before, except maybe around the marshes of a certain decayed Massachusetts seaport.

"Come on," Caddy said. It squatted there loathsomely until Jason crooked his left hand in the shape of the elder sign.

"You touch it you turn into a Deep One," Quentin said. The frog hopped away, and the hops of that frog were longer than any of us Compton kids liked. I started to cry.

"Hush now," Caddy said. "Come on."

"They got company tonight," Quentin said.

"How do you know?" Caddy said.

"I seen a veritable army of footprints or claw-prints near the house, by some of Paw's footprints—footprints that faced toward them. I bet Paw's invited them Outer Ones to a party."

"Damuddy been mighty poorly lately," Jason said. "I say it's a funeral."

"Well, it's not," Quentin said. "It's a party. You don't know anything about it. Let's go around to the front."

"Could be it's both a funeral and a party," Caddy said.

We started to go. Quentin took me up and we went on around the kitchen. A snake crawled out from under the house. Jason said he wasn't afraid of snakes, unless they were like the rattlers in Grandma Compton's tales of Yig, the Father of Serpents. Caddy said our name was Compson, not Compton, and not to worry our heads over it.

We stopped under the tree by the parlor window. Quentin set me down in the damp and strangely luxuriant grass. There were lights in all the windows. *The trees were buzzing, like the drone of some loathsome, gigantic insect. The boughs surely moved, and there was no wind.*

Caddie went to the tree nearest the window.

"Push me up, Quentin."

"Paw told you to stay out of that tree," Quentin said.

"Push me up, Quentin," Caddy said.

"All right," Quentin said. "You the one going to have your brain removed and stuck in a tin can for a trip to Yuggoth. I aint." He went and pushed Caddy up into the tree to the first limb. We could see the fearsomely muddy bottom of her drawers. Then we couldn't see her. We could hear the tree thrashing.

"What you seeing," Jason whispered.

We could hear something snapping and tearing around.

"What you seeing."

Caddy dropped to the ground, covered in green sticky stuff. *She smelled like trees—or like green sticky stuff.*

"It cant be described," Caddy said.

"Oh, come on, sure it can," Jason said.

"It cant be described."

"I'll give you a quarter," Quentin said.

"All right then," Caddy said. "The parlor is full of giant crab critters with convoluted ellipsoids, covered with multitudes of very short antennae, where a man's head would be. Most of them have martini glasses in their pincers."

"I told you it was a party," Quentin said.

"Oh, and Damuddy is lying on the divan with the top of her head sawed off. Satisfied?"

I started to cry. The front door opened and Father came out with a liquor bottle in his hand. Then one of the crab things appeared in the door, and it buzzed in the door, and then the door was black with the things. Caddy held me and I could hear the whisperer in darkness, and some indescribable stench I could smell. Then the crab things began to take off into the sky, three abreast in disciplined formation, *and one of them held in its pincers a fresh, shiny gray cylinder.*

II.

When Father gave me Grandfather's watch, he said to me, Quentin, I give it to you not that you may remember time, but that you may conquer it and escape its galling limitations. As I lay listening to it in bed I was reminded that the commonest form of my imaginative aspiration is a motion backward in time, or a discovery that time is merely an illusion and that the past is simply a lost mode of vision which I have a chance of recovering. I can form no picture of emotional satisfaction that does not involve the defeat of time, so that one may merge oneself with the whole stream of Southern history and be wholly emancipated like the darkies in the year 1863.

"Hey, Compson, you taking a cut this morning?"

"Is it that late?"

"Look at your watch, dummy."

"I didn't know it was that late."

"You never do. Why you even kept the dean waiting three-quarters of an hour last week. You have no conception of time."

Going to Harvard. It would have been cheaper to send me to Miskatonic. Then we might not have had to sell the pasture. Some day I'll buy back the land and recover the lost heritage of the Compsons, that is, if I don't kill myself first *He lay on the damp and strangely luxuriant grass bellowing at the things in the sky They have sold the pasture so Quentin can go to Harvard and Caddy can get married Mr and Mrs Jason Richmond Compson announce the marriage of their daughter Candace to*

we crawled though the fence when I rose from stooping it was coming out of the trees coming toward us about five feet long with a crustaceous body bearing vast pairs of dorsal fins or membraneous wings and several sets of articulated limbs

this is Quentin

we stood there her face a blur against a dorsal fin or membraneous wing it extended a limb

ia shub-niggurath human

I refused to shake

what do you want

all that we wish of man is peace and non-molestation and an increasing intellectual rapport

Im going for a walk

this latter is absolutely necessary now that our inventions and devices are expanding our knowledge and motions and making it more and more impossible for our necessary outposts to exist secretly on this planet

goodbye

we are perhaps the most marvelous organic things in or beyond all space and time—more vegetable than animal—and have a somewhat fungoid structure, though the presence of a chlorophyll-like substance and a very singular nutritive system differentiate us altogether from true cormophytic fungi

that doesnt make you good enough for my sister

in the woods the fish frogs were flopping, hopping, croaking, bleating smelling rotten seafood in the air they sounded like a grotesque, malignant saraband of fantastic nightmare whatre you going to do Quentin

I think Ill walk a while through the woods

wait for me at the steep-sided gorge that even the black goat shuns

I turned away going

Ill be there right after I say goodnight to N'gah-Kthun

I didnt look back the fish frogs didnt pay me any mind the gray-litten fungi in the trees glowing evilly in the sunset glow when moonstruck poets know after a while I realized I couldnt smell that putrid fish smell and I knew I had come to the steep-sided gorge that even the black goat shuns where she was waiting

wherve you been

in the woods

youre late

sorry

I couldve spent more time saying goodnight

Caddy

what

you cant marry that winged one Caddy

why not

its a foreigner

so

its not even from this planet

at least its from the same solar system

Caddy

its not like N'gah-Kthun is from Yaddith on the Outer Rim or heaven forbid a Yankee

Caddy do you remember the day Damuddys brain was transported to Yuggoth

no

it was the same day you sat down in the flood waters in your drawers

Quentin please no gentleman would dare mention her unmentionables to a lady

what kind of lady gives herself to an alien

you shut up

I guess you got tired of all the earth boys you let

you shut up you shut up

did you appreciate it Caddy did you appreciate it When it touched me with its nippers they tickled

III.

Once a predatory female always a predatory female, what I say. I says you're lucky if her vamping every eligible bachelor at that amateur press convention in Boston is all that worries you. I says she ought to stick to her hat making, instead of wasting time with those no-talent amateurs, printing at great personal expense slick, error-riddled little magazines aimed only at other losers. And Mother says,

"But to have the president of the National Amateur Press Association phone me long distance and accuse me of having no control over her, that I cant—"

"Well," I says, "You cant, can you? You tried your best, getting her a job in that millinery shop, but now that your half-human granddaughter's gone nuts over amateur journalism it's up to me to make sure she doesn't run hog wild."

"She's still my own flesh and blood."

"Yes, then how come she's see-through in photographs, like a ghost?"

"That's the human side trying to express itself. If she took wholly after her pa's kin she wouldn't show up at all!" Then she started to cry again, talking about the terrible consequences of alien miscegenation.

"You're a fine one to talk. You and Father agreed to the match."

"That was your father's doing. He made that bargain with those Outer Ones."

"Yes, Father had to pay for his liquor somehow," I says, "not to mention Quentin's Harvard education and Caddy's wedding."

"I know I'm just a neurotic, overprotective mother to you," she says, crying into her grits.

"I ought to know it," I says. "Here I am thirty-four years old still living at home tied to mama's apron strings."

"Those Outer Ones aint all bad," she says. "After all they gave you a regular nine to five job."

"Yes, well, there's that," I says. "Speaking of which, it's time I headed down town to the mine."

Ask me about those Outer Ones or Winged Ones or Fungi from Yuggoth and I'll tell you that as the manager of their Yoknapatawpha mine I've come to take their inability to settle on a single name for themselves as a sign of racial insecurity. I also have to wonder about their traveling three billion miles through the ether to dig up a load of rocks only to haul those same rocks back across the solar system. Not that I'd raise any of these points to their face, or what passes for a face. Just so long as they let me play golf for half-price on the course that used to be our pasture, and the job's not so demanding that I cant do a little writing on the side on office time—professional writing, I mean, writing that some day somebody's going to pay good money for, not like that amateur junk my niece circulates for nothing or those caustic and satiric eulogies on the locals Father used to compose all day long at his law office.

Mother says I'm her only child who isn't a reproach to her. Well, that's not saying much, not after Quentin shot himself at Harvard, then got reanimated by that Miskatonic-trained doctor. Turning up at Caddy's wedding and running berserk until the ushers had to tear him to pieces with their pincers really took the biscuit. No wonder Caddy's marriage broke up, notwithstanding her child obviously being her husband's when it was born a week later with rudimentary fins or wings. As for Ben, I just hope he's enjoying himself at that stud farm on Yuggoth they took him to after his brain transplant failed.

There wasn't much doing at the mine when I got in, so along about ten oclock I went up to the front office. There was a stranger with a cultivated manner about him there. It was about a couple of minutes to ten, and I invited him into the back office for a mug of moonshine. We got to talking about the writing profession.

"There's nothing to it," I says. "Freelance revision is a sucker's game. The would-be authors send the revisionist their unpublishable drivel and expect him to make it salable for the market. Do you think the revisionist gets anything out of it except a niggardly flat fee? You think the man that sweats over that garbage can afford to pay more than two dollars a week for food," I says. "Let him try to write original fiction on spec; let him break his back and ruin his eyesight two-finger typing a hundred-page manuscript. And what for? So some ignorant jackass of an editor can reject his most ambitious story. You're not an editor, are you?"

"No, I'm not an editor," he says. "I'm an agent of the Winged Ones, Mr. Jason Compson, and it's high time you returned to work."

That evening, when I got home, I went to the dining room. Quen-Kthun was sitting with her head covered by one of her fancy hats. But I could see the antennae sticking out at the edges. She had dyed them again. Her nose looked almost human.

"Do you think Quen-Kthun is ready for supper?" I says to Mother.

"Why don't you ask her yourself?" she says. "I wish the two of you would talk directly to each other once in a while. If you and Quen-Kthun got along better it would be easier for me."

"Grandmother," she says, "Grandmother—"

"Would Quen-Kthun like some meat and rice?" I says to Mother. I helped fill the plates and we begun to eat.

"Why does he treat me like this, Grandmother?" she says. Then she says very low, "He must be jealous."

"What did you say, missy?" I says.

"You're jealous," she says not looking at me.

"Didn't anyone tell you young ladies shouldn't sit at the supper table with their hats on?" I says.

"I'm in print and you aint," she says.

"Well, just keep your hat on," I says. "While I'm eating I dont need to be distracted by any goddamned Medusa."

"I publish my own journal," she says. "My stories and poems get praised by persons of taste and refinement. But what about you? None of those New York houses you've sent that novel you killed yourself typing has sent you anything but a form rejection slip," she says. "Why dont you do the literary world a favor and stop doing something you're no good at and concentrate on your job at the mine?"

"That's enough," Mother says. "Not another word."

"I hear you've been slacking off," she says.

"That's enough," Mother says. "He's the head of this family."

"He may not be for long," she says.

"Just what do you mean by that, missy?" I says.

"Nothing," she says with a sort of half smile.

"You better mean nothing," I says. "And dont preach to me about writing. You only joined the amateur press to meet a man. I know. You're just like your ma—man crazy. Only it's harder for you because you aint fully human."

"Is that right?" she says. "Tell that to the gentleman who's been writing me long letters every day since the Boston convention." She took her time getting up from the table. Then she sashayed out of the room. We heard her flying up the stairs.

"Serious writing is man's work," I says. "Like I say it's not for the likes of female semi-alien predators."

After dessert I told Mother goodnight and went on to the library and got out my manuscript and looked at it again. It's a fine manuscript even if those damn New York editors dont agree. I dont want to make a killing. I just want to see my name on a hardcover book with a color jacket and advance praise from big name authors on the back. And once I've done that I reckon I can quit working for a bunch of stupid aliens and get a position at the university as writer in residence and after a few more books even win the Nobel prize for literature.

IV.

The day dawned with a hideous unknown blend of color, a moving wall of unnatural sparks and venomous particles out of the northeast which, instead of casting shadows, suffused everything with a faint and unhallowed radiance that, when Jason went down to breakfast, crowned his head like the fire of St. Elmo or like the flames that descended on the apostles at Pentecost.

"Where are the servants?" Jason said brushing the sparks out of his hair. "I'm hungry." He joined his mother at the table.

"I know you blame me," Mrs. Compson said, "for letting them go off to the steep-sided gorge last night."

"Go where?" Jason said. "Haven't they come back yet?"

"To the steep-sided gorge that even the black goat shuns," Mrs. Compson said. "I promised the darkies two weeks ago that they could hold a special service there on May Eve. Lord knows when or if they'll come back."

"Which means we'll eat cold cereal," Jason said, "if there's any milk left."

"I know I'm a bad mother," Mrs. Compson said. "I know you blame me."

"For what?" Jason said. "You never reanimated Quentin, did you?"

They heard Quen-Kthun banging into the balustrade as she sailed down the stairs. When she swished into the dining room, she was wearing her travel hat and holding a suitcase in her fin.

"Where are you going?" Mrs. Compson said.

"New England," Quen-Kthun said.

"Mother, would you ask Quen-Kthun to put her suitcase down," Jason said, "and go fix breakfast?"

"Tell him to fix his own damn breakfast," Quen-Kthun said. "I'm not staying in this house another minute."

"That's what you think, missy," Jason said. He reached up and seized Quen-Kthun by her fore-antennae. "I'm going to knock some sense into that squiggly little head of yours."

"Let me go, you hack," Quen-Kthun said.

Quen-Kthun squirmed and Jason's hand slipped on the fresh dye. She flew out of the dining room. Jason ran after her with Mrs. Compson right behind but she got to the library first and slammed the door. He grasped the knob and tried it, then he stood with the knob in his hand and his head bent in a subtle attitude of awed listening, as if to something much further away than the tri-dimensional room beyond the door, as if to something that was scratching on the known universe's utmost rim.

"All I hear," Mrs. Compson said, "is a window sash being raised."

"The key," Jason said, "to the library. Do you have an extra key, Mother? She's locked the door from the inside."

Mrs. Compson reached into the pocket of the rusty black dressing sacque she wore and produced a handy three-in-one device including a skeleton key. "You cant say your old mother aint good for something," she said. He grabbed the three-in-one device out of her hand.

Jason tried the lock and after a few seconds of cautious fumbling the door flew open. The library was still except for a couple of sheets of typing paper fluttering in the draught from the open window.

"By Yuggoth," Jason said, "the predatory female's stolen my manuscript!" He rushed to the window but all he could see was a tiny winged figure disappearing into the clouds of an unknown color to the northeast and trailing sheets of paper. "I'll die before I have to retype that thing," he said.

"I know you blame me," Mrs. Compson said, "for never learning to type."

"Hush, you old fool," Jason said. "I'm calling the police." He went past his mother into the hall to the telephone.

"This is Jason Compson," he said into the receiver. "I want to report—What?—You say the chief's on his way over now?—You already know about the robbery?—Why that's Southern law enforcement for you—I'll commend you to the governor."

A minute later there was a knock on the front door. Jason went to answer it. Outside was a uniformed policeman.

"Mr. Compson?" the officer said. "Mr. Jason Compson?"

"Yes," Jason said.

"Please come with me, sir," the officer said.

"Thank you for coming so quick," Jason said. "I reckon you must have seen my niece flying over the station house with my manuscript and you put two and two together." The officer said nothing. When they reached the patrol car, Jason noticed a couple of bodies inside. They got out of the car. They were Winged Ones.

"Mr. Compson," the officer said, "you're under arrest."

"What do you mean?" Jason said. "What are these hellish fungi doing here?"

"Sorry, human," one of the Winged Ones buzzed. "I'm afraid you're going to have to come with us." They each took an arm with their pincers. Jason roared.

APPENDIX

A Description of the Compson Family, of Mississippi and of Yuggoth

This was not a Compson. It was an alien:

N'GAH-KTHUN. A parvenu Yuggothian. Called "worm face" (and sometimes "crab cake") by its fiancée, the earthling Caddy Compson, who had it not fallen for that round-heeled cutie could have been one of the leading minds in the Milky Way galaxy; who, because it only realized its mistake after marrying her and had to suffer the ignominy of desertion and neglecting to file the final divorce papers, retreated to a basalt pillar on its home planet where it lived out its days in a dour celibate dignity.

These were Compsons:

JASON SR. At the turn of the century the Old Compson place was inhabited by Jason Richmond Compson and his wife, Caroline, with their children, Quentin, born in 1890, Candace (known as Caddy) born in 1892, Jason born in 1894, and Benjamin (Benjy) born in 1895, not counting the colored servants. Compson was a substantial lawyer, and when his fourth child turned out not to be right in the head he blamed the fungi from Yuggoth who had been infesting the Compson square mile since Benjy's birth. He let his practice and property run to ruin, and (it was said) made a deal with the Winged Ones, to whom he sold the pasture for conversion into a golf course. His securing the transport of his mother's (Damuddy's) brain to Yuggoth set a precedent for the family, and in the fullness of time his cerebral organ, already preserved in alcohol, was likewise transported to Yuggoth where it was found to be insane.

QUENTIN. Who rued the sale of the family pasture to a syndicate of alien interlopers to finance his Harvard education. Who lamented the breakdown of a father who took to drink due to insomnia and an over-stressed nervous system. Committed suicide in Cambridge, Massachusetts, a month before his beloved sister's wedding, excepting that a certain unorthodox doctor from Bolton disinterred his corpse and reanimated it in time for him to return home and try to spoil the ceremony. The Yuggothian attendants tore him to shreds before he could wreak too much havoc.

CANDACE (CADDY). Cute as a button and knew it, accepted the cuteness as a way to attract not just boys but an extremely eligible young Yuggothian with whom she was paired in the annual human-alien invitational at the golf club of the Winged Ones. Was fond enough of her brother despite the behavior of his reanimated corpse to name her daughter after both him and her husband. The bridegroom felt otherwise and divorced her shortly after their wedding in 1910. Leaving her child behind at the Old Compson place, she took off for Hollywood and later got to Europe. Although in her travels she happily remarried several times, none of her subsequent husbands seemed adequate in cosmic outlook compared to N'gah-Kthun. And even though she was not his widow, she mourned his eventual passing in a basalt pillar on Yuggoth.

JASON JR. Who in striving to become a professional writer neglected his job as manager of the Yoknapatawpha mine, for which he had to face the consequences. His employers were considerate enough in his case to observe the legal formalities. The first Compson to travel to Yuggoth and remain sane, though he forever regretted the loss of his manuscript in undreamable abysses back on Earth.

QUEN-KTHUN. Who on the morning after May Eve flew off with her uncle's manuscript toward Boston to elope with a fellow amateur journalist. Who during their honeymoon helped her husband revise the manuscript, or what survived of it after her thousand-mile flight, to the extent that it was totally unrecognizable from the original. Who published it under her own name and earned enough money to start her own millinery business and buy back the Old Compson place. They plan to convert the latter to a vacation home for themselves and their brood of quadraliens.

This was a Compton:

GRANDMA COMPTON. Whose tales of Oklahoma snake lore frightened the bejezus out of the Compson children when they were small.

The black servants:

The endured the May Eve festivities in the steep-sided gorge that even the black goat shuns and vowed they would never return.

All Moon-Beasts Amorphous and Mephitic

"Ah, James," cried Siegfried as I came down to the consulting room, "a messenger has just arrived for you from one of your most exalted clients—King Kuranes. His moon-beast is in need of your services." Siegfried was grinning like a gug as he spoke.

I gave my partner a "ghastly" smile in reply. "Oh, swell. You didn't fancy going there yourself, did you?"

"No, no, my boy. Wouldn't dream in the waking world of depriving you of the fun."

I looked at my checkbook. The bill for that last cask of moon-wine I'd bought from the almost-human merchants in Dylath-Leen was overdue. They say in Dylath-Leen that those almost-human merchants have strange and unpleasant ways of dealing with customers whose accounts remain un-settled for too long.

"Remember, James, Kuranes always pays on the nose—in rubies." Siegfried waved cheerfully and climbed onto his yak.

I got my bag and set off on my zebra, relieved to be spared the company of the messenger—a ghoul in the king's employ—who glibbered how he was sorry he couldn't join me on the return trip but he had a further errand to perform at the Celephaïs cemetery. I rode out the eastern gate and across the tract of English countryside—verdant valleys, Norman abbeys, Cornish fishing villages—that had been designed and built for the monarch of the land of dream by the Disney corporation. (It is said that from the sea-cliffs to the foot of the Tanarian Hills King Kuranes had been losing precious gems by the bushel because "Eng-Land" clashed with the local culture. In my view it had been the sheerest folly to ban the sale of wine, even the mild vintages brewed by the zoogs from tree sap.)

Two days later I came to the moat of a gray gothic manor-house, and when I threw a stone in the water there slithered to admit me a voonith in a "Black Magic Kingdom" tee-shirt who spoke as best it could in the unintelligible tones—at least to a native Glaswegian like me—of far Cornwall. After leaving my zebra in the care of that amphibious terror, I walked up the parched path between trees as near as possible to England's trees (which frankly wasn't all that near), and climbed the terraces among gardens neglected since Queen Anne's time. At the door, flanked by stuffed cats (former pets evidently), I was met by an unshaven butler in a bhole skin, and was presently taken to the library where Kuranes, Lord of Ooth-Nargai and the Sky around Serannian, sat on the floor in a sailor suit playing with his blocks.

"If you've come to scold me because my mother's nearly out of patience waiting in the carriage to go to that hateful lawn-party at the vicar's, I'm not ready."

"I beg your pardon, your Majesty, I—"

"Oh, it's you Herriot," exclaimed the king, looking up. "I thought you were my nurse. My apologies, old boy."

"Not at all, your Majesty—"

"Come, come, Herriot, no need to stand on formality. I'm only a humble dreamland despot, you know. Call me Kuranes."

"As you wish, sir."

King Kuranes had a reputation for being something of an eccentric, but I will credit him for his ability to put commoners like myself at their ease.

"I'm awfully glad you're here, Herriot," he said, staggering to his feet and giving the wooden fort he'd just constructed a good kick. "Matilda has not been her usual slimy self of late."

"Have you noticed any change in her eating habits?"

"No, I can't say that I have. She still consumes her weight in fish and fungi like clockwork every day."

"Fish and fungi?"

"Well, mostly fungi."

"Fried fungi?"

Kuranes nodded as if it were the most natural thing in the dream world. While it probably did no harm, fried fungi was about the last food I would've expected a moon-beast to relish. The king's realm boasted a chain of fish and fungi shops, and I had a strong suspicion Matilda was the chief beneficiary of the leftovers.

"Any symptoms of ill health?"

"I'm afraid she no longer plays her disgustingly carven flute of ivory."

"Oh, dear. We better go have a look at her straight away, then."

As we descended a fathomless spiral of steep and slippery stairs to the dungeon, the king sang the praises of moon-beasts, in particular of his prize. Matilda was clearly in a class by herself. Not only was she a champion racer but she excelled at dressage as well as zoog hunting. Personally, I've never been fond of those polypous and amorphous monsters, but thought it politic not to mention the fact to my royal client.

At the bottom we followed a passage lined with torch-bearing slaves until we came to a mephitic pit. Below lay the moon-beast, a great grayish-white toad-like thing, expanding and contracting in its sleep. By the light of a brace of torch-bearing slaves I dropped into the pit, praying to the tame gods atop Kadath that the patient wouldn't suddenly wake up.

Since Matilda's hindquarters were pointed in my direction, I decided to begin my examination there. I rolled up my sleeve and gingerly stuck my arm as far it would reach up her nether orifice. One has to be careful handling these jellyish entities, which can easily burst with results highly offensive to the sight and smell. All seemed normal, normal that is for a carnivorous creature on a diet of fish and fungi—and so primitive that it has only one organ system for both sexual reproduction and waste elimination.

Next I tiptoed around toward the mouth, the beast's business end and by far the more dangerous. I was in luck. I could spot the problem from a safe distance. The curiously vibrating mass of tentacles on the tip of the blunt, vague snout instead of being a healthy pink was a sickly green. It was little wonder flute playing was out. The formless abomination had a cold.

"I think I know what's ailing Matilda, sir," I said as I clambered up a pyramid of torch-bearers to the top of the pit. "I'll have to give you some antibiotic ointment and you must rub some onto her tentacles three times a day. You'll be able to do that, won't you?"

"Actually, I believe I'll have the butler take charge of a gang of slaves to perform that chore, thank you."

"Good, good." As I rummaged in my bag for the ointment I had the old feeling of fraud, but there was nothing for it. I pocketed my fee—a couple of low-grade rubies—and skedadled back to Skeldale House, wondering if my esteemed client's cash-flow problem was as dire as my own.

One morning a week or two later, King Kuranes showed up at our consulting room with the eyeless abnormality in tow. Matilda was no better; in fact, she was worse. Her tentacles and snout were now encrusted with great gobs of greenish-brown mucus.

"You said you'd cure her, Herriot," the monarch of dream sniffed, doing his best to fight back the tears.

King Kuranes showed up at our consulting room . . .

"There, there, your Highness. Bring her into the surgery why don't you and we'll see what we can do. It's only a little discharge."

"Discharge! I don't like the sound of that." The king began to sob.

"Oh, it's nothing to worry about. It'll be child's play to remove it and she'll be right as a bog-wraith afterward."

I spoke lightly because these procedures were routine. A massive injection of local anesthetic and some judicious pruning with a pair of hedge clippers would do the trick, but as I looked at the moon-beast I felt a twinge of unutterable loathing. Things might not be so easy with Matilda.

There was, for instance, the trifling matter of one of us grasping that noxious head while the other inserted the needle into that repulsive snout. Matilda made it very clear that we would share the fate of the black men of Parg if we dared take any liberties with her. Being on unfamiliar ground and feeling hungry, she came waddling, open-mouthed, at Siegfried and me as soon as we tried to enter the room. We retreated hastily and barred the door.

"Looks like one for the nembutal," murmured Siegfried.

"With zoog," I added.

For unapproachable cases we kept a supply of the succulent small brown burrowers in a pen in the garden. Live zoog was a delicacy no moon-beast could resist. It was a simple matter to grab one, force a few capsules of nembutal down its throat, and heave it through the half-open surgery window that faced the garden. It always worked.

When we came back twenty minutes later we expected to find Matilda beyond the Gate of Deeper Slumber, but when we peered in she lumbered against the window, shifting shape like an accordion. On the floor the comatose zoog lay untouched.

"By Azathoth, look at that!" I cried. "No moon-beast's ever refused one of those weird-eyed flutterers before!"

Siegfried scratched his armpit. "What a damned nuisance! Do you think she can smell the nembutal on the zoog's breath? Better try her with a larger creature."

Fortunately, there was a turbaned almost-human in the waiting room who was only too glad to accept the flagon of nembutal-laced moon-wine we were shortly to offer him. As we guided that evil wide-mouthed merchant out to the garden, he muttered something about the wine's bouquet, which reminded him that he hadn't come to avail ourselves of our veterinary services but to collect— He was down the seventy steps to lighter slumber by the time we shoved him through the surgery window.

When we peeked in fifteen minutes later, the picture hadn't changed. The almost-human was sprawled on the floor next to the zoog—untasted.

"What in the Cold Waste are we going to do?" Siegfried exploded. "We can't afford to upset the king any more than he already is."

Inside we could hear Kuranes complaining that it was time for his lunch. He wanted something English, like his favorite food, fish and—

"Just hang on for a minute," I said. "I think I know the answer."

I rushed in the door past Kuranes, who was squirming in his chair, and up to our living quarters, where even then my wife was fixing a mixed fungi salad for our own midday meal. It was the work of a moment to seize the bowl she was preparing and dump the contents into a skillet coated with nembutal-saturated oil. The fragrance of frying fungi must have wafted down to the offices below, for the house soon started to shake with the sounds of some heavy body repeatedly launching itself against an interior wall. It was the work of another moment to run downstairs with the glowing platter of the phosphorescent treat and toss it through the surgery window. Matilda was on the stuff like a shantak and swallowed it whole without hesitation.

As we watched the flabby moon-beast roll over, we knew we had won. When we finally unbarred the door and entered the room, Matilda was dozing, her expression as goofy as a night-gaunt's. We administered the anesthetic and applied the shears; the operation was over within five minutes.

Matilda was still dopey as a Dhole when her master had finished his luncheon—some extra drug-free fungi that my wife had managed to scrape up (or off)—and was ready to go home.

"We've removed that little discharge, your Worship," I said. "Her tentacles will be fine now, but I'm prescribing a course of Lindane tablets to stop any further infection."

As I reached for my 1906 Waterman to write the instructions, I glanced at some of the other labels I had written: "Pepto-bismol for ghoul. To be given in a pint of offal." "Vitamin C for web-footed wamp. To be given in a pint of human blood."

I poised my pen for a moment, then, for the first time in my dream life, I wrote, "Tablets for moon-beast. One to be given three times daily inserted in fried fungi."

"I'm much obliged to you, Herriot. Matlida seems her old slimy self again," the king said, as we exchanged papers. "Say, I'm a bit short of rubies at the moment. I trust, my dear fellow, you won't mind accepting this certificate for a hundred shares of Kuranes Enterprises Limited instead."

"Ah, James," said Siegfried, as we watched our august client ride off on his filthy mount, "our almost-human visitor should be waking up directly. Let's hope he'll be as delighted as you were to be paid in Kuranes Enterprises stock."

The Undercliffe Sentences

Carl Dreadstone, guest of horror at the 1995 Brichester Fantasy Convention, wrapped up his talk about authorship, "Horror: Fantasy or Fiction?," with the usual lies about his childhood. In truth, both his parents had been loving and kind, giving him the sort of enlightened, humanistic upbringing that those raised beneath the yoke of religious superstition can only envy. Nothing had scared Carl Dreadstone as a boy, not even the dark. Happiness *was* a warm puppy in the Dreadstone household. But what self-respecting horror writer is going to let on that his had been a "normal" family? Certainly not a professional like Carl Dreadstone, who was never one to disappoint the fans.

"Finally, after years of intensive therapy, I succeeded in sublimating my fears into my fiction. Any questions?"

Dreadstone surveyed the sea—no, puddle—of moon-shaped faces, hovering above soft, baggy bodies, which lay strewn like discards at a parish jumble sale over the seats of the auditorium. A few flabby arms, like over-ripe cheese, rose balloonlike in the air.

"Yes, you there with the skull earring."

"I've heard rumors that you weren't the con's first choice as guest of horror. Have you any comment?"

"Yes, that's quite true. In fact, I wasn't even the second choice. Martin Amis had not said no when originally invited. You can imagine how the organizers were practically foaming at the mouth at the prospect of roping in a popular mainstream author—an extract from *London Fields* appearing in a 'New Gothic' anthology had given them their opening—but in the end Amis realized he had better things to do. Receiving that record advance went to his head, I suppose. Then they tried to get Jay Ramsey, but he was already booked to go to America. Frankly, I was the best they could scrape up at the last minute. Next question please."

"Do you ever write anything but horror?" piped up another lad.

"Yes, I've tried. Lord knows, I've tried. And failed. How I wish I could write literary fiction and be accepted as a real author—like Martin Amis or

Gwyn Barry, to name two of Britain's top novelists." While Dreadstone would have loved to bare the soul a bit further, from experience he knew audiences could tolerate only so much self-pity. So after an anguished pause he simply said, "But I must do the best I can within my limits as a mere genre writer."

"Do you mind not being famous?" asked another adolescent.

"Yes, I do. I mind it terribly. But then I realize there's still lots to be grateful for in this life whenever wacks like you ask me questions like that."

"What was Errol Undercliffe like?" came the next query.

"Rather indulgent with pushy and self-centered fans, based on our one encounter. I was in the audience at an author talk just like this one thirty years ago, at the last Brichester Fantasy Con. Afterwards I managed to steer Undercliffe into a corner and grill him at length about Roland Franklyn."

And so the inquisition went on for another half-hour. No one could deny that patience—though at times it felt like self-abasement—was Carl Dreadstone's strong suit. For example, his fondness for signing books of his sent from America was legendary in horror circles. These collectors were often considerate enough to include U.S. currency, which he could then change for pounds at the bank before queuing up at the post office to mail the books back overseas. Usually his correspondents provided an envelope and left him a few extra pence for his trouble.

In any event, this one-man performance had been no more an ordeal than the author-signing the night before. One admirer had been pushing a handcart stacked with hardcover copies of Dreadstone's last three novels— *The Itching, They Who Suck,* and *Alien Turds*—all pasted with remainder stickers. He'd cleaned out the stock of the Lower Brichester branch of a national discount chain, the git had cheerfully confessed, and looked forward to reselling them for a profit to his friends. Most had required personal inscriptions. Dreadstone had been only too happy to oblige. Then there had been the many fans with copies of his current novel, *Vampire?!* A joy, as always, seeing and fingering one's new book for the first time.

In fact, Dreadstone's only real regret was that he had missed the panel scheduled opposite him, featuring S. Hutson and S. Hudson. Like Superman and Clark Kent, Hutson and Hudson had never been seen in the same room at the same time. For years he'd suspected that the author of *Heathen* and the author of *Hounds of Horror* were one person—though he wouldn't put it past the man to hire a double to keep the deception alive. Hutson, or Hudson, as the master of contrived plot and perfervid prose, was more than capable of pulling that kind of juvenile stunt, he was sure.

After a good vomit in the gents, Dreadstone headed for the dealers' room, where he hoped to find Richard Royce, editor of True Lite Press. Royce was bringing out a collection of his tales, *The Undercliffe Sentences: Parodies or Pastiches?*, the sort of stuff his regular publisher wouldn't be caught dead doing but ideal for a small press. Dreadstone wanted an update. A pity the book hadn't been ready in time for the convention, but then Royce had been holding the manuscript for only three years. There had been concerns about money, libel, copyright infringement, bad taste— all the familiar excuses for delay. At last, however, Royce had agreed to shake hands on the deal and the project was pretty much under contract.

Dreadstone was in luck. The editor of True Lite Press was sitting alone, free of pesky customers, at a table near the door.

"How's tricks?" asked the author.

"Not bad, I suppose. I've already sold three copies of *Photographed by Lightning*. Undercliffe's always a reliable seller. Even better, one bloke bought a copy each of my two published novels."

Like most specialty publishers, Royce carried a wide range of titles, mainly within the field, but he offered other odd volumes as well—like his own two non-genre novels, *Afterthought* and *Dreams Don't Mean Anything*. Such mention led Royce to expand on his so far unfruitful efforts to place several successor novels. Lately things were looking up, though. The head of the London vanity press where he worked one day a week as Special Director had expressed an interest in issuing one or more of them.

"I see you have copies of *Vampire?!*," Dreadstone finally interrupted.

"Oh, yes. Several potential customers have thumbed through it. Quite the crowd pleaser, from what I hear. Mind autographing my supply?"

"Glad to. 'Til I get my author's copies, this is the next best thing."

As Dreadstone set about this pleasurable task, Royce held forth on his ambitions for True Lite Press, which had had a slightly different name back in the sixties, long before his own involvement. He planned to reissue *How I Discovered My Infinite Self*, by "An Initiate," and was busy trying to track down Roland Franklyn's exceedingly rare tome, *We Pass from View*, bound in bright blue.

"Even if we could find a copy, there's no guarantee the text wouldn't writhe and shimmer across the page." Royce chuckled.

Dreadstone recognized the reference, to an episode in one of Undercliffe's homages to Franklyn, and smiled—thinly. He Dreadstone, after all, knew the tales of these two authors more intimately than any fan, critic, or collector on this planet. Only he could have pulled off such a brilliant send-up as *The Undercliffe Sentences,* simultaneously parodying Franklyn à la Under-cliffe and Undercliffe à la Franklyn. Or was it more a matter of pastiching? Given how closely Franklyn and Undercliffe could resemble each other in style and content, the differences weren't always obvious. Well, readers liked puzzles. Let them figure it out.

"Oh, before I forget. I have something for you." Dreadstone set down the last signed copy of *Vampire?!,* while the editor reached under the table and handed him a bulky envelope. "I think you'll be pleased. We took espe-cial care. No rush to return it, of course."

"Dare I ask? What I gave you six months ago, is it, can it really be . . ."

"Yes, the copy-edited manuscript. As I say, whenever you get around to it . . ."

Eager as he was to check it over, Dreadstone had no immediate oppor-tunity to peruse his manuscript, which he dropped off in his room in col-lege—how economical it had been to hold the convention at Brichester University during the summer vac—since he'd promised to meet Harvey Nadler, of Delta Film Productions, for lunch in the cafeteria.

Usually an important author, in particular a guest of horror, had an en-tourage at these gatherings. Authors of equal if not greater stature hung out with him, stood him lagers at pubs, shielded him from the unwanted ad-vances of the fans. His editor, his agent, stood by his side like a Praetorian guard. But where was Dreadstone's editor? Where was his agent? Well, it just so happened that they were also Jay Ramsey's editor and agent—and because Jay Ramsay was in America on tour they were also on tour in America. With Jay Ramsey. Who'd be signing a four-film deal in Hollywood.

Harvey Nadler was an old friend. Delta Film Productions had consid-ered taking an option on *The Itching,* on *They Who Suck,* on *Alien Turds*—and now they were considering picking up the option on *Vampire?!* Delta Film Productions had yet to pay Dreadstone a penny, but perhaps it would be different this time—the Great Pumpkin would show up on Halloween, Linus would throw away his security blanket forever, Lucy would at last let Charlie Brown kick the ball. Right. And maybe in the New Year he'd re-ceive his knighthood, for services to literature.

Dreadstone joined Nadler at a formica-topped table for two, near the kitchen. It was noisy enough for them to talk without fear of being over-heard.

"Please thank your publicity department, Carl," said Nadler, with a thin smile. "A copy of *Vampire?!* was on my desk a month ago. What I've read looks promising—not as allusive as previous novels, I was relieved to find. Readers can't stand that, you know. It makes them feel dumber than the author. Never condescend to your audience, Carl. It's bad form as well as bad business."

"I made a deliberate effort to be more commercial, Harvey," responded Dreadstone. "Vampires are hot right now."

"Yes, they're hot all right. Very hot. Damned hot. There are more vampire books on the loose today than bats in hell, Carl. Ever try to tell one bat from another? Believe me, Carl, you've seen one bat you've seen them all."

"I appreciate your concern, Harvey."

"Ever think about screenwriting?"

"No, I never have."

"Why not?"

"Oh, I don't know. Maybe because my heroes Roland Franklyn and Errol Undercliffe never wrote screenplays."

"Franklyn and Undercliffe, as if I needed to remind you, Carl, had their careers cut prematurely short. If they'd survived to your age, I'm sure they would've moved to Hollywood ages ago."

"What about *Red Dragons,* Harvey? You know, Harry Chang's adaptation of three of Undercliffe's best tales."

"Come on. That arty stuff?"

"Chang's interpretation of 'The Drifting Face' is beyond anything we've done or could even conceive of in the West. If an independent Korean filmmaker were to express an interest in adapting one of my works, why I'd—"

"Carl, is *Red Dreams* part of this weekend's film program?"

"No. In fact, I was rather surprised to learn it wasn't. I mean—"

"Carl, what was shown last night at that special midnight screening?"

"I believe *A Clockwork Orange* and *Child's Play 3.*"

"Right. There you have it—the kinds of films the public want to view."

Dreadstone had been sorry to have missed these two movies, as well as the subsequent police raid—he wondered if the organizers now regretted advertising their film program in the *Brichester Herald*—but he'd needed his sleep after the long trip from London's Squatney district by lorry. After debating the genius of Stanley Kubrick versus that of the director of *Child's Play 3,* whose name neither of them could remember, it was almost time for the next big event.

"One last piece of advice," said Nadler as they bussed their trays. "Have you ever considered doing novelizations? I might be able to send something your way in that line sometime, if you like."

"No, I haven't, Harvey, but please do keep me in mind, though."

Next on the docket for Dreadstone was an interview with the editor of a local fanzine called *Spirited*. *Spirited's* readership may not have been large, but it had circulated around the Brichester region off and on over the years and Dreadstone was never one to turn up his nose at even the humblest of publicity venues. He met the editor, a pubescent fourteen-year-old who'd recently taken over the position, in an empty classroom.

"Should I have heard of you?" the lad asked as he fiddled with his tape recorder.

"Yes, definitely. I'm a professional horror writer."

"Before we begin, I should tell you I prefer fiction to be about real life."

"Well, I prefer fiction to be about real life, too. But it so happens that what I write, what I'm capable of writing, isn't about real life. It's escapist. It has nothing to do with the everyday cares of ordinary existence, like finding and holding a job, or getting married and staying married. Do I make myself clear?"

"Yeah."

"When you reach my age, my boy, you'll recognize your own shortcomings as keenly as I do mine."

"I should hope not. . . . Oh, here, the mike's on. Ready for the first question?"

"Fire away."

"Does it bother you that none of your work has ever been turned into a film, especially when others, less talented than yourself, have made a packet on movie sales?"

"Yes, it does. Funny you should bring it up. I was just talking to a producer friend of mine about this very subject. To speak plainly, I'm frightfully jealous of toffee-nosed twits like—— and—— who've been paid such obscene sums of money for rubbish like—— and——. Very self-satisfied these hacks are, too, I might add. Hate 'em."

There was an extended pause while the editor flipped through the pages of a loose-leaf notebook on his lap.

"Right, second question. Would you care to comment about how your words have been altered in American editions of your books?"

"Yes, I would. Take the word *randy*. In *They Who Suck* it was turned into a proper name. Yes, believe it or not, there are male Americans named 'Randy.' A shift from lowercase to capitals affected a major sex scene— 'Tiffany was feeling randy' into 'Tiffany was feeling Randy,' with a capital R. I'm afraid some American readers got the impression I sanction three-somes. I'm sorry, but I don't."

"What about foreign translations?" asked the editor.

"I've just placed the English translation of the French translation of a story of mine, 'The Revenge of the Curate of Temphill,' with another French publisher. Mark Twain did something similar once, with that jump-ing frog tall tale of his. It's also like that dinner-table game, telephone, where one person whispers a saying to a person next to him and so on round the table. The results can be quite hilarious. I hope to keep 'Revenge of the Cu-rate' going this way between French and English for as long as I can."

There was another lengthy break, until the editor again found his place in his notes.

"Is Carl Dreadstone your real name?"

"As real as the name Roland Franklyn or Errol Undercliffe."

"Where were you born?"

"Clotton."

"So you grew up here."

"Yes and no. My family moved to Squatney, in London, as soon as they could afford to get out. I was almost able to go to the loo by myself at the time. As a teen I returned to the area for the occasional pop concert."

It was a comfort to Dreadstone that the editor's questions were begin-ning to follow in some logical sequence. As he'd done in dozens of past in-terviews, he covered the familiar biographical ground—ancestry, schooling, jobs, his discovery of the works of Roland Franklyn and Errol Under-cliffe—varying the details in subtle and fiendish fashion. Let future Dread-stone scholars straighten out the mess was his motto. What could be more boring than plodding and unremitting consistency?

Three hours later Dreadstone looked at his watch. He'd missed the tour of the nearby Undercliffe and Franklyn sites, though to be honest he didn't care all that much, unlike some scholarly types he knew, which drab house or grotty street or blitz-bashed neighborhood had inspired his mentors in a slag heap like Brichester. He would have to hustle to make his next ap-pointment, a reading in the college library of his notorious acrostic tale, "The Letters That Spell."

Written in the second-person plural voice, this ingenious short-short requires you to take the first letter of the first word, the second letter of the second word, the third letter of the third word, the fourth letter of the fourth word, and so on, until you reach a word with fewer letters than the number you were up to. Then you count down to one, whereupon you start to count up again, until, as before, the count exceeds the last number of the series, and you once more descend the scale, as it were, repeating the process to story's end. These letters form an anagram concealing a passage from Robert G. Ingersoll's classic *Some Mistakes of Moses,* a favorite text of his freethinking parents. Dreadstone's explanation of all this afterwards took several times as long as the reading itself. He was glad he'd been allotted a full hour.

Back in his room Dreadstone deliberated whether to smoke a joint or pop some LSD in preparation for the climactic con banquet in the caf, billed as the "Feast of Eihort." No, taking drugs was what he invariably did before writing anything important. The complimentary four-pack of Tetley's beer the organizers had been so kind to place on his pillow was all he required to fortify himself for the feeding.

Dreadstone was accorded a chair at the head table, along with such other dignitaries as S. Hutson and S. Hudson, who sat side by side, like Laurel and Hardy—or was it like Tintin's twin detectives, Thompson and Thomson? In the glow of the tepid beverage he'd swilled beforehand, Dreadstone couldn't decide whether the pair resembled each other or not. At any rate, he passed through the alcohol-free meal in an agreeable stupor until speaker time, when horror m.c. *extraordinaire,* Beavis Lampbeavis, rose to his feet.

"Ladies and gents, girls and boys, lasses and laddies, ghouls and goys, may I have your attention please," Lampbeavis announced, tapping Dreadstone's head sharply with a spoon. "We have gathered here at Brichester U. to 'honor' one of horror's professionals. Let me say right off the bat that the rumors running round the con are true. He wasn't our first choice, nor even our second—as I'm sure he'd be the first to confess. Right, Carl?" Dreadstone nodded. "But if there's one thing you can say about Carl— some would say the only thing—he's a jolly good sport."

"Hear, hear!" cried a voice in the crowd, possibly Richard Royce's.

"Others would say that Carl Dreadstone is a modest man, of modest achievements. Just think about it. First he made us scratch our skins in horror with *The Itching;* next he made up purse our lips in horror with *They Who*

Suck; then he made us wipe our, er, wipe ourselves in horror with *Alien Turds;* and now with his latest novel, *Vampire?!* . . . or is that *Vampire!?* Quick, Carl, which is it?"

"It's question mark first, exclamation second, Beav."

"Yes, right, thank you. With *Vampire?!* Carl Dreadstone will, uh, will, uh—drive his fans batty!"

More cheers from the assembled horror hordes.

"It's been my privilege, Carl, to flip through your new novel," the m.c. continued. "It includes so many characteristic touches. On page fifty, for instance, you describe a *Los Angeles Times* crossword clue as being followed by the numbers four and five in parentheses. Carl, you should know in the United States crosswords don't provide the number of letters and words where there's a multi-word answer, as we do in Britain. Nor is the phrase 'eggs and chips à la mode' apt to appear in an *L.A. Times* cookery column. Chips are 'French fries' in America. As for the word *cookery,* I believe it's not in common parlance across the Atlantic. You get the picture."

"Yes, my ignorance appalls even me at times," answered the author, standing up so the whole room could hear. "Forgive me."

"We forgive you, Carl. I promise to supply you with a complete list of your errors in time to correct them for the paperback edition."

"Thank you, Beav. Spoken like a gentleman."

"I think you'd agree with me, Carl, that you've already said enough to-day—at your author chat, at your story reading, at the feast just now. So if you don't mind, why don't we dispense with the customary guest-of-horror speech. Sit down, relax—and get set to enjoy a special personal tribute."

Dreadstone readily complied. He liked receiving accolades. A moment later a young chap appeared beside the m.c., sheets of paper in hand. Lampbeavis introduced him to the audience.

"At the eleventh hour, we on the organizing committee decided that a writing contest would be a smashing idea. As a surprise for you, Carl, we invited your readers to send us stories, no longer than ten thousand words, that mimicked, parodied, or otherwise ripped off your fiction. The re-sponse, I must say, was gratifying. The winner will now read his tale in its entirety."

"This is my version of Mr. Dreadstone's brand of 'televisionary' hor-ror," the fellow mumbled into his manuscript. "It's called 'The Curate of Temphill Goes to New York.'"

Dreadstone thanked his lucky stars he was sitting close enough to catch every word of the lad's low, monotonic delivery: the slow introduction with its antecedentless pronouns; the strings of adjectives run riot and metaphors gone mad; the lengthy expository passages unrelieved by dialogue; the images out of cheap films and comic books; the blood, the entrails, the animal sacrifices; the climax where the narrator realizes the killer's name spelled backwards is—

The crowd roared its approval as soon as people noticed the amateur had stopped reading. Fan fiction. It was Dreadstone's secret vice. He consumed it the way some addicts stuff themselves with bonbons—or fill their veins with crack—or drown themselves in Tetley's beer. But how much of a good thing can one bear? After the winner departed, Lampbeavis introduced the runner-up, who proceeded to read his Dreadstone offering in full. Then it was the turn of the third-place finisher, and finally of the "horrible" mention.

At the end Lampbeavis announced to the few souls still scattered about the caf that these four stories would be featured in the next issue of *Spirited*. "I'll make sure you get put on the comp list, Carl," the m.c. said in parting.

"Thanks, Beav. I look forward to seeing them in cold print."

Back in his room Dreadstone looked forward to a little light reading before seeking the darkness he craved. Another page or two of Gwyn Barry's best-selling *Stumbling on Melons*? No, there was something for him even more thrilling—how could he have forgotten?—the copy-edited manuscript of *The Undercliffe Sentences*.

He pulled it out of the envelope, plopped it on the bed, and dived in. He soon discovered that every page was a veritable Jackson Pollock of editorial markings: commas added and deleted, dashes for semicolons, semicolons for dashes, colons for dashes, words italicized and unitalicized, infinitives split and adverbs transposed, big paragraphs minced into little paragraphs, entire passages rewritten to convey their hidden meanings. In short, he found all the usual changes and corrections he'd come to expect from a thorough copy-edit job. If he'd wanted to punctuate, paragraph, italicize or emphasize in the way that the copy-editor had, he reminded himself, he should have done so in the first place. Fair enough. All this he could and did routinely accept.

There was another class of commentary, however, that took him aback. These had mainly to do with content, scrawled in indelible red ink in the margins, odd queries like: "Are you sure the name of the initiate who travels to Tond is Yohk'khim?"; "Did this occur before or after the yarkdao built the city of Derd?"; "Would this character be likely to use a tok'l container for this purpose?"; "What's the true, hierophantic significance of the phrase *xada-hgla soron*?"; and perhaps queerest of all, "As'lak, Sauron, Daoloth, etc.—do you think it safe to use this incantation?" Did the answers to these nitpicking questions—this was a collection of parodies or pastiches, after all—really matter? He fell asleep pondering the possibilities.

In the morning he woke up knowing he had to speak to the woman who had dissected the ms., performed the autopsy as it were, given how vivid the postmortem had appeared in a dream. (Dreams can and do have meaning, even if Richard Royce might disagree.) There was something insistent about her queries that brooked no delay in response. Perhaps there was still a prayer the patient could, if not be revived, at least be reanimated.

He located a working phone two blocks from the college, slipped in a ten pence piece, and rung the number in Goatswood.

"I say, it's a mite early, Dreadstone. Couldn't this wait 'til the dealers' room opens at ten?" answered the editor of True Lite Press.

"You have to tell me who your copy-editor is, Royce. I must talk to her straight away, and see her if possible. I sense she's local. Not at the con, is she?"

"Yes, she lives in Brichester, but fat chance you'd catch her at a con. She's a recluse, has no phone, scarcely ever goes out."

"Sounds like your typical introvert copy-editor—wide knowledge making up for lack of worldly experience."

"We chose her for your book because of her particular expertise."

"You wouldn't mind my calling on her."

"Not at all, not at all. She welcomes visitors, she gets so few of them. You can walk from the university to her place in Dee Terrace, on Mercy Hill."

"I think I can find that." Then, remembering his manners: "Thanks awfully. Sorry to wake you."

"Quite all right, but please remember, there's no hurry on the manuscript."

Dreadstone consulted a city map, to make sure he could find his way. The most direct route was through Central Park. At that hour of the morning he had the park to himself, apart from the few furtive figures that flitted like loose sacking through the underbrush and the nasty bits of paper that skimmed across the grass like illicit lovers on a lark. He passed the bandstand where the Titus Groans had played a concert in '66. He had come down from London for that one, just as he had a year later to hear Spinal Tap perform at the island beyond Severnford. Ah, the memories! The horned skulls and the devil masks bobbing and weaving in the strobe lights, the lads leaping and prancing through the flaming pentagrams, the night breeze wafting the acrid scent of Wimpy burgers—all now as quaint as Druids and Stonehenge. He'd been heavily into the works of Errol Undercliffe at the time and thought it no coincidence that bass guitarist Derek Smalls had gone on record as having read and liked *The Man Who Feared to Sleep*, while the influence of "Through the Zone of the Colossi" was manifest in Nigel Tufnel's lyrics on Tap's *Break Like the Wind* album. No doubt about it—heavy metal music had helped satisfy his youthful craving to believe in some higher spiritual authority.

From the foot of Mercy Hill he had to climb a dozen or so levels before reaching Dee Terrace. The house was unmistakable—the waist-high weeds in the garden, the cloud of flies above the chimney, the black curtains across every window except a bricked-up one on the ground floor—each eccentric detail bespoke a copy-editor's domain. He knocked at the front door. From inside a woman's voice screamed, "I'm naked. Wait a minute!"

Five minutes later the door opened. She wore a pink nightgown that clashed with the crimson wallpaper of the hall and the carrot color of her hair. The silky garment barely concealed the flabby folds of her aged flesh.

"Hello, I'm Carl Dreadstone."

"Never heard of you."

"I'm a horror writer. You—"

"A horror writer! Of all the nerve!"

"I'm attending the fantasy convention being held this weekend at the university, and was wondering—"

"Yes, I know all about that from the reports on the telly. Shocking, absolutely shocking it is showing filth like those films. Jail is too good for those degenerates!"

"I was hoping you wouldn't mind my dropping in. I've brought—"

"A present. For me?" The woman eyed the package under his arm containing the copy-edited manuscript. "I never get presents anymore. Never. You'd better come in."

He followed his hostess down the hall into a sunken living-room, lit by a single red bulb on a ceiling cord and furnished with a bed, a chair, a state-of-the-art home entertainment center. A dark-skinned girl was dusting.

"Bhaji, we have a visitor. We must play something. What would you like to hear, young man, Debussy's string quartet or Beethoven's opus 135?"

"Either, both. It doesn't matter."

Dreadstone sat down in the chair, the envelope on his lap, while the woman went over to the console and jabbed at some buttons. Nothing happened.

"Miss Arco, the tape player's broke," whispered the girl. "You forget."

"Broke! Why didn't you tell me? Get out, you impudent wog. Out I say. Can't you see I have a guest?"

"Yes, Miss Arco." The girl left quietly, evidently accustomed to such treatment.

"Never mind," the woman said, sitting on the bed. "I shall sing for you. The 'Vissi d'arte' aria from *Tosca*."

"Please don't trouble yourself—"

"Trouble! You talk to me of trouble! I'll tell you about trouble!" Her face took on a scarlet hue that matched neither the pink of her gown nor the orange of her hair. "For years I live alone here. Nobody comes. Then yesterday a busload of those, those *people* turn up at my house. They trample the garden with their clumsy feet. They try to look in windows. They bang on the door. Nobody cares about me—they care only about him."

"Him?"

"My late husband. That idiot. If they want him they can go to his grave, near the school. That other horror writer did, soon after he died, and look where it got him—worse than the grave! I threw out all my poor little Frankla's books after that, including every copy of *We Pass from View*. Disgusting the way they used to ooze through one's fingers, just disgusting!"

"I'm sorry—"

"You're sorry! What about me, Leda Arco? Yes, I go by my own name now. Only that pathetic failed novelist gives a damn, what's his name, you know the one I'm talking about."

"Richard Royce?"

"That's the one, that's the one. Only he appreciates me. He gives me work—"

"Yes, I know!" Dreadstone shrieked. He'd decided he'd better assert himself if he didn't want to spend the rest of his natural days in that house. "Please listen. That's why I'm here. You copy-edited my manuscript. That's what's in the envelope. I wanted to talk to you about your . . . suggestions."

The woman stared at Dreadstone, as if suddenly recognizing him for the first time. Her complexion shaded into purple.

"You! You! You thief! That's what you are. How dare you steal my husband's stories?"

"I didn't steal anything. I wrote *The Undercliffe Sentences* as a way of acknowledging my debt to the influence of my predecessors. It's perfectly normal and innocent."

"Normal! Innocent! How dare you! How dare you use his concepts when you have no idea, no idea you understand, what you're doing!"

"Stylistic concerns aside, I take it you had some problems, serious problems I'll grant, with some of the text."

"I was his wife! If you knew what I know you wouldn't be so glib about the burrowers beneath the Plain of Sound on S'glhuo or what the elder things kept out of later editions of *Revelations from Glaaki*."

"I'd like to put everything right—"

"Come here." Her tone was gentle again. Amazing how she could shift from one mood extreme to another. "Let Ledasha help you."

Dreadstone hesitated. The woman leaned over and pulled him next to her on the bed. He unsheathed the manuscript.

By the glow of the red bulb they went over *The Undercliffe Sentences,* page by page, paragraph by paragraph, sentence by sentence. Bathed in blood, the words seemed to wiggle, to squirm, against the rosy-hued page. They were compelled to read much of the text aloud, including the Daoloth chant, repeating it three times. Discarded manuscript leaves fluttered to the floor, gathering in curiously ordered heaps at their feet.

They had reached the fourth pastiche parody when Dreadstone felt something on his calf, beneath the trouser leg. He scratched the offended area, to relieve the itching of some tiny creature who sucked, depositing its orthographical droppings— He pulled both legs onto the bed, as did the woman breathing heavily at his side. Dreadstone seemed to be viewing the scene through the thin and shifting perceptual haze of an acid trip that was just ending—or just beginning. He closed his eyes as they lay back and embraced, but it did no good. When he opened them he saw her mouth was disappearing—the left side was already gone—for swarming over limbs and faces like flies were the Undercliffe letters, the Undercliffe syllables, the Undercliffe words, the Undercliffe phrases, the Undercliffe clauses, the Undercliffe sentences.

THE ARKHAM COLLECTOR

for Jon White

Of all my friends Sam Lowell takes the prize as the most considerate. Two acts of generosity in particular put me forever in his debt. The first was his adulatory advance review of my novel *The Golden Doom* for *Books Weekly*. All *BW* reviews are of course unsigned, so it wasn't until I'd written the anonymous reviewer in care of the journal to thank him or her, and received his response, that I learned his identity. His second great gift came as an even more welcome surprise quite recently, almost a decade after we first got in touch, indeed during our first face-to-face meeting.

I know such a delay may seem odd, but let me explain. If not for his mother's health we might've met much sooner. Sam had been living in Manhattan, only blocks away from my own West End Avenue address, in fact—so he'd informed me in one of his early letters. Then his mother, who'd always been something of an invalid, took a turn for the worse—the same week his notice of my book appeared, coincidentally—and since he was her only family he packed up his place in New York and within a month was settled back in Arkham.

Yes, that's right, Arkham—the venerable Massachusetts seaport that H. P. Lovecraft fixed on the literary map, so to speak, just as firmly as Nathaniel Hawthorne did his native town of Salem. Like any horror fan, and back then freshly minted horror author, I was tickled to find his response to my initial note postmarked Arkham, Mass. I'd visited there a couple of times myself, during the most intense phase of my Lovecraft infatuation. Miskatonic had been my back-up for college, but once Brown accepted me I'd opted for the more prestigious institution. In truth, as my literary horizons have broadened, HPL and the New England territory he immortalized have lost some of their glamour. As Sam pointed out in his review, *The Golden Doom* chiefly reflects a Dunsanian influence. Perhaps on account of my Celtic heritage, too, I find on balance the gentle mysticism of the Irish *fantaisiste* more to my taste than the eldritch horrors of the Providence gentleman.

Like Lovecraft, I enjoy writing letters, and Sam Lowell soon became one of my most active and stimulating correspondents. At first we mainly discussed horror fiction, debating the relative stature of the greats in the field, but later I learned a fair amount of personal data as well. Fortunately, Sam was able to continue to do freelance work for publishing clients in New York, including *BW*. Though he never more than hinted at it, I guessed he also had another source of income (family money?) to help support himself and to indulge in what I gathered was his principal passion—collecting books.

While I don't consider myself a book collector per se, I do like thumbing through dealers' catalogues and checking out the offerings of used-book shops and library sales. If I own any valuable items it's usually because I chanced to purchase them while they were still in print, like Lovecraft's *Dark Brotherhood* and *Selected Letters III*. Frankly, I'm a lot more interested in reading a book, turning down page corners and making marginal notes if so moved, than enshrining it on a shelf like some goddamn virgin. For others, such as Sam apparently, the pleasure lies less in the text itself than in the physical package of paper and print.

Which is not to say Sam's communications suggested he was anything less than highly literate. Besides the standard authors in the genre, he was clearly well versed in the mainstream tradition of English letters, ranging from Jane Austen and the Brontë sisters to contemporary Americans like John Updike and Nicholson Baker. He disdained the commercial and popular, unless it had literary merit, swearing he collected only those works that would survive the test of time. He possessed nearly a complete run of Arkham House books of the Derleth era, spurning the later science fiction titles favored by the Sauk City sage's editorial successor. While he must've engaged in buying and selling with other diehard collectors, I had the impression that, with few exceptions, he was loathe to part with a single volume. Every acquisition was a treasure. Making money scarcely entered the equation.

Though I was an English major at Brown, I confess I have some big gaps in my knowledge of literature, gaps I never expect to fill. You'd have to put a gun to my head before you'd get me even to consider reading another one of those long and pious nineteenth-century novels, with their mawkish heroines. When Sam inquired if I was familiar with the works of Maria and Elizabeth Brontë, for example, I wrote back to say I wasn't and maybe it was my loss but I doubted if I'd ever get around to them. Unless you're Harold Bloom, who has time for all the classics? One has to be selective, and I'd rather re-read an old favorite than plod dutifully through some so-called masterpiece just because some smart-ass critic tells me I should.

One book much on my mind was, of course, my own. During the first year or so of our correspondence I was full of news of the efforts to publicize and promote my novel. Sam's led the parade in a series of largely positive reviews, while the hardcover advanced enough copies for my agent to make a lucrative paperback sale. As a rule I don't like to toot my own horn, but with Sam it was different. I sensed early on that, with virtually no personal life of his own, he got a vicarious kick out of the tales of my successes, which I always took care to leaven with a healthy dose of self-deprecating humor. (Among my friends I'm reputed to be a bit of a raconteur.) Then again, though he never confirmed or denied it, I imagined Sam to belong to the old New England aristocracy, as rich in blue-blooded ancestors as Lovecraft himself. I, with my humble Irish roots, couldn't help being envious, and therefore was perhaps more intent on impressing him than certain other members of my literary circle, with whom in all honesty I kept up merely to be polite. (For an egotist, I'm very attentive to others, who in gratitude often try to please me in return.)

The only family Sam did mention from time to time, as to be expected, was his mother. She was a sensitive and refined woman who suffered from some degenerative hereditary disease that kept her confined to the house.

Shades of Lovecraft again! When in response to this revelation I jokingly asked if his mother originally came from Innsmouth, he didn't reply for two months. (At times, I admit, in my attempts to be funny I go too far.) Sam hardly left the house himself, other than to shop for necessities or to attend the rare auction in Boston. If his life was limited, however, he never complained. Books were his world, and in provincial Arkham he could house his ever-growing collection under one roof as he could never have afforded to do in cosmopolitan Manhattan.

It was I who for the moment was basking in the limelight of the New York literary set, or at any rate that segment of it that didn't automatically look down its nose at horror fiction. (Incredible what literary snobs people can be.) I reached my peak with the signing of the contract for my second novel, provisionally titled *The Laughter of the Gods,* based on a three-page outline. (My agent, alas, was only too efficient a deal-maker.) With the proceeds I bought a weekend place in Bucks County, where I anticipated settling down with my new Macintosh to a regular writing schedule, free of the big city's distractions. All this I recounted to Sam in great and, judging from his appreciative comments, entertaining detail.

Well, things didn't work out quite as planned. Yes, there wasn't much to do of an evening, or of a day for that matter, in Erwinna, but then the new house required lots of attention and I found myself filling my hours in meetings with contractors and electricians and plumbers. In addition to fan mail, I had stacks of magazines and catalogues to go through, not to mention an assortment of girlfriends whom I brought along for company. In the end, I realized I was doing everything I could think of to procrastinate on writing. The major problem was I'd set myself an impossible task. In my gut I knew that to deliver on the epic I'd so grandly and glibly outlined I'd need to be a genius of the order of Lord Dunsany.

And I was no Dunsany—though I will say I am rather a perfectionist, the sort of compulsive type who can spend hours over proper word choice, preferring to polish existing text than to plunge ahead with a rough draft. I can't let a sentence alone for long without tinkering. *The Golden Doom* had taken me five years of agony to produce, with no deadline pressure. On the due date for *The Laughter of the Gods* I was hard at work cataloguing my video collection. As time went on, I said less and less about the new novel in my letters, instead dwelling on the ups and downs of home ownership. In response Sam sent me a copy of humorist S. J. Perelman's classic work on the subject, *Acres and Pains*—which I'd already read but whose delightful novelty I was careful to relish in my reply.

So the years rolled on. I invited Sam to come visit me, either in the city or the country, but his mother's condition precluded any overnight travel, as well as his receiving any visitors at the house in Arkham. I cut down on all my correspondents, even at the risk of hurt feelings, except for Sam, whose undiminished enthusiasm for this or that new author helped to alleviate my gloom. (I might have dropped letter-writing altogether if it hadn't provided a further excuse for avoiding the novel.) Sam in his turn continued to insist on how much he valued my letters, which he claimed gave him a unique and precious perspective on the larger world—even though, I countered, it was evermore that of a jaded and disillusioned hermit.

As the whole business with the second novel dragged on, about the only person I could bear to see was my agent. After the third extension of the delivery deadline for the manuscript passed, he arranged an incentive plan with my editor. When that didn't work, the publisher started making legal threats. Ultimately, though, neither carrot nor stick could induce me to do much more than fiddle on my Mac with the design for the chapter heads (a grinning Buddha). To boost my income I was forced to go back to substitute teaching in the New York City public schools, with the dreaded prospect of a full-time career in the classroom looming unless I finished the frigging novel.

Then, after an uncharacteristically lengthy delay between letters, word came from Sam that his mother had "made the transition," as he euphemistically put it. For weeks he'd been grief-stricken, but now life was starting to return to normal. He was lonely, he hinted. Was there a chance I might be persuaded to swing by Arkham next time I was in the area? On impulse I wrote back proposing a weekend in August, almost a month away, which just so happened to include my birthday—not that I told him that. I'd been dating a cute but not very exciting girl who I knew wanted to celebrate my (shudder) fortieth birthday in a way that would only bring home to me how little I had to celebrate. That I had to go console a friend whose mother had recently died was exactly the sort of excuse I was looking for.

By the time that August weekend was at hand, however, I can't say I was feeling all that eager. After years of envisioning Sam as this ideal gentleman, I feared that in person he might be a disappointment, rather like a certain female fan who'd written in admiration of my author photo on *The Golden Doom*. (Foolishly, I'd called the phone number she'd supplied in her perfume-scented note and scheduled a rendezvous without first asking for her picture.) Come to think of it, maybe this isn't a fair analogy. Still, I was anxious about our meeting, and wrote Sam to expect me late Friday night, with departure set for Sunday morning. I had to be back in New York, I fibbed, in time for an important dinner with my agent that evening. One full day with Sam should be plenty, I figured.

Deciding in emulation of Lovecraft to use public transportation, I rode Amtrak up the Connecticut coast, through Providence and ending in Boston, once again left to wonder why HPL had chosen in his fiction to disguise these two capital cities under made-up names and not other, less prominent places like Arkham and Kingsport. From Boston's North Station I took the commuter train to Arkham, where Sam did not meet me at the depot. As advertised, his house was an easy three-block walk from the railroad, even in the dark. (I had no sense, by the way, of passing from the mundane into the magical, such as Wilmarth describes in his journey from New Hampshire to Vermont in "The Whisperer in Darkness.")

The real Arkham, in contrast to Lovecraft's romanticized version, is not terribly scenic. Yes, you can find Federal-style mansions in the tiny "old town," but today Arkham, like Salem, is a small industrial city of mostly undistinguished commercial streets and nondescript residential buildings, inhabited by ethnic types such as myself or my relatives. Since I already knew Sam lived in an untouristed part of Arkham, I wasn't surprised to discover at his address a clapboard "triple-decker" of late Victorian vintage.

The guy who greeted me at the door was slight, pale, of indeterminate age though older than myself—in sum, utterly unimpressive. But as soon as he smiled, a sort of mischievous half-smile, I warmed up to him immediately. Since I was exhausted from traveling most of the day, we talked books for only five minutes or so before he showed me upstairs to the "guest room," which judging by the old-fashioned furniture, the floral curtains and carpet, and the antiseptic odor must've been his mother's bedroom. On the bedside table were some women's magazines and a copy of Eldridge's *Tide and Pilot Book*. Sam confirmed that he'd preserved it just as it was when his mother was alive. Truly I felt honored having the most sacred room in the house!

In the morning, after a sound sleep, I met my host downstairs in the kitchen, where he prepared a sumptuous breakfast—eggs, bacon, and fried potatoes. Sam himself only had coffee and a bagel. When I remarked on his abstemiousness, he said he was one of those people who eat to live rather than live to eat. He survived on purely cerebral nourishment.

At any rate, as good as Sam's cooking was, it wasn't the main attraction. We shortly moved into the study, although we could've started the tour almost anywhere, seeing how nearly every inch of wall space was given over to bookshelves. From the study's packed floor-to-ceiling cases there was an overflow, on desks and tables, but Sam was both tidy and systematic, not at all in the mold of the stereotypical eccentric who carelessly heaps volumes any old place and never bothers to dust. The study had a pleasantly musty smell, an air reminiscent of the Strand Bookstore, if without the crowds of pushy customers and rude salespersons. Through the bay window one could tell it was going to be a hot summer day, but an air-conditioner and dehumidifier ensured we would remain in comfort as long as we stayed indoors.

We never did get outside, so enchanted was I to dwell in this second-hand book dealer's paradise. Sam evidently had his own peculiar organization within categories, which ranged from genre literature, mainly horror and fantasy with a smattering of s.f. and mystery (his tastes in this respect were similar to mine), to mainstream fiction, some of it quite obscure.

The first odd volume to attract my attention was J. R. Ackerley's *My Sister and Myself*. Not counting his one play, I knew this minor mid-century author had written only four books. What was this?

"I'm a big fan of Ackerley's *My Dog Tulip* . . ." I began.

"Greatest dog book ever written . . ." my host interjected.

"After Dunsany's *My Talks with Dean Spanley*—"

"Then there's Virginia Woolf's *Flush*—"

". . . but I don't know this one, though it does sound kind of familiar."

"You must be thinking of his autobiographical memoir, *My Father and Myself*."

"Oh, right."

"*My Sister and Myself* was compiled from his diaries several years after his death. It made more of a splash in England. The American edition is quite scarce."

From Ackerley we somehow got onto the subject of mainstream authors who've dabbled in the horror genre. By way of illustration Sam pulled out a recent acquisition, Brad Leithauser's *Norton Book of Ghost Stories,* with the comment, "Mostly mediocre tales by Henry James and other highbrows."

"Yes, how idiotic to exclude writers like Dunsany and Lovecraft."

"I'm not saying there hasn't been wonderful work done by writers outside the field. Take *The Green Man* by Kingsley Amis, for instance. It deserves to be far better known."

"Agreed."

"I'm afraid, though, old Kingsley has of late been overshadowed by son Martin."

"At least John Updike doesn't have that problem."

"Another example is Evelyn Waugh's *The Temple at Thatch,* written while he was at Oxford. Do you know it?"

"Uh, maybe. It was a long time ago . . ." I hate admitting my ignorance, especially when it comes to literary matters.

"Harold Acton was right—most of it's dull—but the parts where the hero practices black magic are superb. I have a first edition. Let me show you." Sam guided me to his Waugh section, which was so extensive it took him a minute to find *The Temple of Thatch*. "Ah, here it is, in between *A Little Learning* and *A Little Hope*."

I glanced at the text of the slim, elegantly bound volume Sam handed me, my eye drawn mainly by the satirist's decadent line drawings.

"Speaking of first novels, have you read Barbara Pym's future fantasy, *Some Tame Gazelle?*"

"Sure." Luckily, *Some Tame Gazelle* was the one Pym novel I had read. Though I wasn't about to tell Sam, it hadn't inspired me to read more of her.

"Too bad she didn't cut out the Nazis."

"Nazis? In Barbara Pym?"

"In her defense, she did write it in the thirties, after a trip to Germany. Later, of course, Nazis weren't so funny anymore."

"Yes, their presence does give it a dated quality." Again, though I had no memory of Nazis in the novel, I wasn't going to admit I'd forgotten.

As I've indicated, Sam had his collection pretty well organized, but it wasn't always obvious to me why he grouped certain things the way he did. In a Mission-style bookcase in the front hall, for instance, I noticed such standard titles as Poe's *Narrative of Arthur Gordon Pym,* Hawthorne's *Dr. Grimshawe's Secret,* Twain's *Mysterious Stranger,* Fitzgerald's *Last Tycoon,* and Capote's *Answered Prayers.* But what was C. S. Forester's *Hornblower During the Crisis* or P. G. Wodehouse's *Sunset at Blandings* or a three-volume set of Thomas Mann's *Confessions of Felix Krull* doing on the same shelf with these American classics? And why weren't August Derleth's *The Watchers out of Time* and Frank Belknap Long's *Cottage Tenant* back with the rest of these authors' works in their respective sections in the study?

Into this Mission-style bookcase Sam put a copy of what he said was his latest acquisition—*Emma.*

"Jane Austen?"

"No, Charlotte Brontë," Sam replied. "A far more outspokenly feminist work than Austen's novel of the same name."

"To each his own, I guess. Or should I say *her* own?"

Sam chuckled. He knew my tastes well enough from my letters not to be surprised by my lack of enthusiasm for certain writers. On the other hand, this didn't stop him from trying to convert me to his own pet authors—like the British novelist Anthony Powell, whose works occupied a large nook in the dining room.

"I remember Anthony Powell was one of your first recommendations to me," I said.

"You mean Anthony Powell?"

"Did you say *Pole?*"

"Yes, *Powell*—rhymes with *Lowell.*"

"Gee, I didn't know that."

"Did you ever read *A Dance to the Music of Time?*"

Over the years Sam had urged me to read the man's twelve-volume saga, supposedly a fascinating portrait of English society from the 1920s to the 1970s, but I'd never gotten beyond the first book in the cycle—too slow, too understated for someone of my Celtic temperament.

"I'll get to it one of these days, I promise."

"Like Lovecraft's, Powell's style can be off-putting. But believe me, he's worth the effort. A related English writer worth the effort, incidentally, is X. Trapnel."

"Never heard of him."

"Like you a bit of a rogue with the ladies. *Camel Ride to the Tomb* is brilliant, but I'm more partial to *Profiles in String*. First printings are hard to come by, especially of the latter novel." These and other Trapnel titles were on a shelf in the Powell nook, but a glance at their spines was examination enough for me. If I was probably never going to read Anthony Powell (excuse me, *Pole*), then almost certainly I wasn't going to get around to X. Trapnel.

With relief I followed Sam to the other end of the dining room, where in a wooden chest he kept his bound galleys and page proofs. These were all modern vintage, both mainstream and genre.

"Say, what should I do with my Stephen King bound galleys?" For a number of years I'd dated the book reviewer of a women's magazine who'd given me her King galleys for free, even after our relationship had turned platonic. It was only after she admitted throwing out the bound galleys of Ian Hamilton's suppressed biography of J. D. Salinger that I dropped her. I have my principles.

"I'd sell them and invest the money in Frank Long paperbacks."

"Like *Cottage Tenant?*"

"Yeah, that's one of the more desirable ones."

In truth I'm not much of a Long fan, but I could see since his death how his paperback novels might increase in value. I assumed *Cottage Tenant* was yet another forgettable piece of hack work ground out in his last years by this pathetic pulp-era survivor.

From the dining room we moved into the parlor, where in a glass-fronted cabinet were displayed the collected works of a no less industrious but infinitely finer author, John Updike. Sam appeared to possess not only a complete set of the Knopf editions, from *The Poorhouse Fair* to *The Afterlife*, but a lot of Updike's small-press stuff as well, including his poetic homage to the female pudenda.

"You know," I said, "looking at all these books, I can understand why Nicholson Baker has such a thing for Updike. It's not just the exquisite prose, it's his obsession with sex. Not a point Baker makes clear in *U and I*, as I recall."

"What do you think of *U and I*?" asked Sam.

"Rather impudent of Baker, I thought, to write a book like that about a living author."

"A case of a lesser talent trading on the fame of a greater."

"Yeah, but to be fair, Baker's almost as amazing a stylist as Updike. I bet you it won't be long, now that Baker's arrived, before someone writes a book about his, or possibly her, obsession with him."

"That's an idea," said Sam, a dreamy look on his face. "I'd love to add it to my collection."

On the wall past Updike was a series of open shelves devoted to postwar American Jewish writers: Bellow, Roth, Malamud, Bech, among others. Again, not an area of literature in which I've done much delving. I listened patiently as Sam held forth on the place of Jewish fiction in our culture.

"Bellow, Roth, and Malamud are giants, admittedly," he said, "but Bech's in a class by himself. After *Travel Light, Brother Pig,* and *The Chosen,* I couldn't wait to read *Think Big.*"

"*Think Big?*"

"Bech's masterpiece. It took him years."

"How many years?"

"Let's see. *The Chosen* came out in '63. *Think Big* didn't appear till '79. So sixteen."

"Jesus."

"Oh, sorry, I didn't mean . . . ." Sam must've sensed he'd touched on a delicate topic.

"It's okay. With any luck I'll have *The Laughter of the Gods* ready by the millennium." As with many such things in my life, I tried to turn this painful reminder into a joke, albeit a feeble one. Sam mumbled some encouraging words, then changed the subject.

So through the morning, the afternoon, and the evening, from attic to basement and all floors in between, with the occasional food or bathroom break, we indulged our book lust. During this orgy we engaged in a sort of friendly one-upmanship, each trying to outdo the other in knowledge of literature—old and new, major and minor, mainstream and genre, American, British, and Continental. For all the vast extent of his collection, Sam owned he could never approach anything like completeness. Such rare Americana as Cotton Mather's *Biblical Commentaries* and Margaret Fuller's *History of the Roman Republic* he feared would elude him forever. In debating the issue of Lovecraft versus Dunsany, I argued the superiority of the Irish lord, despite my innate pessimism, because he had the courage in his fiction to resist despair and hold out the hope of a happy ending.

Finally, near exhaustion, I said, "Tell me, what's your single most prized volume?"

"Funny you should ask," he said. "I've been saving the best for last."

By this time it was close to midnight and we were in the kitchen, nodding over the remains of some Cantonese delivery and an empty bottle of Chardonnay, my house present, all of which I'd imbibed since it had turned out my host, like HPL, never touched alcohol. With no little effort we got up and staggered into the study. There Sam lifted the cushions off the seat of the bay window, ignoring my facetious guesses as to the title of this most awesome of tomes.

"I keep the really esoteric stuff hidden," he said as he raised the hinged seat. I was suddenly aware of a strong musty odor.

"Esoteric? How Lovecraftian."

"You're getting warm."

"You don't mean you have—"

"Yes—"

"No, it'd be too much of a cliché!"

But, yes, there it was, in a compartment below the window seat—the *Necronomicon*. Or was it? Maybe it was a fake, like the Neville Spearman edition or the one that merely repeats a sixteen-page signature of Arabic script.

The oversized copy that Sam now held in his hands, however, looked authentic—dark, worn, centuries old.

"Personally, I prefer Edward Casaubon's *Key to All the Mythologies,*" Sam said with an elfin smile, "but by any objective standard this is the all-time winner. Care to take a peek?"

With trembling hands I took Abdul Alhazred's fabled volume, which felt strangely light.

"Go ahead, open it," my friend urged.

I undid the clasp. A moment later I'd dropped it and let out a scream—at the thing that had leapt at me from the book as soon as I'd lifted the cover. Sam laughed. On the floor was a crude octopoid creature on a spring. The *Necronomicon* was hollow. It had been a joke. Cthulhu-in-the-box.

"On that note," I said, doing my best to hide my irritation, "let's go to bed."

Later, under the sheets, I felt less annoyed. I had to give Sam credit for a sly sense of humor. Something else, though, vaguely troubled me as I teetered on the verge of sleep, from earlier in the day. I recalled that there was a link between Updike and Bech, the Jewish writer. I've by no means read all of Updike's massive oeuvre, but it struck me that our leading living novelist had written a book about Bech—and while it approached its subject with a certain mock reverence, somewhat akin to Baker's in *U and I,* there was one extremely crucial difference . . .

In the morning I was all set to ask my host some pointed questions about Updike and Bech, along with a few other anomalous authors who'd stalked my dreams. I was distracted, however, by what I found at my place at the breakfast table—a bulky, gift-wrapped package.

"Happy birthday, Sean!" exclaimed Sam, who was smiling by the stove.

"How the heck did you know it was my birthday?"

"No problem. I have *Contemporary Authors* online as well as the Necro Press 1995 Dunsany calendar. Most of the standard references still list you."

"Gosh, after last night I'm not sure I dare open it."

"Go ahead. I don't think you'll be disappointed."

I gingerly hefted the package. Whatever it was, it was too loose, too soft to be a book.

"Okay, but I warn you, if this is another trick—"

A few days after my visit to Arkham, I sat down to write Sam a quick note:

Dear Sam,

Many thanks for your hospitality over the weekend. It was truly a thrill for me to share in your fantastic collection. As for your birthday present, what more could an author ask for? I've now read the manuscript of *The Laughter of the Gods* three times, and it's perfect, right down to the grinning Buddha chapter heads. The ending's more upbeat, a trifle more Dunsanian than is my usual style—but who says the protagonist always has to get his comeuppance? I'll be sending my agent a chapter a week starting tomorrow. He'll be ecstatic. Again, you Wasps are too kind.

        As ever,
           Sean

Old Man

That spring, following an extended and inconclusive trip to help settle the estate of the Boston dreamer Randolph Carter, Ward Phillips returned home to Providence. There he took the upper floor of a venerable dwelling in a grassy court off College Street—on the crest of the great eastward hill near the Brown University campus and behind the marble John Hay Library. It was a cozy and fascinating place. Beneath his study window, across a little garden oasis of village-like antiquity, huge, friendly cats sunned themselves atop a convenient shed and adjoining fence. This refined and sedate club of felidae seldom numbered fewer than one or two sleek old Toms with as many as five or six or seven junior attendants. In view of the prevalence of fraternity-houses in the neighborhood, Ward Phillips came to call this pleasing sodality the Kappa Alpha Tau.

The K.A.T. president was a handsome black-and-white gentleman of patrician lineage, Peter Randall. President Randall's aloofness from ordinary mortals both human and feline was proverbial, but after about a month he permitted Ward to break through his reserve, so that he would roll over and kick and purr like a kitten upon his new admirer's approach. The vice-president, Count Magnus Osterberg, was a gigantic tiger with a white face and gloves and boots, whose aristocratic reserve was quite equal of President Randall's. He and Peter were very close friends, but neither would ever pay the slightest attention to any other feline. When one was out alone, he always looked about for the other; and when they had found each other they generally took up permanent stations about two feet apart on the club-house roof—dozing, surveying the semi-rural scenery of their back-garden oasis, or exchanging courteous and affable glances.

Casual approaches of other cats went unheeded, but when any outside Grimalkin became actually obtrusive or overbearing, Count Magnus displayed the hardier side of his nature. Magnus would never *pick* a fight, and often went to considerable lengths of tact to avert a vulgar brawl—but when the other guy became insistent, so that a gentleman must either fight or bear the imputation of tarnished honor, then the fur that flew during the ensuing battle was not often the tiger-and-white miniver of Count Magnus Osterberg! As for President Randall, he had outlived his combative years, hence repelled foes only with chilling glances.

The secretary was a great Maltese with white spots, elected to replace a gray part-Angora, who had withdrawn from the fraternity. The treasurer was also newly chosen, supplanting a small tiger who had resigned. Other members included a titanic coal-black warrior with a stentorian voice, a pale yellow gentleman of fairly martial tastes, and one very sprightly young fellow, another Maltese, smaller than the rest of the boys, who was undergoing initiation. By summer's end Ward himself had achieved honorary membership, assuming the post of third assistant undersecretary, whose duty it was to handle the wide and voluminous correspondence of the Kappa Alpha Tau. He was also charged with maintaining a supply of catnip, which he sprinkled on newspaper for the benefit of any K.A.T. member who might deign to drop in at his museum-like eyrie overlooking the garden.

While this feline fraternity served to delight Ward Phillips during the day, at night he dreamed of... Old Man. Good Old Man! He had belonged to the market at the foot of Thomas Street, where he was often to be seen curled up on the sill of a low window. Occasionally, he would stroll up the hill as far as the Art Club, seating himself at the entrance to one of those old-fashioned courtyard arches for which Providence is noted. At night, when the street lamps make the street bright, the space within the archway would remain pitch-black, so that it looked like the mouth of an illimitable abyss, or gateway of some nameless dimension. And there, as if stationed as the guardian of the unfathomed mysteries beyond, would crouch the Sphinx-like, jet-black, yellow-eyed, and incredibly ancient form of Old Man.

Ward Phillips first knew him as a kitten and used to pat him and remark what a fine boy he was. Ward was but a boy himself then. The years went by, and Ward continued to see him off and on. The youngish cat grew mature—then elderly—and finally cryptically ancient. Ward, who had grown to manhood and had a gray hair or two himself, began calling him "Old Man." Old Man knew Ward well, and would always purr and rub around his ankles and greet him with a kind of friendly conversational "e-ew," which finally became hoarse with age. Ward came to regard Old Man as an indispensable acquaintance, and would often go considerably out of the way to pass his habitual territory, on the chance of finding him visible. In fancy, Ward pictured Old Man as a hierophant of the mysteries beyond the black archway, and wondered if the furry gentleman would ever invite him *through* it some midnight . . . and wondered, too, if he could ever come back to earth alive after accepting such an invitation.

More years slipped by and still there by the antique archway Old Man lingered! He was no longer very active, and spent most of his time sleeping—but he still knew his fellow elder, and never failed to give his hoarse, amicable "e-ew" when he chanced to be awake. He seemed a trifle feeble, but his purring friendliness was unabated.

Around the time of the disappearance of Ward's human friend, Randolph Carter, Ward began to miss Old Man. Always when turning the corner on the hill he used to look down ahead and see if he could discern a familiar lump of black by the archway or at the market. He feared the worst—and dared not inquire at the market. Finally, he did inquire and found that his fears were all too well founded. After more than two decades, Old Man had gone through the archway at last, and dissolved into that eternal night of which he was a true fragment—that eternal night which had sent him up to earth as a tiny black atom of sportive kittenhood so long ago!

Ward had dreamed of Old Man and the mysteries of the archway before, but now he began to do so with redoubled vividness. Old Man would greet Ward in sleep on a spectral Thomas Street hill, and gaze with aged yellow eyes that spoke secrets older than Aegyptus or Atlantis. And he would mew an invitation for Ward to follow him through the archway—beyond which lay the unreverberate darkness of the abyss. In no dream had Ward actually followed Old Man through—but he often wondered what would happen if ever he did, whether in such an event he should ever again awake in this tri-dimensional world. Ward was sure, however, that no world Old Man would lead him to would be a world of horror. He was too old and true a friend for that!

In the meantime, in the waking world, summer shaded into fall, and as the days grew shorter the horror of cold weather descended on the hill. Meetings of the Kappa Alpha Tau became rarer and with the the first heavy snowfall they ended for the season. Abnormally sensitive to low temperatures, Ward Phillips settled into virtual hibernation—though he did venture out once, early in the new year, to accept an invitation to tea from a friend of a friend, a female member of the human species, who had come to Providence to visit relatives. Joining them for tea was the young woman's aunt, who at first seemed to be a harmless old lady. Then, when he spoke of how peculiarly uncomfortable the recent cold snap had been, she was reminded of how hard near-zero temperatures and deep snow were for the wild birds. In the brisk little lecture on ornithology that ensued, she compared the birds' winter hazard of harsh weather with their summer hazard of city cats left to roam hungrily at will. Something should be done about that, she felt. There were too many cats in Providence. They should either be belled or done away with altogether.

Ward Phillips experienced all the thrills of a spy unexpectedly stumbling into the camp of the enemy. For weeks he had been noting with growing uneasiness letters to the editor of the Providence paper from some bird-lover wishing to bell roving cats or worse. But until he was face to face with her and heard her express such offensive views in similar language, he had not identified the writer as the young woman's aunt. He hastily changed the subject back to the weather, declaring how happy he was to be living in a charming old Georgian house with plenty of central heating courtesy of Brown University. He particularly thrived when he turned the temperature up to the nineties. The old lady was scandalized, for she was a staunch believer in fresh, cool air and plenty of it. "Young man, you should harden yourself," she said firmly. He shivered as she outlined a regime of brisk wintry walks, wide-open windows at night, and cold baths in the morning. He drained the tepid dregs of his tea and announced that it was time he headed home.

Ward Phillips may not have been terribly hardy for a native New Englander, but he knew that there were black zones of shadow close to our daily paths, and now and then some evil soul broke a passage through. When that happened, the man who knew had to overcome his weaknesses and strike before reckoning the consequences.

The following spring evil stalked the Kappa Alpha Tau. First President Randall and then Count Magnus Osterberg succumbed to some malady which was afflicting all the local felidae—a thing which might have been an obscure epidemic, yet which might have reflected the malign activities of some contemptible poisoner. The sad end of the K.A.T. leadership seemed connected with some digestive disorder. Fearing that this was the mark of some wretched neo-Borgia, Ward prayed to Bast that somebody would feed that fiend a slow poison a thousandfold more painful than that which he had subtly supplied his furry victims!

The cat-headed goddess answered his prayers, for the night after both the secretary and the treasurer entered the great unknown, Old Man appeared to him in a dream, seated in the darkened archway. Good Old Man! That jet-black, yellow-eyed heirophant of the cosmic mysteries left his post and trotted up the hill, far beyond his customary range, until he reached upper College Street. There, at an hour when the streets are usually empty of human forms, Old Man mewed plaintively while a furtive figure, oblivious to his spirit, went about her business—scattering from a box a flaky substance that could have been mistaken for catnip, except that the box was marked with a skull and crossbones. Ward Phillips saw red. . . .

At the stately old brick court and colony house on North Court Street, on the advice of his lawyer, Ward Phillips pleaded innocent. But when he took the stand in his own defense, he could not help telling the truth. The cat-hating, cold-weather-loving old lady richly deserved her fate, he proclaimed. He was sure her soul was freezing in a polar hell, perpetually pecked and scratched by the beaks and talons of innumerable and unnamable wild birds.

In the end the jury found him innocent—on the grounds of insanity. For some time, in what may have been a case of psychosomatic sympathy, Ward Phillips had been suffering from serious digestive trouble himself, so he anticipated with some relief his imminent transfer from jail to Butler Hospital, where he knew he would receive the kind of expert medical attention both his parents had enjoyed in their latter days at that venerable and distinguished loony bin.

But the night before he was due to be removed, he dreamed again of Old Man. Good Old Man! The archaic animal sat in the pitch-black archway and mewed for his human companion to join him. This time Ward Phillips did not hesitate. He realized that if he passed beyond the archway he would never return to the waking world, but in truth there was little now to hold him there. Into the ancient archway he walked, close on the heels of his four-footed guide.

After a short distance the blackness abruptly dissolved, and before him was a realm reminiscent of his own oasis-like garden, lying under the sunshine as far as the eye could see. And on a myriad of shed tops and fences there basked a host of cats, Manx and Maltese, Siamese and Burmese, Angoras and American short-hairs—every imaginable representative of the feline tribe. And as he strolled through this Eden, Ward Phillips received welcoming purrs from old friends, notably Peter Randall and Count Magnus Osterberg, together with other late officers of the Kappa Alpha Tau, as well as dozens of other cats he had known and lost down the long years.

The dreamer Randolph Carter welcomed him too, though Ward did not recognize the Bostonian at first with his whiskers and tail. Then Ward looked down at his own gloves and boots and understood that he was now truly one of the elders, a full member of the fraternity—and so he bounded after Carter onto the nearest clubhouse roof, to assume his rightful place among his peers in that world of eternal summer.

Nautical-Looking Negroes

Negro, n. The pièce de resistance in the American political problem. Representing him by the letter n, the Republicans begin to build their equation thus: "Let n = the white man." This, however, appears to give an unsatisfactory solution.—AMBROSE BIERCE

I.
The Testimony of James F. Morton

My knowledge of the thing began in the winter of 1926–27 through my contact with George Gammell Angell, Professor Emeritus, of Brown University. On the recommendation of a mutual friend, a writer in Providence with whom I was in regular correspondence, the retired professor had sent me a rather unusual item for identification. As the curator and sole proprietor of the Paterson (N.J.) Museum of Natural History, I am reputed to be the leading expert in the East on arcane minerals, and I hoped the artifact (I'd been told to expect a kind of bas-relief) would prove of more than ordinary interest. I should never have doubted my sometimes hyperbolic writer friend when he claimed that even I would be stumped. I was. While the football-sized specimen did represent a most curious figure—a vaguely octopoid creature with a crown of stars—what was really striking was its composition. The hard yet light crystalline rock was not sedimentary, it was not metamorphic, it was not igneous, but some fantastic combination of all three, formed under conditions of space and over aeons of time that I instinctively felt were not native to this planet. Though in his letter the professor made no mention of where he'd found it, I was convinced that this bizarre chunk of matter, which in addition showed no sign of weathering, had to be of meteoric origin.

I confess the specimen had an almost hypnotic effect on me, for I could not resist pausing at my desk for minutes at a time to admire its gleaming, translucent surface. In the course of the day I accomplished little else. That evening I took it upstairs and placed it on my bedside table. But

200

that night I dreamt horribly—of a cold, black, nightmare city of odd angles through which a tentacled behemoth resembling the cuttlefish thing on the bas-relief floated with astonishing grace. Attended by hairy, long-armed humanoids of hideous aspect, it presided over nameless ceremonies, routine for that icy city and yet loathsome in their import for any civilized member of mankind. In the morning I brought the object back downstairs to the office and shut it in the safe, where I proposed to leave it until I received further instructions from Professor Angell.

In my reply I expressed my bafflement with the mineral, asking if I might proceed with a spectrographic analysis. This would entail chipping off a small sample from the nearly diamond-hard stone, a procedure requiring more sophisticated equipment than was available at the museum. I decided it best not to mention the dreams surely inspired by the specimen, though I was curious to learn eventually whether the professor himself, or others under its influence, had been likewise affected.

Professor Angell wrote back a cryptic note simply saying to continue my precaution of keeping it locked up and to tell no one of its existence. Further word would follow. Weeks passed and then came the letter urging me to destroy all correspondence pertaining to the "cult idol" (as he now called it), even the epistles from our mutual friend. He had already disposed of my missives to him in order to protect me—though from what he was evidently too frightened to say. I did as he requested, though I was mighty reluctant to burn the letters of a born writer like my Providence pal.

Finally, a month later, the mail brought a letter from my friend the author with a clipping from the *Providence Journal* reporting Professor Angell's death. The cause of death, according to the obituary, was an obscure lesion of the heart, induced by the brisk ascent of a steep hill by the ninety-two-year-old authority on ancient inscriptions. My friend added that the professor had been stricken whilst returning home from the Newport boat; falling suddenly, as witnesses said, after having been jostled by a nautical-looking Negro. In veiled terms my correspondent suggested that he and I never allude again to the you-know-what. Clearly, the fear I had come to associate with the strange stone was contagious. I, at any rate, remained intimidated, unwilling either to go ahead with a spectrographic analysis, which might reveal untold scientific wonders, or to rid myself entirely of its burden by literally throwing it away. And so it stayed in the museum safe, and so for a while I could almost forget it was there.

Then in the spring I received a letter postmarked Boston from one

Francis Wayland Thurston, who identified himself as George Angell's grandnephew. He had come across my name and address in the process of going through his late uncle's effects. He would very much like to question me regarding certain unspecified researches that the elderly professor had been engaged in. He planned to travel to New Jersey soon. Would I mind if he stopped by Paterson for a chat? I wrote back to say he was welcome to visit me at the museum, that I might be able to enlighten him to some small degree on his relative's researches. I left it at that. It appeared Thurston had no clue I held the "idol," or even that it existed, unless he was playing a very deep game, feigning to be more ignorant than he actually was. Clearly, he was on to something, and the stone, I surmised, might just form a crucial piece to the cosmic puzzle, hinted at in his letter, that he was so desperate to solve.

Through a coincidence of a type unacceptable in fiction though common enough in real life, I was to provide Thurston with a vital clue in his quest, if from a wholly unexpected and mundane source. Upon his arrival I had taken him, like every first-time visitor, on a complete tour of the museum, including the storage area in the rear. There his eye had been caught by an odd picture in a two-year-old newspaper spread beneath one of the shelves of reserve specimens. It was from the *Sydney Bulletin* (I have wide affiliations in all conceivable foreign parts), and it showed a carved figure that roughly resembled, now that I studied it, the bas-relief in the safe. My guest became extremely agitated. Without asking my permission, he tossed aside the rocks covering the paper and snatched it up. He acted even more excited after reading the related article. Again without so much as a by-your-leave, he grabbed the phone and rang long-distance to make travel arrangements. At this stage I was in no mood to be generous. If he was too impatient and self-absorbed to bother to ask me what I had to offer, then to hell with him! An hour later, as he hung up the phone, Thurston apologized. He couldn't stay, but had to rush to Newark, to catch the next train to San Francisco, where he was booked on a boat for Dunedin, New Zealand!

To give the fellow credit, he did take the trouble to send me numerous postcards, first from the South Pacific and later from Scandinavia. In them he admitted he was on the trail of a cult of portentous significance. He would supply a full account once he returned to the States. Still smarting from the cavalier way he'd treated me, I wrote him at his Boston address to say I looked forward to another visit when we might resume our conversation where we left off. Again, I did not mention the idol, which I was sure was as important as anything he might have picked up in the course of his globetrotting.

By a certain date Thurston was supposed to be back home, but I heard nothing. Then one day I received an envelope containing a manuscript from my writer friend, who was in the habit of sending me copies of his stories for comment, but this was different. The handwritten deposition, which I might easily have mistaken for one of my Providence chum's more fanciful fictions, purported to be Thurston's summary of his investigations into his granduncle's researches. In his cover letter my friend declined to explain how the document had come into his hands, but he did say the Boston gentleman had disappeared more than two weeks before, the victim of enemies unknown, according to the police theories. I could draw what conclusions I wished after reading the manuscript, which might fairly be titled "The Statement of Francis Wayland Thurston" or "Facts Concerning the Cult of Cthulhu."

It was with a healthy sense of skepticism that I read this story (too long to cite here), and I cannot even now be sure how much of the text to believe and how much to discount. (Thurston's version of his Paterson visit, for instance, led me to wonder what else he might have slanted to make himself look better.) Yet in its essentials I had to admit the account rang true. No doubt there was a worldwide cult that worshipped an entity called "Cthulhu," with an alleged extraterrestrial origin. This unspeakable, or unpronounceable, if you will, "god" corresponded to the totem of mysterious province and uncertain substance that had caused me such dubious and disturbing dreams. But what action to take? Outsiders who became too curious about the cult were liable to meet bad ends. Was I prepared to place my own life and sanity in jeopardy?

What I did finally resolve to do was write Inspector Legrasse in care of the New Orleans constabulary, in an effort to verify that part of Thurston's precis of Angell's research concerning the detective's 1907 raid. As fate would have it, Legrasse in his reply said he was scheduled to attend a police convention in Boston within the month. He would be happy to stop by en route to talk over the "whole delicate affair," as he put it, in detail. (Even he seemed scared to commit too much to paper.) I eagerly awaited his arrival, trusting our get-together would prove more satisfying than my meeting with Thurston.

Legrasse betrayed no disappointment when, instead of offering him the customary tour, I suggested we get right down to business. I showed him a seat in the office and, without comment, handed him Thurston's manuscript. As soon as the aged inspector had finished his perusal—he vouched for the accuracy of his own role despite some overdramatization—I pulled the Cthulhu idol out of the safe. I had not set eyes on the object since I first put it there and wondered what pernicious influence it might still exert. I set it on the desk, and for several long moments the two of us stared in silent awe at the queer octopoid form with its halo of stars. As in my earlier dreams, images of a dark, frigid world filled with floating blasphemies intruded on my consciousness. With an enormous effort I turned away and signaled the detective to follow me out of the office, back into the museum proper.

For the rest of the afternoon we discussed our next steps. Fortunately, Legrasse, being a more intrepid soul than myself, agreed to take the initiative from that point on. He would bear the Cthulhu figure with him, for we both intuited that it might be of some value as a protective talisman. He would drop off Thurston's manuscript at my friend's in Providence on his way to Boston, where in between convention duties he expected to lend the local police a hand in their search for our missing man. His contacts on the Boston force had already shared an important clue: Thurston had last been seen wandering the waterfront—in the company of a band of colored sailors!

II.
The Adventure of Inspector Legrasse

John Raymond Legrasse was not a man much given to philosophizing. As a forty-year veteran of the undercover branch of the New Orleans police force, the old Creole knew it was often the best policy to shoot first and ask questions later. Act on instinct was his motto, and leave the thinking to the sensitive types, like that guy Morton or that even fussier Rhode Island buddy of his. Morton had warned Legrasse he might be subject to bad dreams from that Cthulhu idol he'd agreed to carry—but so far, after three days in Boston, the only disturbance to his sleep had been caused by downing too many slugs of bad Irish whiskey. John Raymond Legrasse, it would only be fair to say, was no friend of Prohibition.

In his spare time he'd been cruising the wharves and warehouses of the Beantown waterfront. Seafaring men from five continents haunted the dives along India and Milk streets, and within hours he was able to finger those establishments that catered to salts of duskier hue. Under his raincoat, along with his Smith & Wesson .38 police special, he'd slung the hard, light stone—which he furtively showed to select members of the clientele he en-countered. Those who recognized the figure he hoped would be surprised into revealing something about the fate of one who had ventured perhaps too far in his cult delvings. A few displayed some reaction, some none. It wasn't until his third day out, at a speak near the Custom House, that the detective hit pay dirt.

Sitting at the bar, he had casually let his raincoat fall open, exposing the stone idol strapped to his belt. The African on the stool next to him took one look at the thing and dropped his glass. "Tulu, Tulu, Tulu," the man started to chant, his voice rising in pitch with each repetition. He slid off his seat and backed away. Two or three of his mates, now noticing what he had seen, took up the cry. Legrasse was soon surrounded by a gang of blacks, who muttered menacingly in their dark language while keeping a respectful distance. When the detective asked if they had recently run into another white man who was wise in the ways of Cthulhu, or "Tulu," eyes rolled. "That thing there's bad magic, suh," one of the Negroes said. "You best done throw it in deh harbor."

"Is that what happened to the other white man, was he 'accidentally' thrown in the harbor?" Legrasse asked.

"We knows nothin' about other white man, suh," the African answered. "Jes like we knows nothin' about folks from deh north, they who's worship Tulu. Or Nof-cays. Same difference. Both bad magic. You best stay 'way."

Before the detective could press his interlocutor further, a tall, gray-eyed man wearing a captain's cap entered the premises. The Negro seamen immediately fell silent. Some seemed almost to cower in the presence of this newcomer, who surveyed the scene with a commanding eye. When he noticed the idol, resting on the detective's thigh, he smiled. Legrasse, who'd been feeling increasingly uneasy among the present company, greeted this fellow Caucasian with relief.

"Ahoy, old-timer," said the man, advancing to the bar. "Say, that's a swell hunk of rock you've got there. Mind if I take a closer peek?"

The detective couldn't help obliging the stranger, with his clean-cut fea-tures and chiseled jaw. Bending over to undo the strap that secured the idol to his waist, Legrasse caught only the flash of a raised arm before the black-jack hit the back of his skull.

John Raymond Legrasse swum slowly back to consciousness. His head throbbed, a nauseous oily smell filled his nostrils. He was lying on a cold metal floor in, as the dimmest of lights showed, a small, empty iron-barred compartment or cell. He staggered unsteadily to his feet. The floor shifted, and he lurched against the bars of the door. He was moving, the whole room was moving. In that instant he realized he'd been shanghaied!

The door, naturally, was locked. Missing from his trousers were both the Cthulhu idol and his revolver. No surprise there either. How long he had been knocked out he couldn't even begin to guess, but it must have been a good while because he was hungry, damned hungry, despite the insidious motion of the vessel and the pervading oily odor. His cries brought no response, other than from the little creatures that scuttled and scurried, for the moment, mercifully out of sight. His head still pounding, he eventually slumped to the floor and lapsed back into oblivion.

The detective next awakened to the delicious scent of hot, fried food. A youthful sailor was standing above him holding a steaming tray.

"Brother, are you saved?" the seaman asked.

"Heck no, near as I can tell I've been captured."

"I don't mean saved in an earthly sense, brother. Let me put it another way. Have you accepted Cthulhu as your personal Lord and Savior?"

"You must be kidding, buster. I rue the day I ever got on the trail of this Cthulhu cult. More to the point, where exactly in tarnation are we, anyway?"

"We are on the ultimate voyage, brother. His coming is nigh."

The Creole had little stomach for such pontificating, but the plate of fish sticks was another matter. He devoured them greedily. He felt a lot better afterwards, apart from his headache.

"Hey, sailor, that wasn't bad, though I could sure use a little aspirin by way of dessert."

"Pain is not real, brother. 'Tis but an illusion, or 'claim' as we call it."

"Then how about a Scotch and soda?"

"The body is the Temple of the Soul, brother, and as such should never be defiled by distilled spirits."

The detective couldn't believe his ears. This was no way for a salt to talk. Then he noticed, despite the rough nautical garb, that the man had soft, smooth hands, a refined visage, like that of a gentleman— Yes, he recognized him now from their one meeting a couple of years before in New Orleans. It was Francis Wayland Thurston!

Too stunned to speak, Legrasse watched helplessly as Thurston shut and locked the door behind him. Once more he slid into blessed blankness.

*   *   *

The next day, or whenever it was, the inspector awoke to find the Bay State aristocrat bringing him another meal. After sating his hunger, he fell into further spiritual discussion with his warder. Thurston admitted that he had forsaken the tepid Congregationalism of his forefathers, that he had recently been converted, or in his phrase "born again." Cthulhuism offered the kind of certainty about the cosmos and man's role therein that he'd come to realize he'd been craving all his hitherto meaningless life. In his prayers he'd expressed the wish that Legrasse might in the course of their voyage also see the light. As for those assertions of materialism in that memoir of his, it was all rubbish meant to mislead his executors.

As a secular and unobservant Catholic, Legrasse was frankly not very impressed. Over a long career in the South he'd heard plenty of fundamentalist drivel. He decided, however, it would be best to feign interest in the hope that Thurston would reveal something of real importance—like where the ship was headed. He suspected it was north, as the temperature had been steadily dropping.

"Say, any chance you could bring me a blanket or an extra sweater?" the inspector asked. "It's getting a mite chilly in here."

"I'm sure, brother, that if you open your mind and heart, Captain Baker will look favorably upon any reasonable request. You may even be set at liberty. But first you must give your testimony. Come and follow me."

Legrasse gratefully accompanied Thurston out of the cell, through a series of narrow passageways and up several flights of iron-runged stairs. The detective assumed the ship was a freighter, though nothing he saw gave any clue as to the cargo. They passed a number of sailors, all of them fine-looking Nordic fellows, tall and fair, with pistols in their breeches. On the quarterdeck he shivered in the wind, drinking in the gray sky and heavy sea. On a bulkhead hung a lifesaver, emblazoned with the name *Polestar*.

"I believe you've met Inspector Legrasse before, sir," said Thurston as they entered the captain's cabin. An authoritative, gray-eyed man looked up from his desk. It was the last person the detective had encountered in that speak back in Boston—and at his elbow was the Cthulhu idol!

"Sorry our first meeting was so, shall we say, abrupt, Inspector. I'm Ed Baker, captain of the *Polestar*."

"And I, sir, am an officer of the law," Legrasse replied. "You have no right to detain me. I order you to steer a course for the nearest port."

"How about a course for the nearest iceberg?" The captain laughed.

"Kidnapping a police officer is a serious crime."

"True, by your worldly standards. But some of us have been chosen to answer a higher call." Baker picked up the fetish and peered at it reverently. "I'm much obliged to you, Inspector, for recovering this particular totem-stone. It was carelessly lost years ago by one of our auxiliary units, reserved for coloreds. It happens to confirm— Well, I won't bore you with such casuistries until you've received the Word."

"The Word?"

"The Word of Our First Lord Cthulhu, of course. Dr. Quimby, the *Polestar's* surgeon, will instruct you in the catechism."

"And if I refuse?"

"Then I'm afraid it's back to the brig for you, Inspector. On the other hand, if you agree to cooperate, you may immediately join the crew with all rights of an ordinary seaman except that of bearing arms. We could use an extra hand in the galley, isn't that so, Thurston?"

"Yes, sir," said the Boston Brahmin.

"It took Brother Thurston here practically no time at all to appreciate the advantages of fellowship among the faithful. I trust, Inspector, you'll look to him as a model."

The Creole realized his choices were limited. Very limited. Even if he could escape in one of the lifeboats with sufficient provisions, he would still be stranded in the middle of the ocean. Who knew whether another boat would come along in time to rescue him. He had a strong suspicion the *Polestar* wasn't sailing in any of the major shipping lanes.

"All right, Captain Baker. You can count me in," said the detective with as much heartiness as he could muster.

"Excellent, my dear Inspector, excellent."

"In return for my cooperation, sir, I have a question or two. Where are we headed and why?"

"I cannot reveal as yet our glorious mission, Mr. Legrasse," said Captain Baker, hefting the Cthulhu totem. "But I can tell you that our compass points north, toward the west coast of Greenland, toward the Land of Lomar."

"What's the Land of Lomar?" the detective asked Thurston as they made their way toward the foc'sle.

"The traditional home of the Lomarians."

"Who the heck are the Lomarians?"

"An ancient and noble race, the Lomarians are a chosen people."

"Chosen for what?"

"I myself have been honored with but a glimpse of the Truth. You also may find the path to the kingdom of the chosen—as long as you're receptive and don't ask too many questions."

In the foc's'le Thurston showed him his hammock and introduced him to the sailors who belonged to his watch. Every man jack, Legrasse was curious to see, had a pair of Colt revolvers in his trousers, specifically the standard .36 caliber Model 1851 Navy, with 7½-inch barrel. These were carried at all times, one seaman explained, for defense. Defense against whom? he wondered. Unarmed citizens like Thurston and himself? The detective was under orders to join them at the start of the dog watch. In the meantime, he had to report to Dr. Quimby in the surgery. Thurston left him at the physician's door.

"Welcome, Pops," said the doctor. "Phineas Quimby's the name. Please have a seat." He gestured at a chair in front of his desk. "Care for a cup of coffee?" A pot was bubbling on a primus stove.

As the detective took the coffee, he noticed something funny. For a ship's surgeon, Quimby didn't seem to possess a lot of supplies or instruments. In fact, a box of Band-aids on his desk was the only sign he practiced medicine. The cabin's most prominent feature was a shelf of books, with titles like *Pnakotic Manuscripts: Vol. I* and *Wisdom of the Zobnarian Fathers*.

"I guess you must be wondering what kind of a doctor I am," said Quimby, taking down one of the books. "Spiritual healer would be a more accurate term, I suppose, though I'll admit I do from time to time minister to those members of the crew still unsufficiently enlightened to realize that ill health is but a trick of the mind." He gave the box of Band-aids a contemptuous shake. "I'm going to start off by assuming you're more open to the truth than those poor saps who work in the galley. Here, take this student edition and you can follow along as I read from the teacher's manual."

The detective accepted the book without comment. It was called *Key to the Watchtower of Thapnen*. The author was one "Alos" (no doubt a pseudonym). His mentor started to read from the opening page.

"'Soul is Cthulhu, unchangeable and eternal; and man coexists with and reflects Soul, for the All-in-all is the Altogether, embraces the All-one, Soul-Mind, Mind-Soul, Love, Spirit, Bones, Liver, one of a series, alone and without an equal. . . .' Is that clear so far?"

"Yeah, that makes sense."

Legrasse quickly drifted off, but was alert enough, thanks to the coffee, to nod in the right places and even repeat passages as if their words meant something. If he was to survive, he knew he had to play along. At the end of two hours Quimby pronounced himself satisfied with his progress, and they scheduled another appointment for the following day. Thurston was waiting outside the surgery to lead him to his next rendezvous, in the ship's galley.

The Beacon Hill blue blood introduced Legrasse to the ship's cook, one Angelo Moroni, who turned him over to a guy named Nephi, who directed him to a stack of dirty dishes from the officers' mess and ordered him to get cracking. After performing his duties, the detective sat down with the rest of the galley detail for a meal of leftover cod cakes and an evil-tasting beverage called Postum. (His request for a dram of grog or other alcoholic brew was politely ignored.) These men, who weren't particularly friendly, were also armed—with Colt .45 double action revolvers, Model 1878, with rosewood grips—though they were careful to protect their weapons with aprons or towels as they went about their chores. Legrasse wondered when and if he'd ever get his Smith & Wesson .38 police special back.

"So what did that quack Quimby have to say?" asked Moroni.

"Not a whole heck of a lot," the detective answered. "Mostly he recited passages from a book about a watchtower by someone named Alos."

"That figures," said Nephi. "I bet he didn't even mention Bliss Knapp's *Book of Gnophkehs,* did he?" The sailor drew a well-thumbed papercovered volume from underneath his apron. "If you want the Truth, as recorded in the original lost 'silver tablet,' this is the goods." The other crew men at the table produced copies of the same text.

"We usually read a few chapters from Bliss Knapp's *Book of Gnophkehs* before we break," said Moroni. "Care to join us, Inspector?"

"Sure," Legrasse replied. Again, he decided he better show the proper enthusiasm.

"Before we start I have a question for our new man," continued the cook. "How come you gave the skipper that Cthulhu idol?"

"I didn't give it to him. He unlawfully took it from me."

"Where did you get it?"

"From this rock collector in New Jersey, who got it from this professor in Providence, who got it from gosh knows where."

The Creole proceeded to explain the business as far as he dared, until he sensed a definite easing of their hostility once they were convinced of his unwitting part in providing the captain with the Cthulhu stone. What they found so objectionable was the crown of stars, a rare variant motif that suggested Cthulhu's divine power was absolute and beyond challenge—or so the detective gathered. The larger spiritual issues that seemed so vitally to concern everyone aboard the *Polestar* still eluded him. He was relieved when the grilling finally stopped, and Moroni commenced to read:

"Behold, I say unto you, that I do know that Gnophkehs will come among the children of men, to take upon him the transgressions of his people, and that he shall atone for the sins of the planet; for Cthulhu, his co-Lord, hath spoken it. For it is expedient that an atonement be made; for according to the cosmic scheme of the Eternal Cthulhu there must be an atonement made, or else certain members of mankind must unavoidably perish; yea, some are hardened; yea, some are fallen and are lost, and must perish except it be through the atonement which it is expedient should be made."

A few more verses about the value of atonement expediently made concluded the service. With relief Legrasse left the galley, though not before accepting a copy of Bliss Knapp's *Book of Gnophkehs* pressed on him by the cook, along with some salve for the bump on his head.

Legrasse grabbed what sleep he could in his hammock before assuming his post with the dog watch. Issued warm clothing, he was despatched up the mainmast to the crow's nest, where he was to keep a weather eye out for whales and icebergs. It was no easy feat at his age to climb the shrouds in the half dark, and from the deck below he could hear his mates shouting that they hoped he wasn't too feeble and given to strange faintings.

The freezing hours spent huddled alone in this sea-going watchtower afforded the detective plenty of time for reflection. Back in New Orleans he'd had some experience of mariners, but none like the crew of the *Polestar*. Since his release from the brig he'd heard no one so much as swear or utter a profane word. There appeared to be neither a drop of liquor nor an ounce of tobacco aboard. When off-duty the men occupied themselves either with cleaning their Colts, an understandable enough exercise in the corrosive salt air, or with studying their sacred books. And yet for all their single-minded devotion to their creed, there were clearly subtle differences of diet and even of doctrine between them. His fellow dog-watchers, for example, scoffed at those in the galley who refused to drink coffee or tea; and as for Bliss Knapp's *Book of Gnophkehs*, they'd merely shaken their heads and smiled condescendingly when he'd shown them his cheaply printed copy.

And what of Thurston? Had the man really repudiated his traditional faith—or was the Massachusetts mandarin only pretending to embrace the gospel of Cthulhu in order to lull his captors into complacency? Even if he was temporarily under their spell, it might not be too late to bring him back to reason. If the two of them ever made it back to Boston alive, the first thing he'd do would be to deliver his companion for treatment to an alienist.

In the meantime, a pallid sun was poking its rays above the horizon. The detective reckoned that the ship must be close to the Arctic Circle, for the "night"—more a kind of orange gloom—had lasted only a few hours. Drift ice now covered most of the sea, reminding him of a tale he'd once read of Arctic ghostliness by that master of the storyteller's art, Sir Arthur Conan Doyle. He shivered, hoping he might be spared the eerie haunting and unearthly wailing that assailed Doyle's doomed hero in similar scenes.

After his morning stint at the galley sink, Legrasse reported to Dr. Quimby's quarters for his second session of enlightenment. As before, the doctor read from *Key to the Watchtower of Thapnen*, but fortunately this time the text was somewhat less soporific, containing as it did some real action.

"I, Alos, was commander of all the forces of the plateau, and in me lay the last hope of our country," the physician intoned. "On this occasion I spoke of the perils to be faced, and exhorted the men of Olathoë, bravest of the Lomarians, to sustain the traditions of their ancestors, who when forced to move southward from Zobna before the advance of the great ice-sheet (even as our descendents must some day regain the Land of Lomar from the squat, hellish, yellow fiends), valiantly and victoriously swept up and embraced the hairy, long-armed cannibal Gnophkehs—"

"Sorry to interrupt, doc, but is 'Gnophkehs' singular or plural? I mean, is the narrator referring to an entire race of cannibals or to an individual?"

"An individual, of course. Believe me, Inspector, once you've become as familiar with *Key to the Watchtower of Thapnen* as I am you'll see there's no room for ambiguity or inconsistency on this or any other scriptural point."

"What's so important about Gnophkehs, anyway? Some of the boys in the galley seem to think he's the cat's meow."

"Cthulhu's avatar would be a more suitable epithet in my view," sniffed Quimby. "I hasten to add that Gnophkehs is, always has been, and *always shall be* subservient to Cthulhu. I'm afraid those who would exalt the hairy, long-armed cannibal to an equal plane risk excommunication—which is not to deny him his status as a very important secondary deity. Your brethren in the galley are not entirely misguided."

The Creole clutched his copy of Bliss Knapp's *Book of Gnophkehs*, which he kept hidden in a pocket of his pea jacket. Best not to flash it, he decided.

Continuing his instruction, Quimby soon shifted to such miscellaneous topics as the evils of animal magnetism and the role of colored people in the ministry. Black men, he asserted, could aspire to the priesthood and preach to their own kind, though there were those—another swipe at Gnophkehs?—who claimed that they were ineligible for such a position of authority. Again, the detective accepted all this and more without argument.

Afterwards Legrasse was ready to saw the proverbial log back in his hammock, but on his way to the foc'sle he noticed an open hatch leading to the hold. No one was about, so on impulse the intrepid police officer slipped down the ladder, hoping he might find some clue to the *Polestar's* mission amongst its cargo. Maybe the ship was a rumrunner after all, despite the Puritanical pretensions of its crew. And the detective could sorely use a man's drink.

Light from the open hatch above afforded a limited view of the hold's contents—stacks and stacks of wooden crates. Here, so close to the engine room, the greasy smell was almost overpowering. Tiny feet scampered in the darkness. Feeling his way from crate to crate, he at last touched one with a loose board. It came away with a popping, splintering sound. He was on the verge of striking a match when he heard a noise on the ladder. Someone was descending into the hold!

"Who goes there?" a familiar voice cried.

The detective, who'd been crouching ready to spring, stood up and sighed in relief. After forty years of service, he appreciated any chance to avoid the rough stuff.

"Thurston, it is I, John Raymond Legrasse!" The detective struck a match, illuminating the startled features of the Yankee patrician.

"Put that out, you fool! Do you want to blow us all to the holy kingdom of our Lord Cthulhu this very instant?"

In the flare of the match just before it went out, Inspector Legrasse saw what was stenciled in bold black letters on the sides of the crates nearest him: "U.S. Army."

"That's right," said Thurston as if reading his thoughts. "The entire hold is packed with boxes of surplus guns and ammunition."

So the men of the *Polestar* were gunrunners! No wonder the scent of oil—gun oil—pervaded the ship! But why in the name of all the saints were they taking such a load to the Arctic?

"Darn it, Thurston, what's going on?"

"You're lucky it was I, brother, who caught you snooping in the hold and not one of the regular crew. The penalty for endangering the ship— Well, as I say, just consider yourself lucky. I won't report you."

Thurston's magnanimity in the circumstances gave the detective some hope as they climbed out of the hold that the Bostonian and he were fighting basically on the same side, despite his companion's spiritual confusion. If only he could break through that outer layer of orthodoxy, expose the depths of the man's soul, then there just might still be some shred of sanity left.

"Thurston, do you really believe in all this Cthulhu mumbo-jumbo?" he murmured from behind. "Have you really taken him into your heart as your personal Savior? And what of Gnophkehs? Isn't Gnophkehs equally worthy of veneration?"

Thurston paused in the passageway and turned to the inspector with a searching look. "You know, Brother Legrasse," he said softly, "this point has lately given me some cause if not to doubt at least to question, well, not actually question but to— Oh, one's faith can be so demanding at times." The convert grimaced, as if torn by some terrible inner struggle. But before he could further express his emotions there came the sound of footsteps from down the passage. "It's best we two not be seen together, brother," he whispered. "Away!"

Legrasse had been asleep barely a minute, it seemed, before he heard a manly voice in his ear. "Wake up, Inspector. The skipper has ordered all hands on deck," one of his mates was saying. "He's going to deliver the Word." The detective rolled over in his hammock. "On the double, sailor!"

By the time the Creole reached the main deck the entire ship's company, apart from those engaged in essential duties, had assembled. The men stood in small groups, silent and expectant. The wan midnight sun hovered just above the horizon. The wind blew in frore gusts off the ice, which the *Polestar*, a former whaler, was now chugging through in fits and starts. A couple of miles off the bow, in stark contrast to the bluish-white of the ice and snow, was a thin dark line—the rocky shore of the west Greenland coast.

Legrasse pulled his fur-lined parka tighter. As a Louisianan, he was not used to such cold. He hoped that the captain would soon emerge and that his sermon would be brief. A moment later the first part of his prayer was answered: Captain Baker, accompanied by Dr. Quimby, appeared on the poop. In his arm the skipper cradled the Cthulhu stone. All was hushed but for the soughing of the wind through the shrouds and the distant call of a sea bird.

"Shipmates! Fellow exiles! Men of Lomar!" cried the captain, his gray eyes gleaming. "I bring you glad tidings." He swung the bas-relief aloft; cheers rose from a hundred throats. "The stars are right!" He caressed the crown of stars on the Cthulhu image. "The Second Coming is at hand!" More lusty cheers, and in spite of himself the detective realized he was joining as heartily as the next man in the chorus.

"For untold generations we of the Lomarian diaspora have wandered in the wilderness. But tomorrow our long journey is over, for tomorrow we strike land—Daikos—Lomar—Home!"

"Hurrah, hurrah!" the sailors yelled in delight. "Say it, brother!" piped a lone voice, possibly Thurston's.

"Our cause is righteous, but the fruits will not be easy to pluck; yea, I say unto you, it is easier for a man to submit to laws restricting his purchase of handguns than for a Lomarian to return to Lomar. Our ancient enemy, the sneaky, slant-eyed Inutos oppose us still. We must be prepared to stain the snow red with the foul blood of the yellow devils. Our cause is righteous, I say unto you again, for as the Zobnarian Fathers have taught us, the Esquimaux diabolists had the audacity in the ancient days to worship Cthulhu as their own. Furthermore, these members of an inferior race boasted that we, the Men of Lomar, were not a chosen people. For this sacrilege they must be punished!"

"Kill, kill, kill!" chanted the crewmen, as if they could almost taste their enemies' blood.

"When the Inutos occupied Olathoë, despite the vigilance of the brave Alos, they seized a certain image of our Lord—the very image that came down from the stars which you now behold. The fact that we have recently recovered it is yet another sign that Providence favors our enterprise."

The captain proceeded to invoke at length past military and theological conflicts, a trifle defensively it seemed to the Creole, who found himself stomping his feet in an effort to keep warm. Finally, this discursive part of the peroration concluded.

"Shipmates, fellow exiles, Men of Lomar, are you prepared to fight our final and most glorious battle?"

At these words two dozen or so zealous souls pulled out their revolvers and started firing in the air. Captain Baker lifted a restraining hand. "Don't waste your bullets on the birds, boys," he shouted. "Save them for the inscrutable usurpers." The shooting gradually subsided.

"You may wonder why," the captain continued, "at this stage in the great cosmic drama, in the year conventionally designated 1927—but which in the new era ahead I suspect will be hallowed as the year 1—you may wonder why we chosen few of pure Lomarian blood have gathered from all the corners of the globe to fulfill our people's destiny.

"I shall reveal to you now a secret that has been known to but a handful of our leadership. Months ago, embedded deep in the Greenland ice-sheet, there was discovered a figure as foretold in the sacred writings. In the summer thaw that glacier has been slowly melting. The figure is growing ever more distinct beneath the ice. Yes, he is coming again, Cthulhu's avatar, the mighty Second Lord, the hairy, long-armed cannibal of ancient lore, the unique and marvelous Gnophkehs."

A veritable frenzy of cheers and whistles broke out at this news, some more ardent than others.

"Gnophkehs remains locked within his icy prison, but the sacrifice of fire will soon see his release—after, I repeat, after we have defeated those hounds from hell, the Inutos."

As another roar went up from the assembled seamen, Dr. Quimby leaned over and said something in the ear of the strong-jawed captain.

"Dr. Quimby has reminded me that I ought to address the matter of the differences in our own ranks. Most are too petty to bother to enumerate here. On one issue, however, I must speak up. A not insignificant point of doctrine threatens to divide us on the very eve of our last crusade. I know there's a sizable minority among you who'd prefer to regard Gnophkehs as Cthulhu's co-partner and equal. I must emphasize that there is absolutely no legitimate scriptural basis for this claim."

This remark prompted some grumbling, mainly from that part of the deck occupied by Angelo Moroni and his galley crew. Some of them didn't hesitate to pull out and brandish their copies of Bliss Knapp's *Book of Gnophkehs*. Others, like the men on Legrasse's watch, were heard to mutter such words as "blasphemers" and even "heretics."

"Peace, shipmates, peace," the captain called. "Let me remind you that we are all Lomarians. As such we stand united against the common foe. Let us take comfort in the knowledge that Gnophkehs himself, I'm sure, will shortly resolve the issue of his own semi-divinity to everyone's satisfaction.

"And now let us close by singing that joyous ancestral anthem, 'Lomar the Beautiful.' Dr. Quimby, will you do the honors?"

"Oh beautiful, for empty skies, for somber wastes of ice," the physican began, soon joined by a hundred husky Nordic voices. While he didn't know the words, the detective again could not help being deeply moved. By the second stanza he was humming the melody. How could anyone resist such an electric appeal to the emotions? What hope was there for clear, rational thought in the face of such an irresistible assault on primal feeling?

By anthem's end, Legrasse was considering whether his forced cruise aboard the *Polestar* was turning him from a man of action into a man of passive contemplation. Perhaps it was time to retire.

Thurston broke into the detective's reverie to say that they were both ordered to report to Captain Baker. The New England nabob said he had no clue why the skipper wanted to see them, but the grim foreboding of the Creole as they proceeded to the captain's quarters proved not unwarranted.

Two brawny blond sailors stood at attention at the skipper's door. Inside Captain Baker looked as if he were in no mood for pleasantries. He was fiddling with a tiny object in his hand. "Boys, I'm disappointed in you." He held up a burnt match. "A reliable witness saw you both leave the hold, where this was found a short time later. In addition, one of the cases of cargo had been disturbed. I'm inclined to take the charitable view and regard it as an act of reckless endangerment rather than deliberate sabotage. Nonetheless, at this crucial juncture of our mission I'm taking no chances. You're both under arrest." With a toot on a bosun's whistle, he summoned the pair of sentries. "Guards, take these seamen to the brig."

"Well, my lad, what do you make of your mighty Men of Lomar now?" the detective asked, rattling his fetters. The Dartmouth Street dilettante, weak and dispirited, responded with a dismissive wave of a steel-clad wrist.

"I tell you, Thurston, that Captain Baker is a maniac! He makes Captain Ahab look like a schoolmarm our for a Sunday sail. This quest is mad! What person in his right mind would want to take over a polar wasteland like Lomar?"

"You're still too concerned with material illusions, Inspector," said his companion, though without much conviction.

If the truth be known, time passed slowly within the all-too-material confines of their cell. Their rations were nothing to write home about, while their only amusement was taking turns while the other slept swatting at small furry intruders with a copy of *Key to the Watchtower of Thapnen*. The jailers who brought them their meals and emptied their slops ignored their requests for information, but they could tell that the ship was reducing speed. Finally, it stopped and the engines died. The *Polestar* had reached its destination.

For the next several hours the prisoners could hear a lot of commotion from the direction of the hold. The cargo was being unloaded as rapidly and as safely as its explosive nature would allow. Thereafter came the sound of shooting, at first sporadic then growing into a veritable torrent of small arms fire. The reconquest of the Land of Lomar had begun.

It was soon over, apparently. The seaman who next delivered them their grub couldn't help boasting of the landing's success. The vintage Civil War weaponry of the Lomarians had proven deadly against the knives and fish hooks of the Inuto women and children defending Daikos. The few survivors had fled the settlement for the frozen plateau to the east, leaving the field to the victors. Captain Baker had already proclaimed their triumph as a sign of almighty Cthulhu's favor.

Legrasse and Thurston didn't have long to wait for the sequel. A squad of burly sailors barged into their cell, unlocked their chains, and dragged them up top, where they were given a minute to walk around and get their circulation going. A great damp fog muffled the ship. Through the mist the detective could barely tell that the *Polestar* was moored to a rocky jetty, which stuck like a narrow finger into the pack ice.

In another minute the two were frog-marched down the gangway to the jetty, past a row of empty wooden gun crates, and along the shore into the gloom. As rough as their treatment was, Legrasse had to be grateful that they'd been allowed to put on their gloves after the removal of the irons. Fortunately, they were already wearing thick-soled, insulated boots.

They passed through the remains of Daikos, which appeared to have been nothing more than a rude fishing village. Scattered cartridges, some dark marks in the snow, a smattering of bullet-pocked igloos were the only evidence of the day's carnage. Here they turned inland and headed for a distant spark, twinkling like a crimson star. As they drew nearer, this spark grew into a flame. The acrid scent of some burning fatty substance carried across the thin Arctic air.

Eventually, they could discern men at work around the bonfire—for such it proved to be, with the flames arcing twenty or more feet into the sky. Using discarded crating, the crew of the *Polestar* were constructing a wooden platform between the bonfire and the face of the glacier, in which could be seen a blurry humanoid form.

Captain Baker, his face glistening with sweat from his labors, smiled at the newcomers. "At last our party's complete," he said. "What do you think, Dr. Quimby? How should we most expediently atone? Shall we offer up both captives to Gnophkehs?"

"May I remind the captain that Inspector Legrasse is of Mediterranean descent, while young Thurston is of northern heritage, more like ourselves."

"In that case let's just go with the inspector. Seize him, boys."

John Raymond Legrasse was not about to surrender without a fight, but in the event he was no match for the half-dozen brutes who grabbed him and started to tear at his heavy protective garments. Within moments the hapless officer of the law was stripped to his union suit and tied spread-eagled to the wooden platform. Although next to naked, he did not suffer from the cold, so intense was the heat from the bonfire—which was shortly to grow even hotter.

"A little more kindling there, boys," ordered the skipper.

With the bonfire behind him the detective had to crane his head around to see what was going on, and what he glimpsed was not pretty. The men of the *Polestar* were fueling the flames with the corpses of the slain enemy! The suddenly strong stench of burning flesh nearly turned his stomach. Weren't the roasted bodies of the fiendish Inutos sacrifice enough for Gnophkehs? Or did the hairy, long-armed cannibal prefer his prey *alive?*

The face of the glacier, which Legrasse could regard easily from his prone position, was now beginning to melt in a stream. As the outlines of the fair figure encased therein grew ever sharper, it seemed to the terrified Creole almost as if the thing were licking its lips at the sight of his pendulous white belly, exposed through rips in his longjohns.

"Wait a minute," he could hear Captain Baker crying. "We almost forgot! Dr. Quimby, if you please . . ."

Moments later the physician was on the platform, setting the Cthulhu idol on the detective's ample midriff.

"Stop wiggling, Inspector," said Quimby. "Let's give Gnophkehs a decent view of the image of his Lord and Master."

Legrasse ceased to struggle, for his attention had in a delirium of fear turned from the monster in the ice to the totem-stone resting on his paunch. The surface glistened with a thousand points of light, particularly in the region of the starry crown. As Morton had warned him might happen, the detective started to have strange visions—first of a cold nightmare city, then of an enormous tentacled abomination being dragged from the sky by its feelers and devoured by a race of—

He was brought back to earth by the jabbering of a group of men who were clustered in front of the glacier, excitedly gesticulating at Gnophkehs.

"I tell you, he's holding the original silver tablet," cried Angelo Moroni, "just as Bliss Knapp predicted!"

"Nonsense!" shouted Dr. Quimby. There's no sign of any tablet. That's matted fur, you moron!"

"What did you call me, doc?"

"Never mind. Look, the ice is almost completely melted. Stand back!"

Legrasse's view of the thawing entity had been obscured by the quarreling crew members, but at that moment the human wave parted and the blond, soaking body of Gnophkehs toppled forward—falling neatly between the detective's legs, his long hairy arms stretched out in supplication.

"Look there, he's paying homage to Cthulhu! He's praying to his Lord and Master," shouted Dr. Quimby gleefully.

"No, he's not," yelled Nephi. "He hasn't woken up yet, you sanctimonious simp. After thousands of years in the deep-freeze you'd be groggy, too!"

"How dare you, a common seaman, address me in such a disrespectful fashion. Captain Baker, I hope you will—"

When those first shots rang out, Legrasse thought they had to be coming from the direction of the icy knoll to his left. Whatever their source, a bullet to the shoulder cut Quimby off in midstream, while Nephi must have been dead before he hit the ground, judging by the quantity of blood that gushed over the detective. Though on his knees, the doctor with his good arm was able to extract his Colt and blast away at Moroni as the cook bent over his fallen comrade. Before he was cut to pieces by the return fire, the wounded physician was able to reload once, without a single yelp or moan. Ah, the power of faith! marveled Legrasse.

The full-scale gun battle between the opposing factions of Lomarians lasted longer than it might have because all parties were using old-fashioned black powder. The air, misty enough as it was, was soon opaque from the smoke of two hundred revolvers. The detective, straining at his bonds, could no longer see Gnophkehs sprawled over his lower limbs. Perhaps Cthulhu's avatar was wise enough to know when to continue keeping his head down.

John Raymond Legrasse had been in his share of tight fixes over the decades, but even the toughest veteran has his limits. When he regained consciousness, the bullets were still flying—and someone was tugging on his extremities. Had Gnophkehs finally awoken from his slumbers? No, it was Thurston, who was cutting the thongs that secured him to the platform!

"Let's get out of here, Inspector."

"But where the heck to?"

"How about the ship?"

"Yeah, maybe it's deserted, and we can radio for help from there."

The two men crawled along the ground, away from the still roaring bonfire, in the direction from which they reckoned they'd originally come. Legrasse noticed that his companion was clutching the totem-stone—which remarkably had not been shattered.

Out of the immediate range of the fire, the detective suddenly felt very cold. Luckily, there were several bodies in their path, and it was the work of a moment for Legrasse to remove and don the furs, gloves, and boots from the least bloodied specimen. They also retrieved a couple of 1851 Navy Colts, in case they encountered any living *Polestar* crew men or— Though neither dared voice his fears, neither man had noticed Gnophkehs on the platform at the time of their flight.

As the sounds of firing receded behind them, the two rose to a crouch. They began to trot. Visibility was still poor, but it wasn't long before they hit the outskirts of Daikos, or what was left of it, and they knew they were on the right track. Once they reached the shore they would be home free, though who knew what reception might await them at the *Polestar*.

Beyond the ruins of Daikos, the fog was rising. From some distance now they could make out the outline of the ship. Figures were running on the deck. Had a guard been left behind? No, there was something odd about their shapes—they were too short, too round. Voices could be heard—a series of gruff, guttural grunts. Theirs was not the language of the Men of Lomar.

"Cunning devils!" Thurston cried.

"You mean—"

"Yes, the Inutos! They've outflanked us."

The men who'd been rushing about the deck were now racing down the gangway. They were not alone. Legrasse and Thurston were just close enough to see that the two heavy hawsers that secured the *Polestar* were streaming—with the slithering forms of countless vermin!

An instant later the ship blew up like fireworks on the 4th of July; the concussion knocked them flat. They shielded themselves as best they could from the falling debris—spars, shrouds, crispy little corpses, smoking copies of *Key to the Watchtower of Thapnen* and Bliss Knapp's *Book of Gnophkehs*.

"The Inutos must have set a larger charge than they realized," groaned the Bostonian. "Probably inexperienced handling explosives, though you have to hand it to 'em. They got the job done."

"Rats, we'll never escape now!"

"Courage, Inspector. Follow me."

"Where to?"

"Back to Daikos. It's the one place for miles where we're likely to scrape up any provisions."

"Then where?"

"South. If we can keep our strength up, I bet you we can make it as far as Godthåb. There we can catch a boat back to civilization."

Both men agreed that flight was preferable to falling into the hands of the savage Inutos, and this scheme seemed their only hope. Inside one of the less damaged Daikosian igloos, they found some fishing line, dried whale meat, and fur blankets, which they secured in sealskin packs. Inland, toward the glacier, the bonfire glowed hard and gem-like in the lifting haze. Was it still being fed? And if so, by whom? At any rate, they could no longer hear gunfire. Soon, as they tramped south along the gravel shore, they would no longer be able to smell the faint yet unmistakable aroma of burning flesh.

In the days and weeks that followed, Legrasse and Thurston were too concerned with basic survival to reflect much on their ordeal. Using the Cthulhu idol as a kind of compass or talismanic lodestone, they worked their way down the rugged coast, often hiking for miles around the many fjords that emptied into the Davis Strait. After the whale meat ran out, they succeeded in catching fish and even shooting the occasional Arctic fowl or fox, though since their ammunition supply was limited, they always tried first to club or stone the creature to death. They quenched their thirst with ice or snow. More than once they observed a ship offshore, but it was always too far out to spot their feeble signals. They never lingered in one place, for they lived with the constant fear that someone—or something—was on their trail.

At night—and after a month they experienced real darkness, having crossed the Arctic circle—one would sleep while the other kept watch, though Legrasse suspected Thurston spent more time gazing into the shimmering surface of the Cthulhu stone than on lookout. When questioned, the Red Sox rooter would merely say the visions therein were guiding them to a safe haven. It was clear to the detective that his fellow refugee remained at least in part under Cthulhu's spell. A person who could mumble under his breath such nonsense as "Cthulhu, All-God, God-good, Good-god, Truth, Bones, Liver, Kidneys" still had a long way to go toward evangelical maturity.

Finally, their trauma sufficiently behind them, the two were able to talk freely of the events leading up to their flight.

"One point still sticks in my craw, Thurston," the detective began during a rest break about forty days into their trek. "Do you have any idea who fired those first shots? Could you tell from you vantage point?"

"I'm sure there was a lone gunman, Inspector. A lone *Inuto* gunman," answered his companion. "The sly dog."

"Do you think Captain Baker of any of his crew survived?"

"Doubtful. My hunch is the Inuto warriors who blew up the *Polestar* finished off anyone still left alive in the vicinity of the bonfire."

"And what of Gnophkehs? Do you suppose he was in some sort of hypnotic trance?"

"Careful, brother, hypnosis is not real."

"Sorry, my boy. More to the point, do you think Gnophkehs could be after us now?"

"If he is, Brother Legrasse, we have the Cthulhu totem to protect us. Gnophkehs wouldn't dare challenge his superior deity."

The detective considered voicing the argument that Gnophkehs was in fact Cthulhu's co-equal, but he decided it best in the circumstances to avoid controversy. "Amazing how that thing wasn't even scratched after being struck by two ounces of lead with a velocity over 800 feet per second."

"Yes, the mineral composition must be quite extraordinary."

About a week later, when they came to large fjord, Thurston insisted that they follow its course into the interior rather than ford it and continue south. Cthulhu had told him this was the right route. In truth both men had been growing steadily weaker, despite every effort to secure adequate nourishment. Unless they found an outpost soon they were in real danger of slowly starving to death, or falling prey to the ever more numerous polar bears who were hovering at ever closer range. Any Inutos they ran into at this latitude were not likely to hold them responsible for the slaughter farther north—they hoped. The detective, close to delirious, acquiesced.

Cthulhu must indeed have been looking down on the weary travelers, for they had gone but a few miles before spying the smoke from a village—the first human habitation they'd encountered since Daikos. Neither was in a state to be circumspect, and they staggered boldly up the fjord-side path into its center. They were soon surrounded by a bevy of curious villagers. As natives went they weren't especially squat or slant-eyed; indeed, there was something comfortingly Nordic in their fair, hirsute visages. When Thurston flourished the Cthulhu stone, the hitherto silent crowd started to jabber excitedly. A few even laughed and pointed at the idol as if it were the source of some colossal jest.

Legrasse and Thurston were given their own stone hut, where they were left to rest but mainly to eat. They were amply supplied with all manner of fish, both fresh and saltwater, as well as rich reindeer meat. The Creole drank flagon after flagon of an unknown fermented beverage, while the Bostonian settled for spring water. Since their hosts spoke an utterly alien tongue, which they decided wasn't even Indo-European, they had to express their appreciation through nods and smiles.

All this food was prepared elsewhere, but one day a group of tribesmen entered their hut bearing an immense iron cooking pot. A fire was started on the hearth. When Thurston declined the fermented beverage the men offered them, they acted a bit hurt. The detective, for his part, eagerly downed his portion of the potable potion. Then one of their visitors picked up the Cthulhu stone and casually tossed it in the large kettle. The Ivy League elitist was on his feet in an instant. In response one of the beefier men rolled up his sleeves and raised his fists. In the final moment before he passed out, Legrasse noticed how striking the firelight was on the fellow's lanky, hair-smothered arms.

III.
The Testimony of James F. Morton (Continued)

Mineralogy, I confess, is far from my sole passion. I have, for example, campaigned for Negro rights all my life. The treatment of these poor suffering people is a national disgrace, from the stereotypical darkies of pulp fiction to publicly sanctioned lynchings. They are human beings like the rest of us, and it is only through the sheerest ignorance and the blindest prejudice that so many otherwise intelligent and decent white folk view them as inferior—like my writer friend in Providence, with whom I've exchanged some heated words on the subject. If only they would get to know educated Negroes as I have, then they might regard the whole matter differently. But I'm afraid I'll be long gone before there's any real progress on this front, so ingrained is the antipathy to the black race in the American character.

Another interest, developed since my involvement in this Cthulhu business, has been comparative mythology. After reading James Frazer's *Golden Bough* and Jung on dreams, I recognized that the story of Cthulhu outlined in Thurston's account fit the archetypal pattern of cosmic creation myths. While these revelations may seem to be about fear in the face of a cold, indifferent universe, they really concern the terrors that lurk in the human soul. To put it another way, Cthulhu and his ilk have no outside, objective reality, inspired as they are by man's profound desire to believe in something greater than himself. Freud, in my opinion, is all wet when he attacks religion as some sort of immature delusion to be grown out of.

At any rate, philosophical reflections such as these helped console me in the months following the disappearance of Inspector Legrasse—not that I didn't try to locate him. The venerable detective, like Thurston, had last been seen in the vicinity of the Boston waterfront, and it was my theory that both men had been kidnapped and taken aboard ship by persons in some way linked to the Cthulhu cult. I can't afford to travel much, but as I've said, I have wide affiliations in all conceivable foreign parts. I began a letter campaign inquiring of my far-flung correspondents, especially those based in seaports, whether they'd heard report of two Americans answering the descriptions of Thurston and Legrasse showing up suddenly on their shores. I received leads from contacts in places like Indochina and Abyssinia, but in the end all came to naught. Whatever their fate in the interim, I reluctantly concluded that after two years both men were almost certainly dead.

Then, in the fall of 1930, I received a communication from an adept from Benares, one Swami Chandraputra, who revived my hopes. A colleague of his in Poona had told him of my quest. The swami, newly arrived in the United States, claimed he had important information on the missing men I'd been seeking. He was vague about just what he knew and how he knew it, but he promised I wouldn't be disappointed. Since he expressed a willingness to come to Paterson, I wrote back to his Boston address to invite him to visit any time. By return post he announced his arrival that evening.

Over the years many strange and eccentric guests have passed through the portals of the Paterson Museum of Natural History, but I have to say that the swami, with his turban, ill-fitting clothes, bushy black beard, almost irisless eyes, large white mittens, and hollow, metallic voice, outdistanced the field for oddity. Somewhat mitigating this exotic impression, I should say, were his normal European attire and his easy, correct, and idiomatic English.

"How do you do, sir," said the swami with a bow.

"Welcome, Mr. Chandraputra, to my humble museum. We can start here with the main exhibit hall, or if you like we can get the rear storage room out of the way first."

"Thank you, but a tour won't be necessary. I confess I'm not one to indulge in idle pleasantries. I suggest we get right down to business, if you don't mind. I have lots to do while I'm here . . . here in America, I mean."

"All right by me. In that case, why don't we just move into my office."

I showed the Indian mystic the same seat that poor Legrasse had occupied some three years before, while I took my accustomed chair at my desk.

"Are you by chance familiar, sir," my visitor said in his queerly alien voice, "with the couplet by the mad Arab Abdul Alhazred that goes: 'That is not dead which can eternal lie / And with strange aeons even death may die'?"

"Yes, that does have a familiar ring," I said, though in all honesty I couldn't quite place it.

"Well, sir, the words of the prophet are true. Death is but a dream, and I have done much dreaming, which we in India have always done."

"But what does this have to do with Legrasse and Thurston? Are they, have they . . ." I couldn't bring myself to ask the question outright.

"The gentlemen whose welfare so greatly concerns you," continued the Hindoo, "have not utterly passed beyond our ken, you may take heart in knowing. No doubt you are acquainted with spiritualism, championed most famously by the late Sir Arthur Conan Doyle."

"It so happens, as a student of world mythology, I've read Sir Arthur on the subject, books like *The Vital Message* and *The New Revelation*."

"Good, good. Then I can dispense with the usual background explanation for the uninitiated. Let me begin by assuring you, sir, that I can establish communication with both of your dear disappeared ones through my control."

"Your control?"

"Ah, I see some explanations are in order. A control is an intermediary between the waking and the spirit worlds. Mine is an entity known in earthly terms as Gnoph-keh."

"Gnoph-keh? What the hell kind of name is that?"

"Have you not in the course of your studies run across references to the horned and hairy myth-thing of the Greenland ice that walks on two legs, sometimes on four, and sometimes on six?"

"No," I admitted, "I'm just an amateur, not a professional like yourself."

"Gnoph-keh is the key to the gate beyond which your friends can be reached. If you'll allow me to demonstrate . . ."

The swami insisted I pull the window shade and turn off the desk light. The darkness was total. His unnatural voice droned on in invocation, then abruptly shifted to unintelligible gibberish, as if he were speaking in tongues. The next thing I knew I was hearing two men talking, as if through radio interference. Their voices were familiar.

"Hold on, Inspector, I think someone's listening in."

"How can you be sure in a place like this, my boy," his companion answered, almost jovially.

"Don't be shy, sir," said the swami in his normal mechanical tone. "Ask a question."

"Inspector Legrasse," I cried. "Is that you?"

"Of course it is I, John Raymond Legrasse, of the New Orleans police department. Who are you?"

"James Ferdinand Morton, the person who sent you in search of Francis Thurston, of Boston—"

"I'm here, too, in case you're interested," came another voice from the void.

"What happened to you two?"

"It's a very long and not very pleasant story," answered the Bostonian.

"Yes, I'd prefer not to go into it," chimed in the detective. "How, may I ask, did you find us here?"

"Where's here?"

"Let's just say it's a spiritual plane that the mundane physical world, with its notions of Western dualism, has yet to discover."

"Well, to answer your question, I found you through the kind offices of a psychic medium who calls himself Swami Chandraputra. Or maybe I should give credit to his control."

"Control?"

"Yes, the entity who actually acts as a sort of cosmic telephone. His name is Gnoph-keh—"

"What!?"

"Gnoph-keh."

"How do you spell it?"

"I don't know. Better ask the swami."

Clearly, both speakers from the other side were perturbed. The Indian, like some cosmic phone operator, obliged them with the spelling.

"So that's with a hyphen and no final 's,'" said the voice that had identified itself as Legrasse.

"Does it make a difference?" I asked

"All myths contain variants," the Hindoo rasped. "One tradition suggests that Gnoph-keh is an individual entity, while another posits an entire race of hairy, long-armed cannibal semi-humans called the Gnophkehs."

Suddenly, there was a shriek, as of a phonograph needle being dragged across a record.

"It's him, Inspector! He's speaking the ancient Naacal language, just as Churchward—"

"Oh, no, he's seen us, Thurston! Good thing they gave me back my .38!"

"How many times do I have to tell you, Legrasse, that material objects, even here—" The shriek grew to a cacophonous roar. "Yikes, he's after us! Away!"

The screams tapered off, as if receding down a long tunnel. The rest was silence. It was with incalculable relief that I heard the swami ordering me to turn on the light.

"Well, sir," said the mystic, "are you satisfied?"

"I guess, though I wish they'd been a little more forthcoming. I don't suppose there'd be any point in trying them again."

"I suppose not. The connection is probably permanently broken. In any case, it is time for me to go. Shall we settle up?"

"Are you saying you expect payment?"

"Naturally, sir. You don't suppose I'd come all the way from Boston just to perform my services for nothing, do you?"

"I'm not a rich man, Mr. Chandraputra—"

"No matter, sir. I do not require cash. No, if you could please hand over the Cthulhu idol that I've been told you keep in your safe."

"Who told you that?"

"Your writer friend in Providence, with whom I've been in touch since my arrival."

"Sorry to disappoint you, but my friend's information is out of date. I gave the totem-stone to Legrasse three years ago. It disappeared with him."

"I don't believe you."

"The detective himself could've told you that a few minutes ago."

"As we both realize, there's little chance we'll be able to raise the inspector again."

"That's not my problem."

"I'm afraid, sir, I must insist you open your safe. That stone was fashioned on Yaddith, on the Outer Rim. It is essential to my operations on this plan— I mean in New England that I retrieve it."

My visitor had risen from his chair. Those irisless eyes seemed to be glowing from deep within his skull with dark menace. I decided it would be wiser to do his bidding than not. Perhaps he'd calm down once he saw the Cthulhu stone wasn't in the safe.

"There!" I said, after working the combination and swinging open the door. "Except for a few papers and semiprecious gems, there's nothing of value inside. See for yourself."

The Hindoo, who'd been leaning over my shoulder, too close for comfort, I might add, quickly inspected the open safe. Then he turned, black eyes blazing. The next thing I knew those clumsy white mittens that covered his hands were on my throat. I struggled, but the Indian mystic appeared to possess preternatural strength. Those white mittens squeezed tighter . . .

* * *

I awoke to the sound of the doorbell. Daylight streamed through the window. I was slumped in my desk chair. The safe was closed. There was no sign of Swami Chandraputra. On the desk was a magazine open to one of my Providence friend's otherworldly tales of supernatural horror. I must have fallen asleep. I must have been dreaming.

The doorbell buzzed again. I hurried to the door. It was my favorite postman, an affable Negro fellow whom I often run into at local N.A.A.C.P. meetings. He had a large package for me postmarked Providence, dated January of this year, 1927. The return address showed it was from one George Angell.

"I'm sorry, Andy," I said on impulse. "I can't accept this package."

"That's okay, Mr. Morton. We at the p.o. is always happy to oblige, especially a white man that's been so kind to colored folks like you been, Mr. Morton. I'll be glad to mark it 'return to sender.'"

"That's fine, Andy, though if that package should just happen to get lost . . ."

"I read your meanin', Mr. Morton."

"Just make sure it's really lost—like in the ocean."

"I got a cousin in the merchant marine we be seein' next week in Hoboken. Say no more, Mr. Morton."

"Thanks, Andy. You're a credit to your race—and my race, too, for God knows beneath the skin we're all brothers."

THE MADNESS OUT OF SPACE

(Found Among the Papers of the Late E. Phillips Winsor at the Innsmouth Home for the Indigent)

I.

Friends and family have wondered at my abrupt return from college a full week before the beginning of the Easter vacation. Explanations of an unforeseen, early termination of school work I hope have satisfied them; for I dare not hint as yet as to the real cause. Eventually, I realize, I must tell them—and the world—of the fate of my roommate and closest friend, Howard Wentworth Anable, who disappeared in the early morning of March 15, 1929, into the densely forested, still winter-frozen hills that extend west of the university town of Arkham, Massachusetts—or so people believe. How much of the "truth" I will reveal remains for me to decide, as I run the risk of being declared as mad as that singular individual whose bizarre and lamentable history I am here about to disclose. I admit that relations between us had been strained in those final months, an unhappy consequence of his physical and mental deterioration; but this in no way affected the underlying fondness and respect I had always held for him.

I fear that I have seen the last of my comrade; for certain evidence— certain damnably conclusive evidence, which for the sake of mankind's collective sanity I hesitate to reveal—indicates that he has ventured into terrible cosmic realms from which no mortal can ever return.

Duty required that I inform Anable's mother and grandmother, who live near the center of the old colonial town, of my gravest suspicions; but without giving away anything of the specific horror I had observed. The Anables had half anticipated a climax of this sort, and bore their grief with admirable Yankee stoicism. There ensued a discreet investigation, which received no publicity other than a short notice in the *Arkham Advertiser*.

The police theorize that Anable was forcibly abducted, the broken window and the disordered furniture and books in his bedroom supporting this

conclusion. Anable's relatives had known of his association with an undesirable band of cultists, who, camped out in the Arkham hills, may have
taken revenge on the youth for some imagined transgression of their laws.
Search parties discovered no trace of Anable or his suspected abductors
(who, in any event, may have left the area months before), and after several
days they abandoned their trampings through the woods.

Naturally, the authorities questioned me closely, but I was able to demonstrate to their satisfaction that I knew little of Anable's dealings with any
queer characters living in the hills. Through an extreme effort of will I managed to suppress my feelings of awful horror and show only normal shock
and dismay. Indeed, until the last mind-shattering revelation, I had dismissed Anable's ravings as nothing more than a lot of theosophical hocus-
pocus. A rational man could easily have taken his strange pronouncements
toward the end as the phantasies of a psychotic. But now I know otherwise;
and because I do I may myself fall a victim to those same dread forces that
claimed my friend. Therefore, for the written record, I am presently setting
down, during these days of early New England spring, while events are still
fresh and there is still time for me, an account of this frightful matter—of
the madness out of space.

II.

I met Howard Anable our freshman year at Miskatonic University,
which is not Harvard, nor is it even Ivy League, but whose unparalleled
reputation as a freewheeling, "progressive," co-ed institution attracts un-
conventional and original minds who care little for prestige. It is located in
the glamorous old, gambrel-roofed town of Arkham, renowned along the
North Shore as a place especially sensitive to adumbrations of the para-
normal. Both he and I enrolled in an advanced course in Colonial American
literature. (Miskatonic's Pickman collection of early American documents is
justly famous for its size and completeness—second only to that of the
John Carter Brown Library at Brown University in Providence, Rhode Island.) I was immediately impressed, as were the other students and Professor Waggoner, by his profound and encyclopedic knowledge of the subject.
Anable boasted that he had read Cotton Mather's *Magnalia Christi Americana*
in its entirety, and would quote lengthy passages from memory to illustrate
all sorts of nice points in class discussion. It appeared that he had done ex-

tensive research from his earliest years into the history, folklore, culture, and architecture of New England.

Physically unobtrusive on first sight, Anable really cut a remarkable figure the more one studied him. He had a frame so excessively spare that, although he stood an inch or two above average height, people usually took him to be much taller. A spectrally pale complexion, set off by strikingly deep, intelligent brown eyes and short-cropped, mousy brown hair, combined to give his face a perpetually startled expression. (That he was fairhaired and blue-eyed as a child, Anable never tired of repeating when I knew him better.) He wore conservative clothing, a dark suit with a plain, dark knit tie being his preferred dress.

Although I frequently engaged in academic debate with Anable, I knew practically nothing about him outside the classroom, other than that he lived at his family's home on Valley Street. Fellow students remarked that they never noticed him at any of the usual campus haunts; rumor had it that he spent his free hours taking long, solitary walks beyond the town. His rapid stooping gait soon became his distinctive hallmark.

An independent figure, Anable ignored the voguish crowd of campus "sophisticates," who courted him as someone whose eccentricities and tastes would have made him immediately welcome among their select circles. Instead, his high-handed disdain of their "immature indulgences," as he put it, won only their resentment. I myself, being by nature more gregarious and eager to be accepted by the elite, was at first given to mixing with the "wild set," but by the Christmas holidays I had grown weary of their superficial pseudo-decadent thrill-seeking, and ceased associating with them altogether with the start of the second term in January.

I think Anable observed this shift in my social preferences. He began speaking to me on his own initiative after the honors American literature class, devoted to a thorough study of those classic if largely neglected authors—Cooper, Irving, and Charles Brockden Brown—of the early Republic, that we shared in the new term. A casual friendship developed between us that I was pleased to cultivate; for I appreciated in Anable his genuine erudition and sobriety of manner—indicative, I sensed, of a special understanding of things outside the ordinary in life.

We soon discovered that we held a good many common interests, as Anable's outward reticence gave way to a voluble stream of talk about himself and his ideas. I already knew him to be an enthusiastic student of the New England scene; now I learned the personal side.

Howard Wentworth Anable was descended from a line of well-to-do Arkham merchants who had flourished during the days of clipper ships and the China trade; the family since the turn of the century, however, having been reduced to the state politely known as "genteel poverty." As a boy of nine, soon after the death of his father, he had moved with his mother from his family's Anawan Avenue mansion, built in the 1820s by his great-grandfather, Captain Adoniram Anable, celebrated in Arkham history for his daring exploits in the South Seas, to the less than grand neighborhood of Valley Street. (The log of the *Miskatonic*, the vessel in which Captain Anable made his most successful voyages, is preserved in the archives of the Arkham Institute.) His first American ancestor, of Northumberland stock, had sailed on the *Arbella* in 1636, Anable proudly told me once; adding that his people were among the very earliest settlers of Cape Cod. Of his father Anable rarely spoke—and then merely to say that he had worked for the 'phone company.

I visited Anable at his home, a privilege granted to few, and was much impressed by the Chinese plates and vases, Polynesian wood-carvings, and scrimshaw still in the family's possession—surviving relics of a more prosperous age that seemed so sadly out of place in the undistinguished, Victorian frame house, divided into apartments, that now formed the Anable abode. With no brothers or sisters or congenial playmates to divert him with the usual childhood activities, Anable had grown up with only the memories and dust of the past to occupy his imagination. A voracious reader, he had mastered the family library with its shelves of mouldy Essex County histories and other quaint, antique volumes. Anable sometimes spoke wistfully to me of someday recovering the family mansion and restoring it to a semblance of that departed glory of his forebears. Alas, that shall never be!

Anable detested cats, and in his youth used to throw rocks at any feline so foolish as to prowl into the Anable backyard and wander within range. He also hated ice cream, amazing as it may seem that anyone could become nauseous at even the slightest taste of this universally loved treat. On the other hand, staunch New Englander that he was, Anable adored seafood—lobster, clams, fried or steamed, mussels with butter, cod, scrod, sole, flounder or haddock, chowder of the Boston variety, he relished them all.

In his devotion to this vision of a purer, happier past, he had, with the advent of his teens and less parental supervision, become increasingly drawn to the countryside beyond Arkham—to the pine, maple, and birch forest that covers the undulant, ravine-intersected hills as far as the sparsely populated regions of the upper Miskatonic valley. It had been on extended walks through the woods that Anable had felt his most exquisite and poignant sensations of wonder and adventurous expectancy—caught especially at sunset in the vista of golden roofs of the town laid out below.

That spring Anable took me to his favorite spot for viewing Arkham and its sunset effects—Satan's Ledge, an outcropping of sedimentary rock on one of the higher hillsides (part of a vast tract of public land), well-nigh inaccessible from the Arkham direction save for a difficult ascent up its steep slope through uncommonly thick vegetation. Believing me not up to the strenuous climb, Anable suggested that we ride the Bolton bus, which drops off passengers during warm months at a roadside picnic area on the westward fringe of the hill, where the slope is considerably gentler. From this picnic area the ledge was but a walk of a half mile along a well-marked path.

Indeed a scenic viewpoint, Satan's Ledge formed a level surface of moderate extent, upon which rested granite boulders arranged in a disturbingly symmetrical pattern—one that no retreating ice sheet was likely to have left, in my opinion. Peculiar ideographs, most badly eroded, were graven on these imposing rocks—no doubt the work of the vanished Indians. Ethnographers had conjectured them to be of cabalistic or magical significance, Anable informed me, but who could say for sure with so few discernible details. Analogues are to be found on rocks in the remote mountain regions of Vermont and Maine and in the decadent hill country around Dunwich.

At the end of the school year in June, our friendship firmly fixed, Anable asked me if I cared to share lodgings with him for sophomore year.

"I've noticed, Winsor," he began, as we sat in the Ratty, the undergraduate refectory, over coffee (his heavily laden with sugar as was his custom), "that you're a fairly sensitive fellow. I think you're someone who understands, who sympathizes. Living with my mother and feeble old grandmother while going to college I've found 'restrictive,' to say the least. It's time I got out on my own, and I don't mean into one of the hideous dormitories with the herd. I'd like a companion—partly for financial reasons, I admit—who'd be willing to go halves with me on a place.

"You see, Winsor, I feel I'm on the verge of making a 'rift in the horizon's wall,' so to speak—but just where or how I cannot begin to tell, let alone explain to you. It has something to do with the sense of adventurous expectancy that hits me on occasion whenever I view scenes of particular aesthetic appeal, such as old gardens, antique harbors, or Georgian steeples topped with gilded vanes." Anable's great brown eyes glowed, as if he were gazing at a Bulfinch cupola and not at a student cafeteria.

"I'm afraid that if I become too absorbed in my search I may lose all sense of proper proportion, act rashly. I may well need a friend close at hand, someone stable whose good judgment I can rely on—a pal such as you to point out to me when I'm going astray."

Flattered by his proposal, I was nonetheless taken aback by his last cryptic remarks. My uneasiness must have been obvious to Anable, for he suddenly shifted back to the main point.

"I've found decent furnished rooms at 973 Hale Street near the end of the trolley line at the north end of town. The location may be far from campus, but the trolley stop is just two blocks away. I've been there once, when I answered the ad in the *Advertiser*. The landlady, Mrs. Delisio, would provide meals. If you're free, we can go take a look right now."

I could not help being intrigued by Anable's offer; here was a unique opportunity to increase our intimacy. His baffling comments forgotten, I readily assented to examine the place. We drained our cups and headed out for the trolley stop in front of Miskatonic Hall.

The building at 973 Hale Street proved to be a small, eighteenth-century clapboard house, which retained much of its antique charm despite its overall dilapidation. I was particularly struck by the isolation of the address, right at the outskirts of Arkham proper. A stretch of dreary marsh land bordered the modest backyard.

The "upstairs suite"—two bedrooms separated by a common sitting room—was clean if bare and severe, containing the basic minimum of furniture. From the windows, which faced the rear, one could look out over the acres of marsh to where the wooded hillsides rose, brilliant with spring green—and to Satan's Ledge, which Anable pointed out to me, just visible as a gray protuberance.

The price Mrs. Delisio cited was only too reasonable, and we signed a year's lease on the spot. Mrs. Delisio, an elderly widow, seemed glad to have engaged two Yankee boys as lodgers. Anable announced his intention of taking up residence for the summer, agreeing to pay the whole rent until I joined him in the fall. He said that his mother would probably disapprove, but there was nothing she could do. Her policy had never been to oppose him when he was adamant enough in his wishes—within certain limits. Besides, he had recently secured a job stamping and addressing envelopes and doing other petty tasks for a local bookseller, and thus he figured he could almost cover this new expense with his summer earnings.

III.

After transferring my few belongings to our new quarters on Hale Street and helping Anable move his possessions there, I rode the B. & M. home to Boston, not expecting to return to Arkham until September. I lingered briefly at our residence on narrow, cobbled Acorn Street, before repairing with my family to our house in West Chop, on the island of Martha's Vineyard, for the summer. After the academic rigors of the past year at Miskatonic, I looked forward to the idle months of sailboat racing, tennis playing, and sun bathing. A part-time volunteer job at the Dukes County Historical Society, conducting tours at the venerable Richard C. Norton "Reading Room," would form my excuse for useful employment. My father's harpsichord factory in Cambridge had thrived mightily in recent years, and he was in a position to spend the entire summer on the island, much to the delight of the rest of us, leaving his business to the care of junior partners.

As I settled into the pleasant routine of healthy athletic activities by day (when not at the museum) and gala social events by night (in particular the weekly dances at the Casino), I began sending Anable cheery postcards, urging him to come pay me a visit. His staying in that stuffy apartment all summer, pursuing his esoteric researches in the university library (in between stuffing envelopes and his usual rambles in the countryside), struck me in my agreeable environment as more and more dubious. A change of scene, a little "fun," would be good for my scholarly friend.

These accounts of my idyllic existence elicited a response from Anable that plainly revealed to what an advanced degree he had already become immersed in the offbeat historical lore he had made his special province. (Puzzled at first by the "1728" at the head of the letter, I eventually realized that Anable—antiquarian that he was—affected to date his correspondence two hundred years earlier.) Here is the complete text:

26 June 1728

My dear Winsor:—

How infinitely gratifying to hear from you of your tennis and dancing, and I do appreciate your invitation to come join you in said frivolous diversions. Quite frankly, however, in the light of an exciting development here, I am afraid I haven't the time to indulge in such things. I think you'll understand when you absorb what I say below.

While you've been burning in the sun (by the way, I don't care to tan), I've made an important discovery. You may remember I told you that I intended to read all the material available at the library on those queer Indian ideographs at Satan's Ledge? (Of course, I already knew the general background—but, I must confess, I was rather weak on the more recent history of the formation. Post–Civil War history has never really interested me.) Well, in the course of digging through the stacks, I came across a very curious monograph, "Satan and His Works in Latter-Day New England," printed privately in 1879 by one Thomas Hazard Clarke of Arkham, concerning an odd religious sect that had a settlement near Satan's Ledge in the latter part of the last century. Originally a Shaker splinter group, which Clarke belonged to, this motley assortment of pious fanatics came gradually to fall away from orthodox Christian practices. It seems the more lunatic of them began to assimilate elements of the pagan myths surrounding Satan's Ledge from the few surviving Indians in the region, and took to holding ceremonies at the ledge surreptitiously—"in which the Christian deity had no part." Many of the members, several dozen men of all ages, were dim, stupid folk, degenerate from generations of inbreeding. Clarke and others who continued in the pure faith were naturally alarmed by this ominous conversion among a sizeable portion of the community. The apostates grew in number, as it devolved that somehow their gods or "Old Ones," which they called by the exotic names of "Azathoth," "Nyarlathotep," "Yog-Sothoth," and "Cthulhu" ("agents of the devil" to Clarke), were more receptive to their worship than the aloof-from-the-petty-affairs-of-men traditional God. At last, with the defection of the chief minister, Everett G. Hartnett, to the new "Cthulhu cult," as it became known, they began to practice the blasphemous faith more openly, using the ideographs apparently to aid in "calling down from the sky" some mysterious entity which Clarke guardedly refers to as "the madness out of space." During certain times of secret worship at night among the degenerates, Clarke could detect a horribly foul odour emanating from the direction of the ledge, along with a muted white glow in the atmosphere above it—but he never tried to witness these repulsive ceremonies for himself. When finally the situation became intolerable, Clarke, as leader of the few members remaining true to the original faith, organized his followers into a campaign to suppress the heresy. Unfortunately, at this point in his, hitherto detailed narrative, he becomes vague, hinting merely that after a "great trial," in which he and his men had to resort to means derived from the unclean rituals of the Cthulhuists—and with the assistance of selected Arkham town officials—they succeeded in eradicating the evil. He is specific about a "cataclysm of God" occurring on October 31, 1878, which utterly destroyed the Cthulhu cult—a fire that swept the settlement and burned to the ground every dwelling (tents and flimsy shacks). Most perished in the conflagration, including Hartnett, the few survivors scattering into oblivion. Clarke retired to Arkham, a badly shaken man, but his solid faith along with the help of an alienist, as he candidly admits, sustained him. He warns others of the dangers of deviation from Christianity, closing with a long, pedantic section extolling the virtues of the Congregational Church to which in the end he converted.

Clarke is reasonably precise about the location of the community, and I'm confident that I can find it somewhere to the west of Satan's Ledge when I go look for it tomorrow after work. That fire he speaks of must have thoroughly effaced the site, since undoubtedly I've passed over it in my exploration and not noticed any remains. In fifty years the forest can wholly reclaim a cleared area.

I'll let you know what my search turns up. Until we meet again, and wishing you luck in the forthcoming holiday races, I am

Yr. Humble Servt, HWA

My reaction to this incredible missive can scarcely be imagined. As I studied its substance, the initial indignation I had felt at Anable's cavalier dismissal of my invitation and aspersions on my summer lifestyle gave way to an ambivalent sense of skepticism and wonder. This Cthulhu cult business was indeed an intriguing mystery, but evidently this Thomas Clarke was some kind of half-baked religious crank who had made up most—if not all—of this wild story. (Funny that Anable seemed to accept the narrative almost at face value.) Yet, even if the element of truth was small, here was a peculiar historical footnote of the sort to satisfy Anable's longing for the *outré*.

I did not have to wait a week before hearing the sequel.

1 July 1728

Winsor:—

Eureka! Success! Forgive this uncharacteristic outburst of elation, but truly marvel grows upon marvel. I've discovered what I believe is the former cult site. I'll concede my conclusion isn't based on any direct evidence, for I found no charred relics—rather in a part of the woods a quarter-mile northwest of Satan's Ledge, where the trees are relatively sparse, there stands a makeshift hovel, which could only have been erected within the last couple of weeks. I can tell someone is living in it from the rough mat and store of supplies inside. No, I haven't met its inhabitant. But I've caught glimpses of him, an elderly man in tattered, nondescript garments, in its vicinity and at Satan's Ledge—where I nearly surprised him in the act of carving fresh ideographs into the rocks, in an apparent effort to restore those obliterated by weather and time. These, when I examined them, proved, crude as they were, not to be mere copies or tourist graffiti—but new designs consistent with legible existing ones. I'd evidently interrupted him in the midst of his work, because when I returned the next day there were several more carved into the brittle granite. I've not come close to catching this individual since our near encounter at the ledge, try as I might—and lately I've been thinking that maybe it's a bit unwise for me to attempt it alone.

To speak plainly, would you mind coming up to Arkham to help me run this fellow to ground? If we could only talk to him I suspect he could tell us a fascinating story or two about the ledge and the ideographs and, who knows, perhaps the cult. Surely after the 4th celebrations Wednesday you could take some time off. Possibly this coming weekend? Anxiously awaiting your reply, I am

Yr. Servt. H.

I reacted to this second letter from Anable, received on the 3rd, with a great deal of confusion. Where before he had simply outlined a fanciful if disquieting story from a pamphlet in a library, now he had ventured into the physical reality of the Arkham woods and found a real mystery—an innocuous one on the surface to my mind and yet a touch sinister, if one could credit the Clarke monograph at all. Reluctant to miss the Fireman's Ball in Edgartown on Saturday night but eager to assist my friend, I wired him to say that he could expect me Thursday, with the condition that I had to be back on the island by the evening of the 7th. I departed the morning of the 5th, a successful Fourth of July race series behind me.

Upon my arrival, Anable impatiently rushed through the civilities and described his plan to me. We would get up before dawn, the idea being that our chances of catching the inhabitant of the hovel were better the earlier we reached the site. An inveterate night owl whose natural tendency was to stay up to three or four in the morning and then sleep well past noon, Anable was grateful for my presence if only to ensure his waking up at the appointed hour. Accordingly, we set the alarm for 5:00 A.M. and retired. Anable was glad I had been exercising regularly, since we would be approaching the ledge by the steep route. As I was weary from traveling much of the day—by ferry, by motorcoach, and by train—I fell asleep instantly on the bed my chum had thoughtfully made up for me.

The next morning after a breakfast of coffee and crackers and cheese (standard fare for Anable), we stole silently from the house in the half-light of an already warmish day and going a block east hit Route 127, the main north-south road that follows the coast of the North Shore. At this point in its sinuous course, just north of Arkham, 127 swings to the west and runs through an unpopulated stretch of woods, bordered by salt marshes on its eastern fringes. (Though Satan's Ledge was only about a mile and a half away as the crow flies from 973 Hale Street, these marshes prevented us from reaching it directly.)

Farms had prospered in this region as late as the early nineteenth century, but had gone into rapid decline during the War of 1812 and the succeeding period of economic stagnation. One could hardly believe that where white pine and birch now stood once waved fields of corn, beans, tomatoes, and carrots, acre after acre in the rocky New England soil. Stone walls, in want of mending or in places simply heaps of rubble, ran nowhere through the trees and brush, mute testimony to the old property lines.

We did not keep for long to this main thoroughfare, however, but shortly took a left turn onto one of the occasional dirt roads leading into the forest interior. We must have followed this for a couple of hundred yards before coming to a fork, where Anable selected the more overgrown path (for it no longer could be properly called a road). Though the branches of the trees we passed under blocked much of the little light there was, Anable never faltered and showed no hesitation in his choice of direction when we encountered other forks in the course of our journey. Midges and other flying insects pestered us, and we swatted at these without much effect. As the ground rose perceptibly, I started to perspire.

Finally, we were picking our way along what was at best a faint animal trail in the thick of the woods. All at once a steep slope, more nearly accurately a cliff, emerged before us and we began the precipitous climb Anable had warned me about. Above loomed the gray eminence of Satan's Ledge.

After many minutes of toil we stood, panting on the flat surface of the ledge. The sun was above the horizon by this time, and we admired the view of Arkham below and the sea beyond shimmering in the dawn. A lovely sight, but nothing, averred Anable, like its appearance at sunset.

Before showing me the new ideographs and checking for any more recent carving, Anable pointed out in disgust the "signs" that other, undesirable types (certainly not our man) had left to advertise their visits. Debris littered the rock floor; cigarette butts, paper wrappers, a beer bottle or two, and—upon part of the ledge covered by a smooth layer of soft earth or humus—several flattened, translucent balloons with wide mouths, resembling the hydra or some other primitive marine animal. (I had noticed this same peculiar detritus washed in great numbers on Martin's Beach near

Gloucester, where my family used to summer in the days prior to our acquiring the Vineyard house.)

We surveyed this sorry spectacle but for a moment before Anable directed my attention to what was of prime importance. On the great, most easterly boulder stood out four rows of bizarre figures—a sequence of alien hieroglyphics whose outlines vaguely suggested odd animal forms rather than abstract characters. These incised figures, each six inches or so in height, proved on closer inspection to be highlighted by a dullish red pigment ground into the contours. They ran roughly in horizontal lines, about a dozen to each line, as regularly as the irregular surface of the granite allowed. Anable calculated that they had been created over a period of two weeks, at the rate of three or four a day. Original, worn figures had been carved over to form a kind of palimpsest. Other boulders had many fewer inscribed markings, we noted.

Once I had satisfied myself with my first view of these astonishing glyphs, Anable led me deeper into the trees in a northwesterly direction. Nature was very much evident at this hour—a rabbit scampered out of sight ahead, squirrels and chipmunks chattered at us as they scurried along branches, and above the pine tops I spotted the distinctive, "flying cigar" forms of chimney swifts gliding soundlessly, along with a stray green heron aimed for the marshes behind and below us. Fallen tree trunks white with fungi oozed the odor of decay—a not unpleasant scent.

After a fifteen-minute trek the woods and undergrowth thinned and we came out into a clearing. Wild flowers grew in spectacular clumps here, covering any sign of former human habitation—for this, conjectured Anable, was where the religious colony had been planted almost fifty years ago.

We crossed the expanse of clearing to where the trees began to grow thick again by a stream, and there beneath a great pine bough was a lean-to, or more accurately perhaps, tee-pee about five feet high. Peering cautiously inside, we saw a tarpaulin and blankets, a small cupboard, an ax, and other camping gear. A pile of ashes and blackened wood circled by stones in front bespoke the remains of a fire. Nearby on the ground rested a chisel and mallet, plus a stick of red chalk.

"Hello, young fellers," cried a hearty voice. "Up kind of early, ain't you, for a nature walk?"

We both turned around at once to observe, coming out of a pine copse about fifteen yards to our right, a short, thickly built, elderly man—smiling at us and tugging at his pants. He wore what amounted to a suit of earth-colored rags, and more than a touch of redness rimmed his eyes, the only part of his face visible in the great, gray mass of hair and whiskers that covered his head. He reminded me of the sort of slovenly rustic one tried to avoid noticing loafing around the Arkham Trailways station. Despite his decrepit clothing, he appeared to have a robust physique, and showed none of the faltering slowness of the aged as he advanced a few steps toward us, then halted. If not for his cheerful tone of voice and ingratiating manner, I would have thought him a very threatening fellow.

"What business have you boys in this stretch of the woods?" he asked. Anable answered that he often took walks in the Arkham hills, and had done so most of his life. Shifting to the offensive, my friend asked in turn what he was doing camping in these parts, and whether he had a permit.

"Well, my lad, I must tell you I'm no newcomer to this beautiful country," said he, looking appreciatively about, "though it's been a good many years since I set foot here—long before you youngsters were toddling around nosing into your elder's affairs. I was camped on this land when a person didn't need a permit to set up a house. Least we didn't bother with one . . . Maybe that's why we had to leave all of a sudden." He chuckled, enjoying his private joke.

Anable asked if he had had anything to do with the "Shaker" community that used to be located at this site—and was he around at the time of the "cataclysm of God" that had destroyed it.

"Oh, you've heard of that, have you? Thought folks had hushed that up ages ago. Not something people in polite circles in Arkham would talk about, even at the time."

Anable said that he had studied the Clarke monograph, "Satan and His Works in Latter-Day New England," and persisted in his questioning.

"So you've read that packet of lies that parsimonious prig slandered our memory with. . . . Yeah, I guess I was a part of it. But before I say more, who be you? And who be your quiet friend?"

My comrade introduced himself as Howard Wentworth Anable of Arkham, Massachusetts, and me as his fellow Miskatonic student, E. Phillips Winsor. Did I detect a happy gleam in the old man's eye, an abrupt perking up, at the mention of Anable's name?

"Glad to meet you, Mr. Anable, Mr. Winsor," he said, nodding to each of us, with a certain mock deference. With an enthusiasm lacking before he said, "Harper is my name. Jay Harper." I was grateful to be at a distance, as

I had no desire to shake the paw of this unkempt vagabond.

"Yeah, I did belong to the sect. I was a youth then, not much older than you boys. In '76 it was. My people, they come from far up the valley—of good sound stock, mind you. My governor practiced law when he wasn't running the general store—sent me to Yale College for a spell, but Yale and me didn't hit it off and so we parted company.

"I had a hankering to wander, and came to Arkham since I heard the mills needed strong, healthy chaps like me. But I guess I was too late, 'cause I couldn't find a job right away. In the meantime, I became friendly with some of the members of this religious community in the hills who said it was okay for me to make my home with them—not that I was ever a devout churchgoer, but it was a lot cheaper than staying in lodgings in town. Later, when I got a mill job, I kept where I was. I had a wild streak then, and I came to see that what those folks were up to was kind of exciting. . . . If that self-righteous blockhead Tim Clarke hadn't meddled in business he had no understanding of . . ." Harper glowered. "Satan's Ledge, huh! Clarke with all his Bible learning could only figure things in Christian terms. We called it by a more suitable name, of course."

Harper smiled wistfully, adding sadly, "Well, if you've read that stupid 'treatise' of his you know the upshot. Poor Hartnett, he meant no harm. I was lucky to get away from that burning mess alive. I went back to Dunwich, where I've worked ever since for Whateley's Tree Service. Never been back to Arkham till now."

Harper paused, casting his eyes down on the chisel and mallet waiting for use. Anable asked why he had returned—and why he was carving new ideographs—and what was their significance.

"Now, son, don't be overinquisitive—one question at a time. Let's just say that I'm indulging myself in a show of sentimental reminiscence. Preparing the stage the way we used to before performing the rituals. I'm carving them from memory for old time's sake, you understand. There's no harm in it—we weren't bothering anyone outside the cult. As for their meaning, I might tell you another time . . ." His throaty chuckle after this remark made me flinch.

"See here, lads, maybe . . . maybe you can help me out. If you do, I'll tell you some secrets about the old cult that few persons alive today could begin to guess at. . . . I'm running low on supplies, and would be obliged to you if you would buy me some groceries. In my state I'm afraid I'd draw too much unkindly attention if I was to go into town myself." He pulled out an oily sheet from his jacket, along with some dollar bills more brown than green. "Here's my list of what I need, and to show you how much I trust you boys"—he was looking straight at Anable—"I'm giving you the money now, no collateral. Do this for me and come back here in a few days and I promise I'll tell you some tales I think you'd like to hear. . . ." So saying, he passed the bills to Anable, who nodded in apparent assent.

Jay Harper retrieved his chisel and mallet, along with his red chalk stick, and escorted us back to the ledge, explaining that he could only get his work done there at odd hours—when snoops like ourselves were not around to disturb him.

"Our mysterious character-carver should reveal a thing or two of real interest, I think," declared Anable as we clambered gingerly down the slope. "Doesn't seem to be a dangerous sort either—though I was glad to have you standing by, Winsor. My impulse is to help out the old geezer, buy him his groceries. Too bad you can't stay around to see for yourself what happens."

My reaction to our meeting with this queer hill person was somewhat less enthusiastic than my companion's. When I told him so, he simply laughed and dismissed me as an old maid.

At my departure for Arkham the next morning, Anable renewed his vow to apprise me of further developments. Making the right connections, I was back on the island in sufficient time to attend the Fireman's Ball.

IV.

A month passed before I heard from Anable again, a longer interval than I might have expected in view of his eager anticipation of revelations to come when I left him. Had the old ruffian disappeared on him? Or had Harper's tales turned out to be so disappointing that Anable was ashamed to report on them to me? In any event, this Harper character was clearly a demented fool who was not to be relied upon as far as I was concerned.

Anable's letter (dated normally for once) read as follows:

August 8, 1928

My dear W:—

Pardon the delay, but I've been so absorbed in matters here that I've not been able to concentrate long enough to write even the briefest note. Between the necessary drudgery of licking envelopes at Dawber & Pyne and my conferences with Harper, I've hardly had a moment to eat or sleep!

Let me begin by assuring you that our forest friend has proved informative beyond my wildest imaginings.

I returned with the groceries two days after our initial encounter, taking the more roundabout but easier route from the picnic grounds considering my load. A bottle of bootleg whiskey I'd included as a surprise did much to encourage Harper's natural garrulousness, and he spoke to me for hours about the cult while I listened in wonder. Gad, what this man knows! What he has experienced! Harper informed me that he had had vivid dreams, growing in persistency, that drove him back to the settlement site—and in those dreams a cultivated young man figured prominently. When I'd said my name that first meeting, he'd known instantly that it was I he'd seen in his dreams! He interprets this as a sign that I can be of invaluable service to him. When he asked for my help (and not just in supplying him with groceries), I readily agreed. Forgive me for not being specific on the nature of his purposes—even I'm not really sure—but Harper has made it a condition of our "pact" that I confide in no one, not even you, dear fellow. Already I say too much. The potential reward for me is tremendous, and I trust you'll understand when I tell you I don't want to jeopardize my chances to earn it.

Suffice to say that now that Harper has finished engraving the glyphs (the ones he hadn't remembered from his youth came to him in visions), he requires the consultation of certain arcane books available in the locked stacks of the Miskatonic library. In particular, he wishes me to transcribe passages from Abdul Alhazred's *Necronomicon*, perhaps the rarest and most marvelous tome in the collection. As a Miskatonic student, I of course would be granted access to this volume more readily than he. I applied to the head librarian, Dr. Henry Armitage, who permitted me—albeit reluctantly—to copy from it. Harper could only provide me from memory with approximate locations of the pertinent passages, with a vague outline of their content. (The cult's copy was lost in the flames of '78.) My Latin proved fair enough, however, for me to determine from the context which lines were relevant.

Harper was pleased with the material I collected, and wanted me to make a second trip to the library for further transcription. Unfortunately, the next time I went to continue my research, on the 3rd, I was disappointed. Dr. Armitage, who has gone into seclusion at his house and refuses to see a soul, has left instructions forbidding anyone to be shown the *Necronomicon*. Harper greeted this ill turn of fortune with dismay, but thinks what I managed to get copied down before may be sufficient. Our progress is delayed, yet other resources do exist.

Looking forward to catching up in person fall term, I remain

Yr. Servt. HWA

So, Anable had taken to humoring the old half-wit in his crazy pursuits. I was beginning to grow alarmed, recalling that the *Necronomicon* had been furtively discussed among the decadent circles I had spurned as a book of colossal, cosmic evil. For the first time it struck me that Anable might be losing sight of reality. His account of his servility to Harper served to confirm my distrust of that scruffy creature. When I wrote Anable back, I told him as politely as possible that I disapproved of Harper and that he ought to keep away from him. In reply I got a short note from Anable, pervaded by a wounded, defensive tone, saying that I was regarding the situation in the wrong way and would understand better when he could explain things to me face to face in the fall.

The remainder of the summer passed pleasantly for me. It culminated spectacularly in an all-night Labor Day weekend aboard our yawl, *Arethusa,* anchored off the West Chop light. With this fête fresh in my memory, I anticipated the return to Miskatonic and reunion with Anable in a gay, trouble-free mood, the very opposite of the one I had sunk into at the time of receiving his unsettling letter.

V.

To say that Anable had subtly changed by the time I arrived back in Arkham in mid-September would be an understatement. As I stepped off the B. & M. coach at the station, he greeted me with an energy and effusiveness that I was wholly unaccustomed to. His usually languid brown eyes were animated, almost mirthful. He exhibited none of the somber demeanor so characteristic of him, and his pace was quicker than ever.

"Great and wonderful things are in the offing, Winsor," exclaimed my buoyant buddy as we settled ourselves on the trolley. "I've gotten to know our friend Harper pretty well in a couple of months. He's really quite a respectable fellow—a decent, middle-class Yankee, and a college man to boot (at least he was for a while). A pity he's had hard luck. But with a few changes of clothing I've provided him—well, it's made a big difference, as you'll see. . . ."

Anable paused a moment slightly embarrassed. "I have to warn you, Winsor, that I've allowed Harper to use your room, to stay overnight from time to time during damp weather. But of course now that you're back, he'll return to the woods for good. Besides, he now has company."

I looked quizzical.

"Yes, others have joined our survivor. There're presently several of his former cult members living on the old site. They, too, have heard the call—in their dreams just as Harper did—and have gathered from disparate parts of the country. They've set up a regular small camp—nothing like on the scale of the original, of course."

I watched the houses become sparser as we approached the end of the line, and for the first time regretted my decision to move out of the comparative civilization of the university dorms. I was not at ease as we tramped the short length of the front walk and marched up the stairs to the second floor of 973 Hale Street.

As we entered the sitting room, a gentleman arose from the sofa whom I did not immediately recognize as the bedraggled individual I had met in the woods in the summer. His shock of hair was combed, and his sturdy frame was decked out in a clean checked shirt, denim trousers, and brand new work boots. This time I shook hands with Jay Harper. Apparently, he had been reading, for next to him on the end table and on the sofa itself were scattered a number of battered, dirty-looking books.

"Well, Howard, I thank you again for letting me read at your place," said the old man. "Fine titles these books are. It'd be a shame if I had to store them in the tee-pee where the moisture'd get at them. Good day to you both." He picked up his jacket and strode out the door.

Glancing down at one of the more modern volumes on the sofa, I saw that it was the shocking *Goblin Tower* by Frank Belknap Long. A quick survey revealed that the rest were just as dismal—among them *Melmoth the Wanderer*, R. W. Chambers's *The King in Yellow*, Bierce's *In the Midst of Life*, and Lord Dunsany's *A Dreamer's Tales* in the Modern Library pocket edition.

Noting my look of distaste, Anable made a half-hearted effort to allay my worries.

"While working at Dawber & Pyne this summer," he began, "I had the chance to search through their stock of secondhand books. Amazing what they kept lying around in dusty cartons in the attic. Because of their poor condition, I was able to pick them up for a steal. Harper made a few suggestions on what to keep my eye out for and choose. His knowledge of the literature in the field is truly profound. I discovered more interesting works than I thought existed. They've been a great help in filling in the gaps in the data we culled from the *Necronomicon*. Just because an author writes 'fiction' doesn't mean he doesn't put some important truths into his books, whether intentionally or not.

"Don't be alarmed—we're not out to destroy the world," he said, smiling. "It's all simply a personal concern that doesn't affect anybody else."

I was not persuaded by these arguments to disarm me. I said nothing, and went into my bedroom to arrange my effects that had been shipped in advance of my arrival.

Despite his initial show of friendliness, Anable displayed little interest in me or my affairs in succeeding weeks. I resented this behavior, and now and then told him he was involved in a lot of rubbish—but he continued to ignore me. Harper came to the apartment twice in the next month for conferences with Anable, held in his room with the door shut. (Had there been a lock on it I have no doubt he would have used it.) My roommate made frequent trips to the vicinity of Satan's Ledge—or so I assumed, for he rarely bothered to tell me of his plans before going out. He never asked me to join him. When I ventured to mention my feelings of exclusion, Anable assured me that he would reveal what he and Harper were up to at the appropriate time. I must remain patient.

In any event, I had my course work to absorb me. "Eighteenth-Century Gothick Taste in England," "Literature of the Restoration" (with an emphasis on Shadwell), "Differential Equations," and "American Transcendentalism" (taught by Professor Albert N. Wilmarth, who started the class a week late owing, rumor had it, to an upsetting, overnight visit to Vermont shortly before the term began) kept me immersed in my books for long hours. Anable, on the other hand, scarcely opened a text, his dubious collection of the weird forming his chief reading material. He often cut classes, an evening course in "Medieval Metaphysics" being the only one he attended faithfully. In sum, he was no longer the conscientious student of the previous year. I feared for his scholarship status.

At the apartment Anable alternated between extremes of moods. Either he would shuffle about in a state of suppressed agitation, or else would lounge around the sitting room in his dressing gown, sunk in lassitude. In this latter condition he seemed to be daydreaming, utterly oblivious of me or his surroundings.

I felt compassion for him just once, when he announced to me that his mother had had to sell two ornately carved, Jacobean chairs that had been in the family for generations in order to buy a new refrigerator. He moped for a week, and I was genuinely sorry for him.

VI.

When, out of kindness, I asked Anable if he cared to accompany me to a Halloween party the 31st, he shook his head.

"I appreciate your concern for my social life, Winsor," he answered, "but I'm afraid I'm going to be busy with Harper and his friends that night. You might say we have a party of our own to attend in observance of the Hallowmass. If it turns out as I have every expectation it will, I can assure you— at long last, my dear fellow—of a complete and satisfactory explanation."

Of what Anable did not specify—and I did not inquire further. The truth is, I had become intimidated by Anable's actions. I faced the painful fact that by now he was not in his right mind—he was already far gone in his involvement in these outlandish pursuits, and it would do no good to confront him head-on. Recalling his injunction to me to help him retain his "sense of proportion," I resolved at that moment to go on Halloween to Satan's Ledge, where surely he and his unsavory companions would be congregating, and observe their goings-on in secret. This would be a risky business to be certain, but I felt given Anable's evasiveness that I had to obtain information first-hand and assess how dangerous this evidently revived cult was to him. I no longer had confidence in his promise of revelation.

During the week prior to the 31st, Anable spent more and more time away from 973 Hale Street, presumably with his comrades in the forest hills. When I returned to the apartment after classes, he would be gone. I would be in bed asleep before he came back, his closed door in the morning the only indication he had done so. I saw him once or twice, and then fleetingly.

The day before Halloween I noticed a brown bag on the sitting room desk. Anable must have brought it in earlier that afternoon. Thinking it contained groceries, I casually looked inside. To my surprise I found a curious assortment of chemicals in glass jars as might belong to a boy's chemistry set: uniodized salt, sulphur, iron filings, compounds of cobalt, magnesium, nickel, zinc, and mercury. Among his other solitary childhood pastimes, I remembered Anable once saying that he had been passionately devoted to chemistry. Was this evidence of a resurgence of interest in that hobby? Again, I hesitated to ask.

That Wednesday around 3:00, when I got back from Miskatonic, Anable was pacing about the sitting room, as intensely agitated as I had ever seen him. He scarcely acknowledged my entry. "The dreams, Winsor, the magnificent dreams!" he exclaimed and rushed into his room.

An hour later Anable emerged dressed in his worn winter coat and carrying his sack of chemicals. "Please bear with me," he pleaded, his brown eyes begging my understanding, as he ran out. For a second I softened and forgot my annoyance with him, overcome by a surge of pity for the fellow. I should not really blame Anable for his deplorable state—Harper and his disreputable cultists were the ones responsible. They had taken in my unworldly friend with their elaborate Cthulhu mumbo-jumbo. If I could catch them this night causing him any harm, psychological or otherwise, I would blow the whistle on them in a minute and call in the Arkham authorities. I had already confided my fears to Mrs. Anable, who agreed that her son was under bad influences.

Leaving at dusk for my party, I drove the Model J Duesenberg my father had given me for my birthday earlier in the month into Arkham center. A paper bag with cut-out eyes would serve me as a simple costume. I spent several agreeable hours drinking cider and bobbing for apples at the Zeta Psi house, then set out on the serious mission of my Halloween night.

Since it would be hopeless for me to try in the dark to follow the forest trail Anable had led me on in the summer, let alone scale the steep slope to the ledge, I decided to take the more roundabout route of my original visit there. Besides, now that I was in possession of a motorcar, distance was no obstacle. I headed inland out Miskatonic Avenue, which runs along the river, to where it hits the Bolton Road. The moon had risen, and the beams of my headlamps illuminated the autumn leaves swirling and eddying in the cold breeze. An exhilarating and magical air suffused the landscape. In high spirits from the quantity of cider I had imbibed, I approached this uncertain rendezvous free of any apprehension. It was almost a lark.

My watch showed a little past 11:00 by the time I parked at the picnic area. In the moonlight with foliage above thinner than in warmer months, I had no trouble locating the path to Satan's Ledge. I kept to this at first, but not wishing to encounter possible sentinels, I strayed to the left and began a cautious circling movement through the woods, which were dense enough to afford adequate concealment. I was able to make my way with a minimum of stumbling as I worked up to gradually higher ground.

I was acutely aware of the noises in the brush and trees—the rustle of swaying boughs, the trickle of a distant stream, an owl hoot, a jay's cry. But soon I heard another sound, an unfamiliar one, a soft, rhythmic moaning, as if the forest itself was breathing. Ahead of me I began to catch glimpses through the branches and undergrowth of flickering, bobbing points of light—but it was too late in the season for fireflies. They seemed to be receding at the same rate as I advanced. As I continued my slow, upward progress, I realized that these were flames—candle flames. As I approached nearer still, I could perceive that each candle was held by a dim human form. A half dozen men were walking in Indian file toward Satan's Ledge— for now at last in the faint light of the moon and candles I could make out the rough, Cyclopean boulders on the ledge's inner rim. I lay down behind a fallen birch trunk about thirty yards away, not daring to go closer.

The men proceeded across the rock floor of the ledge and arranged themselves very deliberately in a semicircle in front of and facing the great easterly boulder with its graven ideographs. From my low vantage point I had an unobstructed view of this scene. All of those in this strange procession (though I could only see their backs) appeared to be elderly folk, except for one—from his hurried, stooping gait I could not mistake Anable. The air was curiously still on the ledge, the flames stirring hardly at all—and the surrounding woods now seemed unnaturally quiet, the continuous, monotonous chanting the only sound.

Abruptly, the cultists crouched down, bowed before the rock. One figure remained standing—the mass of hair and beard marked him as Harper. He moved to the center of the semicircle, set down his candle by the boulder's base, and drew from his jacket an object that I thought at first was a mallet—but it was a pipe, for he raised it to his mouth and blew three low, loathsome notes. The others ceased the moronic chanting instantly in response. Harper next pulled from his jacket a small, glittering container and started methodically to march around behind the huddled group and scatter a powdery substance from it with his fingertips. Soon emptying its contents, he withdrew another and repeated the process, and so for several jars until he had covered the length of the semicircle and enclosed the band from one edge of the great boulder to the other. Thus were the chemicals Anable had purchased put to use.

Done with this seemingly pointless ritual, Harper rejoined the congregants, squatting down with them at one end of their semicircle. They then raised their heads in unison to the rock and commenced to pour out, as if reading the blasphemous glyphs, an uncouth string of syllables in a language that not only bore no relation to English but to no sane human tongue on this planet.

"*Cthulhu fhtagn,*" they recited over and over.

With the cry of "*Iä, Iä, Shub-Niggurath,*" an indescribably foetid odor swept down upon me from the direction of the ledge. I almost swooned as

I closed my eyes in disgust. My nausea stemmed from not only the ghastly stench itself but also from the sudden remembrance of Anable's description of certain events outlined in Clarke's monograph. Here these crazed cultists—and my brash friend—were reënacting an unholy ceremony of the sort practiced fifty years ago on this spot! I trembled, no longer the bold spy of a short time before.

I had barely mastered my nausea, the vile odor having passed within moments, when I opened my eyes to see, atop the graven boulder, a shrouded human figure—who must have scaled the rock from behind and emerged in the instant I had them shut. A great wind had sprung up and whistled and howled around this apparition, blowing his immaculate white robe in billows and nearly extinguishing the flames of the candles of the worshippers clustered below him. Emanating a brilliant glow of purest white, this luminous, lithe-limbed being glided down the nearly vertical granite face to the ledge floor, while the hideous glyphs burned a dark red as if reflecting his radiance. I could clearly discern his dazzling features—he was smooth-faced, delicately boned, and boyish, with the almond eyes of an antique pharaoh. From his crown luxuriant, silken, gold hair flowed as if electrically charged. I was more in awe than frightened—indeed, overcome by the unearthly beauty of this personage. I was transfixed.

One of the crouched celebrants rose—it was Anable—and approached this exquisite, godlike creature. Harper and the rest remained prostrate. Anable knelt before him and raised his face and clasped his hands in supplication. The gorgeous youth began to speak, to murmur to Anable, but the wind had built to such a frantic pitch that I could catch nothing, though I believe he was using English. After communing with Anable for what seemed like aeons, he bent over and embraced and enveloped my friend in his wavering folds. They blended into one writhing, amorphous mass, Anable invisible in the voluminous robe—then they almost poured back to the graven rock and began effortlessly to ascend its steep face.

At this point I could endure it no longer. I lurched forward from my hiding place and ran screaming, "Anable! Oh, Howard! Watch out!" Perhaps emboldened by my liquor, perhaps driven by some mad, selfless instinct, I hastened to try to save my chum. Damn the risk! What had I to fear after all from a half-dozen old people, whom I could fast outrun if need be? As for the fragile fellow who had swallowed up my friend, I was suddenly overwhelmed with rage and hatred for him. I didn't know whether to kiss it or kill it! All that mattered was rescuing my companion from his willowy clutches.

I had barely mastered my nausea . . .

Incredibly, I succeeded in my immediate attempt to cause disruption. The celebrants turned around in bewilderment, then hurried to their feet, extinguishing their tapers, and raced off in panic into the woods as I charged them, brandishing a stout birch limb and wearing my paper bag mask for added effect. The white-robed youth hesitated, then lowered the inert form of my friend gently to the rock floor, finally mounting the boulder again and swiftly disappearing over its top edge—he would have a difficult climb down the steep slope beyond.

Only Harper of the fleeing cultists paused. "Curse you, boy!" he bellowed. "You've spoiled his initiation. Woe be to you, my lad!" Then he slipped with the rest into the darkness.

Guided by the moonlight, I rushed to where Anable lay prone on the rock. He was stunned and babbling: "The Great Old Ones . . . Cthulhu's Ledge . . . I was so close . . . Azathoth." Sheer nonsense, of course.

Frightened that the Cthulhuists might regroup and come after us once recovering from their surprise, I hoisted Anable to his feet, first ascertaining that he was in no pain. To my relief I found him ambulatory and was able to lead him by the path quickly back to the picnic grounds and the safety of my Model J.

During the frenzied drive back to Arkham, Anable continued his wild mutterings. At first incoherent, he abruptly began to speak in lucid sentences, albeit rapidly and with a terrific intensity, his brown eyes glazed.

"Yes, Winsor, I have met the Old Ones' avatar . . . who told me of marvels beyond the galling limitations of time and space as we conceive of them. I learned where Henri Rousseau had obtained his models for the jungle creatures in that curious and unsettling painting of his, 'The Children of the Kingdom.' And the primitive tribes of Guatemala and the Dutch East Indies archipelago are not the only repositories of secrets that would drive the mass of mankind mad if they were known. The woods of New Jersey, just a few miles from the Pest Zone euphemistically called New York City, contain creeping, insidious, eldritch horror, which threatens at any moment to erupt and spew over the land (a result I wouldn't mind seeing if it meant the destruction of that hateful burg). Nor even are the Connecticut suburbs safe . . .

"I learned, too, of those dark and dangerous forces that flop and flounder at the galaxy's rim. . . . This goes infinitely beyond man's feeble morality. We're no more significant than the least bacterial scum in the larger scheme of the universe. The Old Ones have spared us worthless wretches so far because we count for so little. They may appear 'malign' to certain self-blinded earth-gazers, but are in fact indifferent—except to the occasional exceptional individual, to whom They may give the opportunity for the realization of and *participation in* the awesome secrets of time and space. There is a chance for human transcendence. Many hear the call, but few will heed it and be chosen. *Iä! Iä! Shub-Niggurath,* the Goat with a Thousand Young!"

At this last burst of insanity Anable trailed off again into gibberish, only to cry a minute later: "Oh but, Winsor, you fool! So much more could I have found out, unimaginable wonders, if you hadn't interrupted. Damn you!" With this imprecation he lapsed into permanent silence, slumped down in the seat beside me. His lack of gratitude stung, but I could hardly judge him harshly in the circumstances. Surely now it was essential that he sever all ties with Harper and company, who had brought him to this woeful condition.

Barely conscious or able to walk, Anable with my help staggered up the stairs and into his room where I eased him onto his bed. Thank God our dreadful Halloween night was over.

VII.

Anable spent the next several weeks in a state of utter collapse. Naturally, the morning after our harrowing misadventure at Satan's Ledge, I notified Mrs. Anable that her son had taken seriously ill, sparing her the worst of the details. She arranged for the family doctor to come to examine him at the apartment as soon as possible. Dr. MacDonald could find no signs of physical injury, but in the light of my guarded account concluded that Anable must have suffered some kind of severe nervous shock that had rendered him powerless. When after two days Anable did regain consciousness, he was too weak to speak or get about on his own. It was clear that he could no longer remain at 973 Hale Street. With the aid of stalwart Dr. MacDonald, I succeed in transferring Anable in my vehicle to his family's Valley Street home. Mrs. Delisio, tearfully watching the doctor and me carry the patient outside, remarked what a pity that such a polite, mannerly young man should be so grievously afflicted.

Mrs. Anable was reluctant to call in the authorities, but she worried about the cultists who had harmed her son lurking still in the woods, and requested that I and some friends scout around the Satan's Ledge area. A week after Halloween, I persuaded three classmates—Messrs. Haiblum, Sullivan, and Klein—to accompany me on a "bird walk" (such was my excuse) during the day to see if Harper and company were around or not. In the course of our bird sighting, I discovered no trace of human habitation other than discarded garbage. Perhaps with the onset of colder weather they had dispersed, returning to their places of origin. Nevertheless, a clever woodsman like Harper could easily evade detection and survive the winter outdoors if he had to. Mrs. Anable was relieved to hear my report that they had apparently pulled up stakes and departed.

I visited Anable at least once a week during his confinement at home. Sitting by his bedside, I filled him in on campus news and the progress of my courses—careful not to mention the cult or Satan's Ledge or the disturbing doings Halloween night. Though capable of speaking for brief intervals (according to his mother), Anable chose to keep silent at these interviews. Indeed, he often closed his eyes, as if overcome by weariness, and turned his head to the wall away from me. When his luminous brown eyes were open, they seemed to stare at me, as if with—could it be?—resentment. I was generous enough not to take this as a personal slight, but rather attributed it to the grave mental strain he had undergone, perhaps coupled with a resumption of that natural reserve that shut out even his best friend.

Anable's physical health did improve steadily, however, and he regained sufficient strength to walk unassisted by the end of November. By early December he could leave the house on short trips. But, having a constitutional aversion to cold weather, aggravated by his present weakened condition, Anable could not remain outside for very long. This was one fortunate complication, for he had begun to express a desire to revisit the ledge, so Mrs. Anable confided to me. She did not wish him to return to the scene of his traumatic experience, and made me promise to do everything in my power to prevent him from doing so.

His mental state, alas, did not change much for the better. Anable continued to be withdrawn and apathetic—as if he had expended all the tremendous energy that had been building within him since summer in one shot that Halloween night, with none left to sustain him for the rest of the year. The dean of the university showed his understanding when he allowed Anable to take incompletes in his fall subjects, at no penalty to his scholarship status.

When I returned to Arkham following the Christmas vacation, I was pleased to find Anable had resumed residence in our Hale Street apartment.

His greeting was effusive, yet somehow perfunctory, lacking the warmth of the previous reunions. At least he was displaying more liveliness.

"Ah, Winsor," he exclaimed, "trust you enjoyed the holidays. Happy 1929! Dr. MacDonald has judged me well enough to get back to my studies at Miskatonic—which I can tell you I'm eager to do. An invalid's existence is a terrific bore.

"As for the cult business, let me put your mind to rest on all that. You needn't feel anxious for me anymore. I realize now I was fooling with forces that no person with his wits about him should ever get mixed up in. I'd become so immersed in arcane lore, shall we say, that I'd lost all perspective—just as I warned you I might. I have to admit you were correct to be suspicious of Harper. He was luring me into the midst of a sinister 'cosmic conspiracy'—but you showed up out of the blue and saved me in the nick of time. I'm through with it now for good, believe me. I'll not bring up the subject again—and I'll appreciate it if you won't say anything about it either. Let's forget about it. It's in the past."

So, instead of a truthful explanation of what he had been involved in, Anable gave me this assurance of his reform. Well, by this point I knew more than I cared to about this Cthulhu cult and was satisfied that it was all a lot of mysterious, mystical claptrap that had dazzled and misguided my friend. I was content to let the matter drop, hopeful that this was indeed the end of it.

Unsteady on his feet as he still was, Anable was nonetheless able to get to and from classes on his own via the trolley. He applied himself more dutifully to his studies than in the first term, yet I sensed his heart was not really in his work. On more than one occasion, I caught him gazing out the sitting room window toward Satan's Ledge. And more than once, I suspect, he attempted to walk to the ledge by the direct, steep route—but the ice and snow must have thwarted him. When he asked me to drive him to the picnic area off the Bolton Road, I refused. He glared at me for a second, then subsided into a disappointed sulk. Unwilling, I suppose, to appear too keen on the idea of a return journey, he never brought it up again.

As the bleak winter term wore on, Anable made less and less of an effort to be sociable. Listless for long stretches, he also displayed at times a certain restlessness. He gave up all pretense of making conversation, except on the most mundane, essential topics. "Pass the salt" was about the most he would say to Mrs. Delisio or me. I forbore, more sorrowed than angered by his rude behavior. Obviously, he had far to go mentally before complete recovery. Despite my protests, he continued to read those trashy, evil books by Chambers, Bierce, and others.

Then in February the dreams came. I began to hear him crying out unintelligibly in his sleep. After one particularly bad night he appeared looking extremely haggard—and yet oddly exhilarated, his eyes flashing with a light I had not seen since before his collapse. When I probed him, he admitted that "distressing" dreams had caused him to sleep fitfully, but his elated expression seemed to belie the notion that they had been in any way disturbing. He would not comment on the content of these dreams.

One night late in the month, after returning from a rush party at the Kappa Sig house, I could hear Anable through his bedroom door talking in his sleep. Pressing my ear to the door, I could make out the following snatches. "He promises to come again . . . Satan's Ledge too far . . . must try one more time . . . I cannot fail Him . . . He shall not fail me . . . chant the Dhol formula . . . Nyarlathotep . . ."

I was profoundly alarmed to recognize the sorts of words and phrases he had not mouthed since our delirious ride back to Arkham on that Halloween night. At last I had to face the fact that Anable's derangement was more serious and lasting than I had guessed. A doctor who specialized in mental disorders would probably have to be consulted soon. But events moved too swiftly for me to act—and, in retrospect, I doubt if it would have affected the ultimate tragic outcome.

The unfortunate climax, when it came, did not catch me entirely off guard. Since Anable had abandoned even an outward show of normality, I was prepared to act forcefully if I had to.

It was a chilly winter evening, a Thursday, with no sign in the air of the forthcoming spring, that I sat on the sofa checking over my notes for a paper on Shadwell's use of irony. Vacation was only a week away. I was feeling quite relaxed after Mrs. Delisio's delicious spaghetti dinner. Anable had retired to his room from which shortly he emerged wearing his heavy overcoat.

"I'm going out, Winsor—into town, to my mother's," he announced.

I offered him a lift in my motor. He declined. I insisted on leaving with him, seeing him to the trolley stop. Grudgingly, he allowed me to accompany him outside. When we reached the street he turned the wrong way—north toward 127 and the woods. I hurried after him as he broke into a run on the slippery pavement. I easily overtook him in his semi-debilitated condition. When he ignored my command to halt, I had no recourse but to seize him and wrestle him gently into a drift at the side of the road.

"I must get out tonight . . . I must break through the Gate, must merge with Him . . . leave me alone," he panted as we struggled.

When Anable realized the futility of further resistance, I let him up and he reluctantly returned with me to the house. We were both soaked from rolling around in the wet snow—it was lunacy to stay out any longer with the temperature falling sharply. Anable was wheezing, gasping for breath.

Ignoring his imprecations against me, I assured him that it was in his best interest not to go to the ledge considering his poor health in this weather at this time of night. Anable, furious, stormed into his room and slammed the door. I kept vigil in the sitting room to near midnight, then went to bed myself.

I did not know what time it was when I awoke (I could not see my clock in the dark), but I soon realized what the cause of my waking up had been—a high wind that rattled the panes had blown over the trash cans in the yard beneath my window. The wind sounded louder than it should have—as if its source were from within the building. I stumbled out into the sitting room to investigate. Judging by the great whistling noise coming from Anable's room I concluded that he had to have his window wide open.

Above the whine, which was like no natural wind I had ever heard, I could distinguish a high-pitched but forceful voice behind Anable's door that I knew could not be my roommate's.

"You know, Howard Anable, that the New England world you have loved and cherished from birth is only the sum of the marvelous sunset cities you have gazed upon (from a height) in your dreams. These have you yearned for with such keen frustration all your years. Ancient Arkham, insular Innsmouth, rumour-shadowed Kingsport, Boston and its ghoul-infested North End, Providence and its jewellers' conventions, these are but ephemeral transcriptions of the real places you have so far only dimly glimpsed—basalt-towered Dylath-Leen, Kled with its perfumed jungles, the Plateau of Leng, Yith, Cyclopean and many-columned Y'ha-nthlei. Your longing for your great-great-grandfather's Greek Revival mansion with its widow's walk and Ionic pilasters is really a longing for a certain windowless, onyx pharos on nighted Yuggoth. When you wish to don smallclothes and periwig you are in truth desiring to wear the unhuman trappings, the extravagant golden tiaras and armlets of the Deep Ones. . . . Soon, Howard Anable, soon you can wander in the Vaults of Zin, and consort with ghasts and gugs."

Someone—some madman—had plainly clambered up from the yard below into Anable's window! Had Harper or one of his cult cohorts returned? I switched on the lamp on the end table. Looking out the sitting room window, I could see that Mrs. Delisio had turned on the light illuminating the backyard.

"I am the Gate," continued the wailing voice. "The Gate that stands open, ready to receive you. Dare you enter? Come, come now. . . ."

I had had enough of listening to this mad drivel. I knocked on Anable's door, then tried to open it and found that some heavy object—possibly the bed—blocked it. I threw my shoulder repeatedly against the door, but it budged not an inch. The wind had increased its daemonic scream—I could no longer make out that piping voice whose youthful owner I now knew, only the thuds of books and furniture striking the floor.

With a strength born of frantic frenzy, I burst through, dislodging whatever was behind the door. I was immediately overwhelmed by a loathsome stench, which caused me to reel back in nausea—but not before I saw a large, white, flowing, viscous mass leap through and shatter the upper panes of the sash window. The flying shards of glass miraculously missed me, as I dashed forward into Anable's empty, suddenly odor-free room—to the damaged window. I looked down, expecting to see Anable and his abductor in a heap in the yard below. But the only person visible was Mrs. Delisio in her dressing gown and shawl, rushing out the back door at the sound of that final crash of glass and wood. Below the window, other than the toppled trash cans and debris, *there was nothing on the ground! In the next moment I looked up—looked up toward Satan's Ledge—looked up into a winter's sky that was alive with motion in unimagined space filled with transcendent whiteness. In utter stillness.*

VIII.

Understandably, I did not linger in that house of horror. I spent the rest of that night and the next at Miskatonic in the dorm suite of Messrs. Haiblum, Sullivan, and Klein. I remained in Arkham only for as long as I had to, to calm Mrs. Delisio (who had apparently not witnessed that last, soul-blasting vision in the sky), to speak with Mrs. Anable and to the police suggesting the theory that Anable had been spirited off by the cult members into the hills and possibly beyond. There was no keeping the authorities out of the matter this time. As already stated, I withdrew to Boston for the remainder of the term, arranging to take my exams after vacation. I spent the bulk of my vacation time composing the above narrative.

There is one more thing. In April when I returned to Arkham, I visited Mrs. Delisio to settle my affairs with her. She had already agreed to terminating my lease short of the appointed year, and I wished to pay her some fair compensation. (Insurance had covered the damaged window.) After negotiations had been concluded as affably as possible under the solemn circumstances, she gave me a sealed envelope that she had found among Anable's effects before their removal. It had my name on it, and contained a hastily scribbled note.

3/15/29

Winsor [it began]:

By the time you read this I'll be far beyond your meddling reach. Despite your best efforts to interfere I should soon be riding through the intergalactic void on the back of a hypoencephalic centipede, frolicking with the night-gaunts and ghouls—or some such. I regret you won't be joining me here, as in fact you aren't worthy to transcend the mundane human world—the mundane human world whose economy within a few months, it's been my privilege to learn from Him, is in for a difficult period. You and your kind are going to suffer, and I can't say I feel very sorry for you. Enjoy what will probably prove to be your last summer on the island. Be forewarned that hard times lie ahead.

Yrs.—HWA

Thus read Howard Wentworth Anable's last—and certainly most unfathomable—communication to me and to the world; the final testament of a once noble mind stolen away from its rightful place among men by a cosmic evil that surely deserves, as I trust my pitiful account has demonstrated, the epithet, "the madness out of space."

Afterword

Back in 1974–75, during the year I was living at home with my mother in Massachusetts, in between my graduation from Brown and my move to Manhattan, I felt the urge to write a Lovecraftian story. Having produced a modest amount of scholarly work, notably a senior honors essay ("A Case for Howard Phillips Lovecraft") and a slim master's thesis ("Lovecraft's New England"), I couldn't resist venturing into the well-trodden realm of Lovecraft-inspired fiction. But I wasn't content to start with something modest, my equivalent of "Dagon" or "The Tomb." No, I aspired to compose my version of one of the later, longer cosmic tales, though "The Thing on the Doorstep" was my immediate model. A sober, sane male narrator would tell of the supernatural misfortunes of his eccentric, brilliant male friend.

Over a period of months, I labored over the first two parts of what I would later run in the Esoteric Order of Dagon amateur press association as "The Thing from the Hills," striving to imitate Lovecraft so closely that the unwary might mistake my prose for the Providence Gent's own. (Indeed, for the publication of the complete story in *Eldritch Tales* I framed it as a "lost" work of Lovecraft's.) But what was the point of a straightforward imitation, however well done? The side of me that had been weaned on *Mad* magazine couldn't resist throwing in more than one in-joke or gag, starting with the hero's aversion to cats and ice cream.

In other ways I followed Lovecraft's example: extended passages of expository prose, broken by the occasional letter extract or monologue; lessons in New England history and geography; no female characters of consequence. I gave my naïve narrator a social life, but it's far less important than his relationship with the Lovecraft-like scholar he befriends.

Working in solitude, as yet unconnected with anyone in the larger Lovecraft community, I decided after a while that my efforts to emulate the master were futile and set aside what little I'd written. Then a few years later, as a resident of New York City, I met horror writer T.E.D. Klein, whose long story "The Events at Poroth Farm" (the basis for his 1984 novel, *The Ceremonies*) I much admired. Ted's enthusiasm for the genre helped stimulate me to resume work on "The Madness out of Space," which I completed in the fall of 1979.

Eager for feedback, I asked Ted to read the manuscript. Rather as Lovecraft so generously lent editorial advice to the likes of August Derleth and other disciples, Ted obliged by providing two pages of handwritten comments. Most of these were corrections of typos or stylistic infelicities. A few were substantive. He didn't think the name "Jay Hand" sounded right, so I changed it to "Jay Harper." I eliminated a reference he noted to Miskatonic University's limiting the admission of Jews, fearing I might offend Jewish readers.

Most significantly, Ted had a problem with the ending. Originally, Anable in his final missive to Winsor informs his ex-friend that he has prevailed on "Him" to cause what will become known as the Great Depression, thus exacting revenge on the smugly well-to-do Winsor. Ted thought this was too extreme. Better would be for Anable merely to learn that this social cataclysm was in the offing and rejoice in Winsor's likely financial ruin—telegraphed, incidentally, in the opening note, analogous to that at the start of "The Call of Cthulhu," that I've restored here.

I changed the ending as Ted suggested. And yet, more than thirty years later, I still am not sure I made the right choice. Why not end on a ridiculous note in a story that for me, at any rate, remains an awkward apprentice exercise, an uneasy and arbitrary mix of pastiche and parody? On the other hand, no less than S. T. Joshi has been kind enough to praise "The Madness out of Space." May other discriminating readers be as forgiving.

A Reading Group Guide to *Forever Azathoth*

A Conversation with Peter Cannon

Besides Mad *magazine, has there been any other significant influence on your work?*

During my otherwise undistinguished career as an editor at Crown, I acquired one comic gem that was published in 1984, *The Beaver Papers* by Will Jacobs and Gerard Jones. Presented as a series of mock screen treatments, this parody mashed up the classic "Leave It to Beaver" TV show, which I loved watching as a child, with literary greats like D. H. Lawrence, Franz Kafka, and Tennessee Williams. As the five star reviews on Amazon attest, *The Beaver Papers* struck many as hilarious—though I will say, I did receive a letter from the actor who played wise-guy Eddie Haskell, a straight-arrow in real life, who made it quite clear he wasn't amused.

Weren't you taking a risk with copyright infringement?

Not really, since parody is protected in the U.S., thanks to a Supreme Court decision involving *Mad* magazine's right to parody copyrighted song lyrics.

But what about using the style and characters of P. G. Wodehouse, an English author?

That was trickier. Paul Ganley, who published my Lovecraft meets Sherlock Holmes mystery, *Pulptime*, was planning to bring out *Scream for Jeeves*, but wanted me first to run the idea past the agent for the Wodehouse literary estate. In reply to my query, I received a letter from the agent telling me in no uncertain terms not to publish, which was enough for Paul to back out. So I published it myself, in collaboration with Marc Michaud's Necronomicon Press. Around this time, as a member of The Wodehouse Society, I was in correspondence with Wodehouse's step-grandson, whose son was temporarily living in New York. By chance, I ended up writing an especially heartfelt seconding letter supporting Wodehouse's step-great-grandson's membership in my club. I like to think that was some recompense for any offense my book may have given the family.

How did you manage to get a self-published work like Scream for Jeeves *reviewed in* Publishers Weekly?

My step-brother's wife, who worked at *PW* at the time, remarked that the finished paperback looked just like a galley. So I marked a phony pub. month on the front of a copy and sending it to *PW*. Several months later, I was thrilled to receive a review in the publishing industry's leading source of pre-publication reviews. Today, I would have the option of submitting the book to "PW Select," the magazine's program for self-published authors— for a fee, of course.

As a reviews editor yourself at PW, *have you ever been fooled by a self-published book trying to pass as legitimate?*

Yes. It was I who decided that *PW* would review Brunonia Barry's *The Lace Reader*, first published by what I assumed was a legit small press in Marblehead, Massachusetts, near where I grew up. That Lovecraft loved Marblehead, the model for his fictional Kingsport, weighed heavily in the author's favor.

What did you think of Alan Moore's mash-up of Lovecraft and Wodehouse, "What Ho, Gods of the Abyss?"?

In all fairness, I think mine reads better. Where I used Wodehouse's light, dialogue-filled style, Moore elected to emulate Lovecraft's dense, expository style. His approach just isn't as funny.

Did you ever consider writing more "Wodecraft" stories?

One criticism has been that the three selections take their plots from non-Mythos tales: "The Rats in the Walls," "Cool Air," and a blend of "The Music of Erich Zann" and a portion of *The Case of Charles Dexter Ward*. The Cthulhu-headed butler that appears on the cover of the new Ash-Tree e-Book edition notwithstanding, these stories don't really address the cosmic.

Years ago, I made notes for a sequel that would be a novel rather than a series of related short stories. In essence, Jeeves would leave Bertie's service after a falling out over some trivial sartorial matter and accept the position of butler in the Ward household in Providence, the previous butler having abruptly resigned, as we know from *The Case of Charles Dexter Ward*. The young master would follow Jeeves to New England, where the two would get involved in all the events of "the great year," 1928, notably those in "The Dunwich Horror" and "The Whisperer in Darkness." For example, Jeeves might have to take a side trip to Vermont to bail out Wilmarth at the Akeley farmhouse, leaving Bertie to lend Armitage a bumbling hand in exterminating the Dunwich horror. Perhaps I'll get around to this project when I retire.

What's the story behind "Nautical-Looking Negroes"? Wasn't it supposed to appear in one of Bob Price's Chaosium anthologies?

Bob had accepted it, but the Chaosium editor axed it at the last minute. According to Bob, he objected to some inauthentic business about weapons being stored in "gun oil" or some such. My guess is the Chaosium editor either didn't get or heartily disliked the religious satire that's at the heart of an otherwise long and pointless story. Happily, the editors at *Lore*, a small specialty magazine, felt otherwise and ran it in their summer of 1996 issue.

Can you be more specific about the religious satire in the story?

Basically, I set elements of Mormon and Christian Science theology at odds, as reflected in the rival factions among the crew aboard the *Pole Star*, the ship headed for Arctic waters. I borrowed in particular from the controversy involving Bliss Knapp, an early Christian Scientist who held unorthodox views about the possible divinity of Mary Baker Eddy, the church's founder.

Incidentally, I was surprised to learn from *Lore* editor Rod Heather when I ran into him at MythosCon in Phoenix last year that "Nautical-Looking Negroes" had caused a controversy between him and a co-editor. According to Rod, this co-editor got worked up to the point where he confessed that he was a fundamentalist Christian, and they soon parted ways.

At one point in "The Madness out of Space," the narrator describes finding what are obviously used condoms washed up on a beach. What's the point of inserting this tasteless detail?

A gratuitous reminder of sordid reality it may be, but I like to think it serves to reinforce the narrator's naïvete and general cluelessness. I can remember as a boy spotting these things one day at the beach where my family and I used to go across the bay from Marblehead. Only years later did I understand why my mother and the other mothers at the beach viewed these puzzling objects with such evident horror. Cthulhu spawn, indeed!

Questions and topics for discussion

In the six "Forever Azathoth" stories, you never learn the ultimate purpose of Ephraim Waite's mind-swapping. Do you wish someone would write a sequel that would lay out in detail what old, half-crazed Ephraim was really up to?

In "Cats, Rats, and Bertie Wooster," Jeeves worries that too much arcane knowledge could threaten his master's sanity. How do you suppose Jeeves manages to maintain his knowing what he does about the horrors below Exham Priory?

Do you think Jeeves was too harsh on Bertie for wearing a checked suit in "Something Foetid"? Would you buy and wear a checked suit if the price was right?

In "The Undercliffe Sentences," we learn that Carl Dreadstone is a big fan of weird writer Roland Franklyn, and yet when it becomes clear that the copy-editor of his manuscript is Franklyn's widow, he has no reaction whatsoever. Don't you think Dreadstone would've started asking a lot of questions about his idol once he realized this?

Does it bother you that the narrator of "The Arkham Collector" refers to a bunch of books and authors you may never have heard of?

In "Old Man," the cat-loving hero has a vision that an old lady of recent acquaintance is poisoning his feline friends. Do you think he should have sought more convincing proof of her guilt before murdering her?

Which of the two rival religious factions aboard the *Polestar* in "Nautical-Looking Negroes" do you think has the sounder theology?

The Lovecraftian narrator of "The Madness out of Space" seems particularly unworldly. Do you really think a 1920s-era male college student wouldn't recognize a condom when he saw one?